About the Author

Peter Aitken has been writing about computers and software for 20 years and has some 45 books as well as hundreds of magazine and web articles to his credit. He specializes in Excel, Visual Basic programming, and XML, but he has also ventured into such varied topics as personal finance, digital imaging, and camera phones. Peter also does technical writing in the medical and pharmaceutical fields and is a part-time faculty member at Duke University Medical Center.

Acknowledgments

An author does not create a book all alone—along the way are many helping hands that are essential to the process. My thanks to all of these talented people: Katie Mohr, my acquisitions editor; Mike Talley, who reviewed the book for technical accuracy; and Sydney Jones, my developmental editor.

Credits

Acquisitions Editor: Katie Mohr

Development Editor: Sydney Jones

Technical Editor: Mike Talley

Production Editor: Kenyon Brown

Copy Editor: S. B. Kleinman

Editorial Manager: Mary Beth Wakefield

Production Manager: Tim Tate

Vice President and Executive Group Publisher: Richard Swadley

Vice President and Executive Publisher: Joseph B. Wikert

Project Coordinator: Ryan Steffen

Graphics and Production Specialists:
Sean Decker, Denny Hager,
Jennifer Heleine, Heather Pope,
Melanee Prendergast, Barbara Moore

Quality Control Technician: David Faust, Joseph Niesen

Proofreading: Susan Sims

Indexing: TECHBOOKS Production Services

Contents at a Glance

Contents

Part IV: Working with PivotTable Components   77

Part V: More About PivotTable Components   111

Part I

Understanding PivotTables and Charts

In this part you learn about PivotTables and PivotCharts, which are powerful data-analysis tools in Excel. They are invaluable for pulling meaning from huge masses of seemingly meaningless data. Given their power, PivotTables and PivotCharts are surprisingly easy to use, but using them still involves many unavoidable complexities. This book teaches you how to use PivotTables and PivotCharts efficiently and effectively. As the first step, you need to understand what these tools are and when you might want to use them.

Tips and Where to Find Them

Understanding How PivotTables Work

PivotTables enable you to extract meaning from large amounts of data. This description is deceptively simple because in fact PivotTables are powerful and sophisticated tools that enable you to do things that would be impossible or difficult to do any other way. A PivotTable enables you to take what seems to be an indecipherable mass of facts and extract any trends and patterns buried in the data. You can organize and summarize your data, perform comparisons, and extract meaningful information that can be invaluable to you and your organization.

Why the term *pivot?* It comes from an analogy between the way PivotTables work and the way you investigate a physical object. Imagine that you have been handed a complex device and asked to figure out what it does. You don't just look at it from one angle; rather you turn it in your hands, examining it from all possible perspectives to be sure you do not miss any important clues. PivotTables work the same way, enabling you to turn or pivot the raw data and examine it from various perspectives to extract the information you need. Then you also have the option of creating a *PivotChart,* a graphical representation of the information in a PivotTable.

Suppose you work for a chain of sporting-goods stores. Every day you receive a report from each store that includes complete details on that day's activities, such as number of customers each hour, sales in each of 30 categories, items returned for refund or exchange, and number of employees on duty at different times of the day. It won't be long before your Excel workbook is chock-full of this raw data, but what good does it do you? You could stare at this information for hours without gaining any useful insights from it. But with a PivotTable you can quickly and easily answer the following types of questions:

- Which days of the week show the highest sales?

- Which categories of merchandise sell best at different times of the year?

- Are more employees scheduled to work when there is the highest customer load?

- Do certain categories of merchandise suffer from unusually high rates of return/exchange?

These are the kinds of questions that a business needs to answer in order to operate efficiently. These are also the kinds of questions that PivotTables are designed to answer. The same kinds of analysis are appropriate for almost any kind of data you can imagine, from political surveys to weather patterns, from quality control in a manufacturing plant to test scores in a high school. That's the beauty of PivotTables — they are powerful *and* flexible.

What About Crosstab Tables?

If you have used older versions of Excel, you may be wondering how PivotTables relate to another Excel data analysis technique, the crosstab table. The fact is that PivotTables are a replacement for crosstabs, which are not even supported in newer versions of Excel. PivotTables are significantly more powerful than crosstabs and are easier to use. If you find yourself working with an old workbook that contains a crosstab table, your best bet is to convert it to a PivotTable report. Then you'll have the power of the PivotTable at your fingertips if you need to change the way the data is analyzed. To convert a crosstab to a PivotTable, follow these steps:

1. Open the workbook that contains the crosstab table.

2. Click any cell in the crosstab table.

3. Select Pivot Table and Pivot Chart Report from the Data menu.

4. Click Finish and then click OK in response to any prompts.

5. Save the workbook in the current Excel version.

Of course you should not do this if you or someone else will later need to open the workbook in the older version of Excel.

Working with PivotTables

I could talk about PivotTables until I am blue in the face, but it's much better to actually show an example. By looking at the kind of data that PivotTables are used for, and seeing the resulting PivotTable in action, you will get a good understanding of the what and why of this powerful tool.

Figure 1.1 shows some data that are typical of the kind you would analyze using a PivotTable. These data are based on the sporting-goods store example I mentioned earlier. As with other examples in this book I have intentionally simplified the data to illustrate the points I am trying to make without confusing you with unnecessary details. You should not think that PivotTables are limited to relatively simple data such as these!

What questions might you want to ask about these data? Here are a few that come to mind:

- What are the sales for the Camping category for each region?

- In each store, which days of the week see the most customers?

- In each store, which category has the highest sales?

- Which day of the week has the lowest total sales?

In the following demonstration you explore the first question. You create a PivotTable report that shows the total sales of goods in the Camping category subtotaled by region.

	Store	Region	Date	Customers	Total Sales	Camping	Fitness	Soccer	Baseball	Fishing	Football
3	2134	Northeast	06-Jun-05	207	$ 6,581	$ 326	$ 1,284	$ 970	$ 1,270	$ 1,488	$ 1,243
4	2134	Northeast	07-Jun-05	162	$ 3,584	$ 901	$ 247	$ 765	$ 1,251	$ 228	$ 192
5	2134	Northeast	08-Jun-05	188	$ 4,713	$ 837	$ 1,260	$ 959	$ 765	$ 179	$ 713
6	2134	Northeast	09-Jun-05	171	$ 5,263	$ 553	$ 1,134	$ 236	$ 1,353	$ 1,011	$ 976
7	2134	Northeast	10-Jun-05	64	$ 4,731	$ 775	$ 294	$ 1,480	$ 160	$ 864	$ 1,158
8	2134	Northeast	11-Jun-05	246	$ 3,853	$ 429	$ 853	$ 773	$ 760	$ 739	$ 299
9	2134	Northeast	12-Jun-05	63	$ 6,077	$ 1,075	$ 1,418	$ 659	$ 1,445	$ 1,340	$ 140
10	2298	Midwest	06-Jun-05	86	$ 4,075	$ 866	$ 399	$ 270	$ 690	$ 418	$ 1,432
11	2298	Midwest	07-Jun-05	234	$ 3,933	$ 1,056	$ 266	$ 781	$ 131	$ 1,376	$ 323
12	2298	Midwest	08-Jun-05	286	$ 3,818	$ 1,330	$ 459	$ 314	$ 1,119	$ 149	$ 447
13	2298	Midwest	09-Jun-05	99	$ 4,923	$ 456	$ 426	$ 368	$ 1,045	$ 1,453	$ 1,175
14	2298	Midwest	10-Jun-05	85	$ 5,084	$ 1,061	$ 729	$ 211	$ 939	$ 939	$ 1,205
15	2298	Midwest	11-Jun-05	218	$ 3,517	$ 1,191	$ 341	$ 123	$ 1,293	$ 300	$ 269
16	2298	Midwest	12-Jun-05	124	$ 4,435	$ 998	$ 581	$ 350	$ 1,249	$ 295	$ 962
17	2166	South	06-Jun-05	215	$ 8,625	$ 1,957	$ 1,995	$ 615	$ 1,623	$ 370	$ 2,065
18	2166	South	07-Jun-05	266	$ 5,902	$ 1,829	$ 612	$ 709	$ 878	$ 1,218	$ 656
19	2166	South	08-Jun-05	92	$ 8,032	$ 1,844	$ 1,099	$ 1,804	$ 1,005	$ 1,509	$ 771
20	2166	South	09-Jun-05	237	$ 7,786	$ 1,470	$ 1,430		$ 787	$ 2,074	$ 1,114
21	2166	South	10-Jun-05	65	$ 7,669	$ 1,377	$ 2,092	$ 364	$ 1,793	$ 502	$ 1,541
22	2166	South	11-Jun-05	263	$ 5,211	$ 1,201	$ 360	$ 655	$ 522	$ 559	$ 1,914
23	2166	South	12-Jun-05	159	$ 9,388	$ 1,663	$ 1,978	$ 828	$ 1,375	$ 1,747	$ 1,797

Figure 1-1: The sample data.

Creating a PivotTable Report

In this section I will guide you through the steps required to create a report that answers the question posed above: What are the sales for the Camping category for each region?

To begin, you must start Excel and open the workbook that contains the raw data, `SportingGoodsRawData.xls`. This workbook is provided for download from `wiley.com/go/excelpivottables/`

Start by selecting PivotTable and PivotChart Wizard from the Data menu. Excel displays the first step of the wizard, as shown in Figure 1-2.

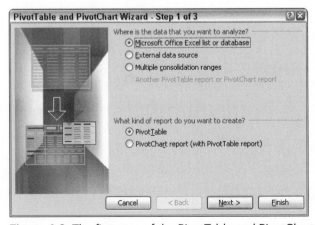

Figure 1-2: The first step of the PivotTable and PivotChart Wizard.

In this dialog box, make sure that the options are selected as shown in the figure:

- Select Microsoft Office Excel list or database.
- Select PivotTable

Then click the Next button to move to Step 2 of the wizard, shown in Figure 1-3.

Figure 1-3: In the second step of the PivotTable and PivotChart Wizard you select the data on which the PivotTable will be based.

In the Range box you must enter the worksheet range that contains your raw data. In this example it is A2:K23. You can also click the Select button if you want to select the data range with the mouse, as follows:

1. Click the Select button. The dialog box collapses to a single line.

2. Drag the mouse over the desired data range. The range will be surrounded by an animated dashed border.

3. Click the Select button again. The dialog box expands to its normal size with the address of the selected data range entered in the Range field.

When you have the data range entered, click the Next button to move to the third and final step of the wizard, shown in Figure 1-4.

Figure 1-4: In the third and final step of the PivotTable and PivotChart Wizard you select the location for the new PivotTable.

In this dialog box you specify where to place the PivotTable. You can also specify the table layout and set some options using the Layout and Options buttons, but that's a topic for a future part. For now just select the Existing Worksheet option and enter the address of a cell that is a few rows below the data, such as A28. Then click Finish to create the PivotTable report. Your screen will look like Figure 1-5.

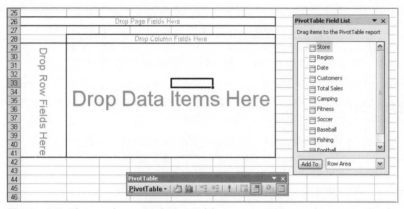

Figure 1-5: The newly created PivotTable report waiting to be customized.

Your screen displays three elements, as shown in the figure:

- The PivotTable itself, which is currently empty.

- The PivotTable toolbar, which provides buttons for commonly used PivotTable tasks and commands.

- The PivotTable Field List, which lists the data fields (columns) that are present in the raw data.

You will be learning all the details of these various elements in future parts. For now just follow the steps required to create the PivotTable report. This requires that you select the data items you want in the report and drag them from the PivotTable Field List to the appropriate location in the PivotTable report:

1. Drag the Region field from the PivotTable Field List and drop it in the Drop Row Fields Here section of the PivotTable.

2. Drag the Camping field from the PivotTable Field List and drop it in the Drop Data Items Here section of the PivotTable.

That's it; your PivotTable report is done and will appear as shown in Figure 1-6. The only remaining step is to format the numbers to display as currency by selecting the cells and clicking the Currency Style button on Excel's Formatting toolbar. You may also need to increase the width of Column B to display the data correctly.

28	Sum of Camping	
29	Region ▾	Total
30	Midwest	$ 6,958.00
31	Northeast	$ 4,896.00
32	South	$10,782.00
33	Grand Total	$22,636.00

Figure 1-6: The completed PivotTable report.

I hope that you are suitably impressed with how easy it was to create this PivotTable report. Yes, it's a simple one, but the same principles apply for more complex requirements. At this time I want to point out a couple of other aspects of PivotTable reports.

When the report is active, the PivotTable Field List is displayed. Fields that are part of the report are displayed in boldface in this list. To make the PivotTable active, click anywhere in it. To make it inactive, click somewhere else in the worksheet.

Note that the Region heading in the report has a drop-down arrow next to it. If you click this arrow Excel displays a list of all the row values as shown in Figure 1-7 — in this case, the names of the three regions, Midwest, Northeast, and South. By checking or unchecking individual items in this list, including the Show All option, you can change what the PivotTable displays.

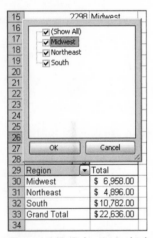

Figure 1-7: Selecting which rows to display in the PivotTable report.

For example, by selecting only the Midwest item and then clicking OK, you modify the report to show Camping category sales for the Midwest region only, as shown in Figure 1-8.

28	Sum of Camping	
29	Region ▾	Total
30	Midwest	$6,958.00
31	Grand Total	$6,958.00

Figure 1-8: The PivotTable report customized to display only the Midwest region.

If you have changed the report to display only a single region, change it back to Show All for the next step.

Creating a PivotTable Report with Multiple Columns

The example PivotTable presented in the previous section was about the simplest PivotTable you can create. It will be useful to go through the process of creating a somewhat more sophisticated PivotTable report, one that has multiple columns as well as rows. The data you will use is shown in Figure 1-10. It is inventory data for a chain of video-rental stores.

	A	B	C	D
1				
2	Popcorn Video Rentals			
3				
4	Store	Category	Titles	
5	Main Street	Action	374	
6	Main Street	Drama	180	
7	Main Street	Childrens	63	
8	Main Street	Sci-Fi	324	
9	Main Street	Classics	203	
10	Main Street	Comedy	145	
11	Northgate	Action	45	
12	Northgate	Drama	287	
13	Northgate	Childrens	320	
14	Northgate	Sci-Fi	36	
15	Northgate	Classics	79	
16	Northgate	Comedy	225	
17	Clarkville	Action	22	
18	Clarkville	Drama	172	
19	Clarkville	Childrens	203	
20	Clarkville	Sci-Fi	324	
21	Clarkville	Classics	251	
22	Clarkville	Comedy	345	
23	West End	Action	310	
24	West End	Drama	369	
25	West End	Childrens	220	
26	West End	Sci-Fi	236	
27	West End	Classics	145	
28	West End	Comedy	296	
29				

Figure 1-9: The video-rental store inventory data.

These raw data are organized differently from the data in the previous example. Each row in this table represents a specific category of video for a specific store. The number is the count of titles in stock for that category. The goal is to create a PivotTable report that presents this information in an easy-to-read form and to display summary information.

To begin, open the workbook VideoStoreRawData.xls. Use your mouse to select the data (but not the heading) — cells A4:C28. Then select PivotTable and PivotChart Wizard from the Data menu to start the wizard. (You saw this first wizard dialog box earlier in Figure 1-2.) Make sure the following options are selected:

- Microsoft Office list or database
- PivotTable

Click Next to go to the second step of the wizard. You'll see, as shown in Figure 1-10, that the range you selected earlier, A4:C28, is already entered in the Range field. This illustrates how you can select your data range before starting the PivotTable Wizard, as you have done here, or select it from the wizard, as you did in the earlier example. The results are the same either way.

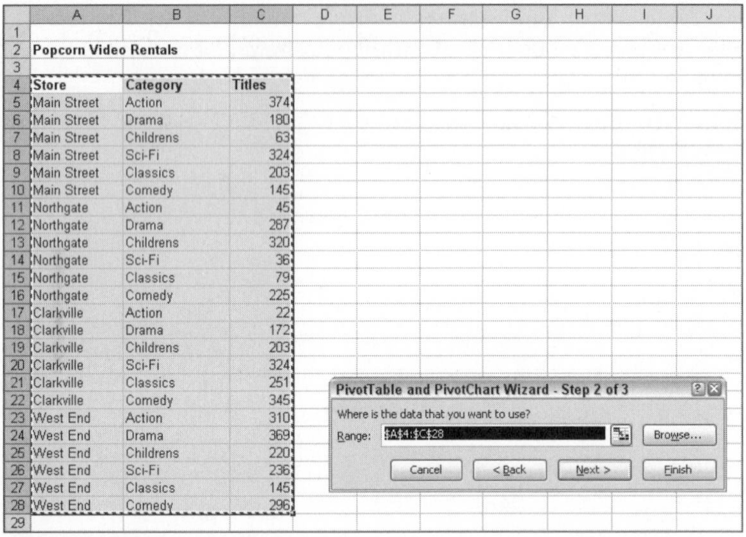

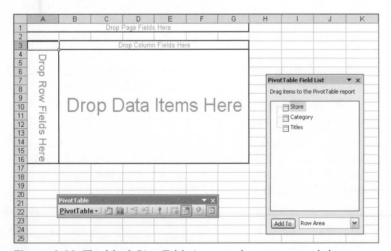

Figure 1-10: If you select the data range before starting the PivotTable Wizard the range will be entered automatically.

Click Next to proceed to the third wizard step. For this example leave the default New Worksheet option selected and then click Finish. You'll see the blank PivotTable created in a new worksheet, as shown in Figure 1-11.

Figure 1-11: The blank PivotTable is created on a new worksheet.

So far this looks like the step you took when you created the PivotTable in the previous example, except that the Field List contains different field names. The differences come in the next steps and are the result of the way the raw data are arranged. Here's what to do:

1. Drag the Store field from the Field List and drop it in the section of the PivotTable labeled Drop Row Fields Here.

2. Drag the Category field from the Field List and drop it in the section of the PivotTable labeled Drop Column Fields Here.

3. Drag the Titles field from the Field List and drop it in the section of the PivotTable labeled Drop Data Items Here.

The PivotTable that will result from these steps is shown in Figure 1-12.

3	Sum of Titles	Category ⌄						
4	Store ⌄	Action	Childrens	Classics	Comedy	Drama	Sci-Fi	Grand Total
5	Clarkville	22	203	251	345	172	324	1317
6	Main Street	374	63	203	145	180	324	1289
7	Northgate	45	320	79	225	287	36	992
8	West End	310	220	145	296	369	236	1576
9	Grand Total	751	806	678	1011	1008	920	5174

Figure 1-12: Excel automatically calculates and displays totals for each category and for each store, as well as an overall total.

Now you can go ahead and create a PivotChart based on this PivotTable report. Make sure the PivotTable is active; then click the Chart Wizard button on the PivotTable toolbar. The resulting chart is shown in Figure 1-13. Each store is represented by a bar in the chart, and within each bar the different categories are differentiated by color.

The Category button above the chart legend and the Store button below the horizontal axis both have drop-down arrows on them. Click an arrow to display a list of fields to include in the chart, as shown in Figure 1-14. (This works the same way as the drop-down lists in the PivotTable itself, which you saw earlier in this part.) Selecting fields to display in the chart affects the PivotTable report too. In other words, the PivotTable report and the PivotChart are linked and always display the same data.

Part I

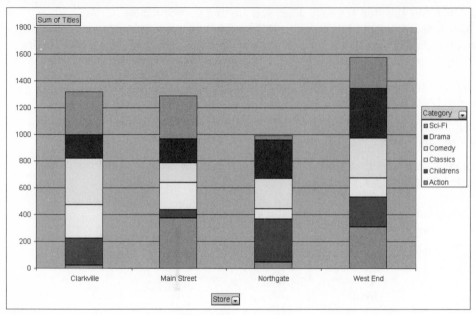

Figure 1-13: The PivotChart breaks the data down by store and by category.

Figure 1-14: Selecting which Category fields to include in the chart.

Creating a PivotChart

A PivotChart is nothing more than a standard Excel chart created from the data in a PivotTable report. In fact there are a few features in PivotCharts that you will not find in charts based on other data — that is, data not in a PivotTable. For the most part, however, a PivotChart is like any other Excel chart and can be manipulated and formatted in the same way. The few differences will be covered as they come up.

Part I

A PivotChart is an Excel chart based on the data in a PivotTable report. It's more than a standard Excel chart; however, because it provides many of the same customization capabilities as a report, it's easy to create a basic PivotChart. All you need to do is make the PivotTable report active and then click the Chart Wizard button on the PivotTable toolbar. Go ahead and do this now and you will see the chart shown in Figure 1-15.

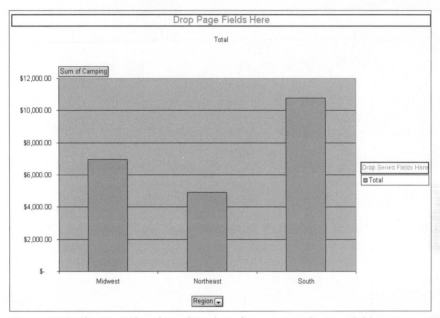

Figure 1-15: The PivotChart based on the information in the PivotTable report.

This chart has some elements that don't appear on standard Excel charts. For example, the PivotTable Field List is displayed and above the legend is a box labeled Drop Series Fields Here. These different elements are all PivotChart tools that enable you to customize which data are shown and how they are displayed. I'll be getting to these features in Part 6. For now you can experiment on your own if you wish.

Part II

Understanding Data Sources for PivotTables

The first step in analyzing data with a PivotTable is, of course, the data themselves. Excel provides you with a great deal of flexibility in this regard. You are not limited to analyzing data that have been entered into the workbook, although that is, in fact, a common scenario. The ability to use external data greatly enhances the power of PivotTable reports. This part explores the various data sources you can use with PivotTables.

Tips and Where to Find Them

Using Excel Data from the Same Workbook

Perhaps the most common way to create a PivotTable is by basing it on data that already exist in an Excel workbook. The data can be in the same workbook as the PivotTable; this technique was used in Part 1. The data can also be in a separate workbook.

Things are at their simplest when you are creating a PivotTable in the workbook in which the data are located. The data should be organized as a standard Excel list as follows:

- The first row contains the field or column names.

- The second and subsequent rows contain the data.

- There are no blank rows, although individual blank cells may be present.

To tell the PivotTable Wizard where the data are located, you can do one of three things:

- Select the data before you start the wizard. The address of the data will be entered automatically in the appropriate place in the wizard.

- Enter the address of the data in the second wizard step. (See Figure 2-1.)

- Use the Select button in the second wizard step to select the data range.

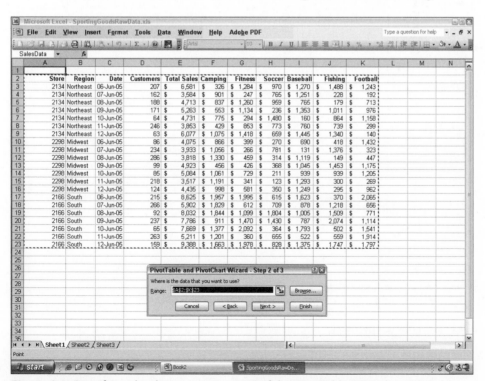

Figure 2-1: Specifying the data range in step 2 of the PivotTable Wizard.

Part II

Actually, there is a fourth and preferred way to tell the PivotTable Wizard where the data are — create a named range for the data. Using named ranges is more convenient than typing the address or selecting the data each time you want to refer to them. Named ranges also provide an advantage in that if you expand the range, perhaps to include additional data, the PivotTable report will automatically include the new data when it is refreshed. Here's how to create a named range:

1. Select the data range.

2. From the menu select Insert ⇨ Name ⇨ Define. The Define Name dialog box is displayed. (See Figure 2-2).

3. Type the name for the range. You should use something descriptive such as SalesData or SurveyResults. It's best to avoid spaces, too; use an underscore if needed to separate words.

4. Click Add; then click OK.

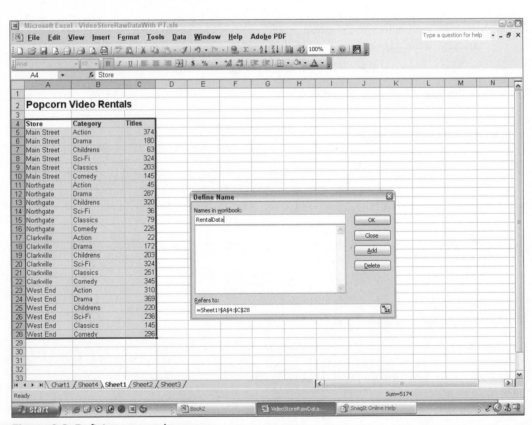

Figure 2-2: Defining a named range.

Then, when you are in Step 2 of the PivotTable Wizard, simply enter the range name in the Range field, as shown in Figure 2-3.

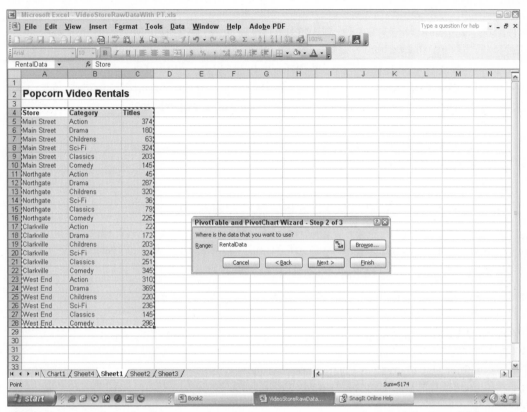

Figure 2-3: Specifying the data range by entering a range name in Step 2 of the PivotTable Wizard.

Of course if you enter a name that does not exist it will not work. Excel will display an error message when you try to exit Step 2 of the wizard so you can correct the entered name.

What About Filters and Subtotals?

If you have applied any autofilters and/or subtotals to your data, they are ignored when you create a PivotTable from the data. If you want to create a PivotTable based on the filtered data, you must copy the data to a new list and use that as the basis for the PivotTable report.

Using Excel Data from Another Workbook

If the data you want to use in your PivotTable are in another workbook, the process is slightly different. You will have to tell the PivotTable and PivotChart Wizard not only the range in which the data are located but also the name of the workbook they are in.

The easiest way to do this is to have both workbooks open; the one into which you want to place the PivotTable should be the active one. Then follow these steps:

1. Start the PivotTable and PivotChart Wizard and in Step 1 select the Microsoft Excel List or Database option.

2. Click Next.

3. In Step 2, click the Select button at the right end of the Range box.

4. Press Alt+Tab or click the Windows taskbar to activate the workbook that contains the data. (The PivotTable and PivotChart Wizard dialog box will remain visible.)

5. Select the data range for the PivotTable.

6. Click the Select button in the PivotTable and PivotChart Wizard to accept the selection and return to the wizard.

7. Complete the wizard as usual.

There's another way to create a PivotTable report based on data in another workbook; this one does not require that you have the data workbook open. You do, however, have to know the name of the workbook and the location of the data, either as a named range or a range address. It is much better to use a range name in this situation, and here are the steps required:

1. Activate the workbook where you want to place the PivotTable report.

2. Start the PivotTable and PivotChart Wizard and in Step 1 select the Microsoft Excel List or Database option.

Why a Different Workbook?

You might be wondering why anyone would put a PivotTable in a different workbook from the data on which it is based. It is actually very useful in some situations to do so. Perhaps you have a huge amount of data and the workbook they are in is slow and cumbersome. By putting the PivotTable in a separate workbook you'll be able to view and manipulate the PivotTable summary without the extra overhead of all those data. Or perhaps you want to summarize data that are located in several different workbooks. You can create a summary workbook that contains several PivotTable reports, each linked to its own external data workbook.

3. Click Next.

4. In Step 2, click the Browse button. Excel will display the Browse dialog box, as shown in Figure 2-4.

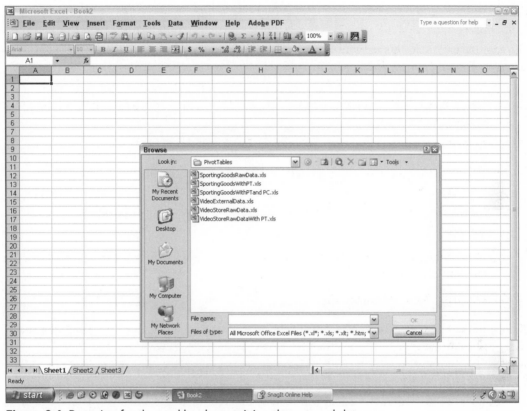

Figure 2-4: Browsing for the workbook containing the external data.

5. Use the Browse dialog box to locate and select the Excel workbook that contains the data, then click OK to return to the wizard.

6. You'll see that a reference to the workbook you selected, followed by an exclamation point, has been entered in the Range field. Type the name of the range that contains the data. (See Figure 2-5.)

7. Click Next and complete the wizard as usual.

Part II

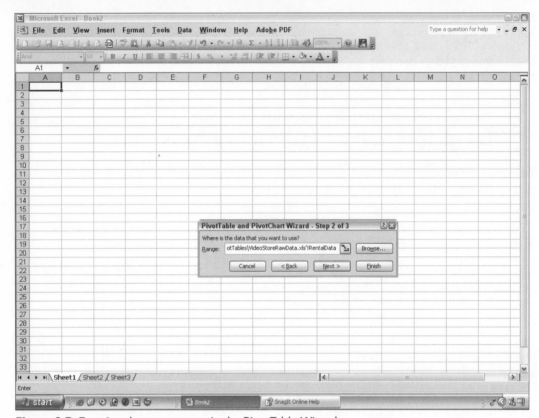

Figure 2-5: Entering the range name in the PivotTable Wizard.

When a PivotTable is linked to external data, you can only update it if the linked data worksheet is available. If this file has been moved, renamed, or deleted, you will not be able to update the PivotTable. Excel will display an error message when you attempt to do so. The original PivotTable data will remain in place, however.

PivotTables and Refreshing Data

It is important to be aware that PivotTables do not refresh automatically. This is true regardless of whether the data are in the same workbook as the PivotTable or in an external workbook. Changes to the data will not be reflected in the PivotTable unless you refresh the data. You do this in one of two ways:

- Right-click the PivotTable and select Refresh Data from the pop-up menu.

- Open the PivotTable menu from the PivotTable toolbar and select Refresh data.

Recalculating the workbook does not refresh PivotTable data.

Using Data from Other Sources

Excel enables you to use data from a variety of other sources for your PivotTable reports. There are two general ways to do this:

- Link to the external data without importing them into Excel.
- Import the external data into Excel and then treat them as an Excel list.

This section covers the procedures for linking to external data. Importing data is discussed in the part tip, "Using Other External Data Sources."

1. To create a PivotTable that is linked to external data, start the PivotTable and PivotChart Wizard and in Step 1 select the External Data Source option.

2. Click Next; the dialog box shown in Figure 2-6 will display. (Note that the caption next to the Get Data button says "No data fields have been retrieved." This indicates that the external source has not yet been selected.) Click the Get Data button to proceed.

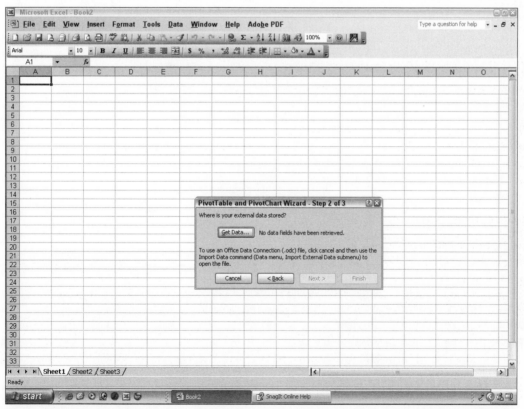

Figure 2-6: This is the first step in selecting an external data source for your PivotTable report.

The Choose Data Source dialog box will display, as shown in Figure 2-7. There are three tabs in this dialog box, representing the three main options you have for external data. I will deal with these in turn.

NOTE

Connecting to external data is a potentially complex process, if only because you have so many options. That's one of the things that make PivotTable reports in Excel so powerful: you can base them on data from a wide variety of sources. Before trying to create a PivotTable based on external data, it is a good idea to have at least some idea of where the data are located and of the type of connection you will use. If you are not familiar with these topics, you may want to ask your network administrator or IT person to lend a hand.

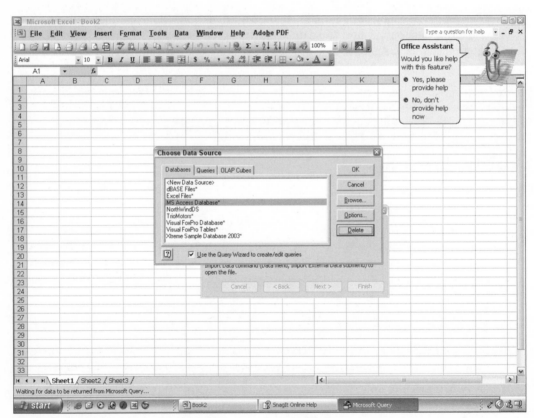

Figure 2-7: The Choose Data Source dialog box has three tabs.

Using Data from Databases

If you want to base your PivotTable report on data from a database, use the Databases tab in the Choose Data Source dialog box, shown in Figure 2-7. (The items that are displayed on this tab will depend on your system; don't expect to have the same items as those shown in the figure.) There is usually more than one way to connect to an external database, and in some cases the results are exactly the same. The items listed on this tab fall into three categories:

- **Existing data source** — Connect to an existing data source.
- **XXXX database** — Connect to a specific type of database file.
- **<New data source>** — Define a new data source.

Regardless of which type of connection you use, you need to define a query that determines what data will be returned by the connection. You won't often want to base a PivotTable report on all the data in a database, so this is an important step. Excel's default is to use the Query Wizard to define queries and this is what I recommend unless you have a specific reason not to. If you do not want to use the Query Wizard, uncheck the Use the Query Wizard to Create/Edit Queries option in the Choose Data Source dialog box. I will use the Query Wizard in the examples; if you turn off this option the precise steps you will take will depend on the type of connection you are using.

Existing Data Source

This is not the place for a complete explanation of the Query Wizard, but these are the basic steps to follow in order to use data from an existing data source:

1. Click the data source's name in the list and then click OK. The Query Wizard will open and display information about the data source, specifically what tables are in the source and what columns (fields) are in each table. An example is shown in Figure 2-8.

2. Open a table to display a list of its fields.

3. Select which fields to include in the query.

4. For each field, define criteria to determine which records are included in the returned data. (This step is optional and can be omitted if you want to include all the data.)

5. Determine the sort order for the returned data (although this is usually irrelevant for PivotTable reports).

6. In the last Query Wizard step, select the option Return Data to Microsoft Excel and then click Finish. The Query Wizard will close and you will return to Step 2 of Excel's PivotTable Wizard, shown in Figure 2-9.

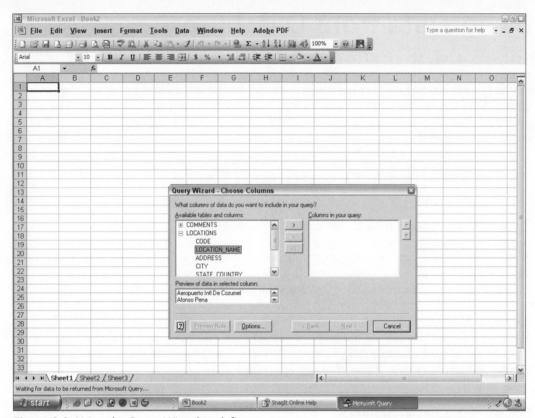

Figure 2-8: Using the Query Wizard to define a query.

Note that the caption next to the Get Data button now says "Data fields have been retrieved." At this point you can click Next and complete the PivotTable Wizard as usual. The result will be the same as if you were using Excel data: You'll have the blank PivotTable and a list of fields to drag and drop. You can go ahead and define the PivotTable as usual. The fact that the data are coming from an external source does not make any difference now.

You may have noticed the Options and Browse buttons on the Databases tab. They have the following functions:

- **Browse** — If you believe the desired data source is defined but not kept in one of the standard locations, click this button to browse for it.

- **Options** — Use this button to specify the folders where Excel looks for defined data sources. By default, Excel looks in the standard Windows locations, but if you have data sources saved in another location, you can add it here so the sources will automatically appear in the list.

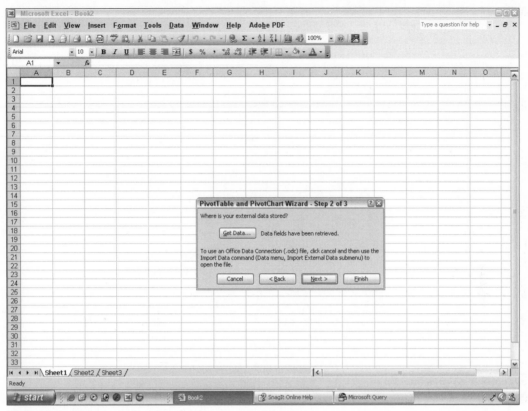

Figure 2-9: After retrieving data from an external source.

XXXX Database

In this case, XXXX stands for the name of a specific type of database such as MS Access or Oracle. You use this option when you want to connect directly to a database without defining a data source. Select the type of database and then click OK. The next steps will depend on the type of database you selected. For example, Figure 2-10 shows the dialog box that will be displayed if you are connecting to a Visual FoxPro database.

I Can't See the Data!

When you retrieve data from an external source, shouldn't you be able to see the data in the worksheet? No — Excel retrieves the data and uses them to create the PivotTable, but the raw data themselves are never displayed in the workbook.

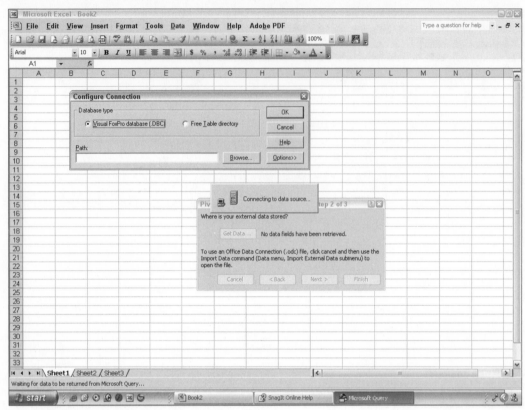

Figure 2-10: Connecting directly to a database file.

The precise steps you will have to complete vary depending on the type of database. In general, however, they consist of locating the database file to connect to and using the Query Wizard to specify which data to retrieve. (The basics of using the Query Wizard were covered earlier in this part.) When you are finished, the empty PivotTable report and field list will be displayed so you can finish defining the PivotTable.

\<New Data Source\>

If you want to use a data source for your PivotTable report but an appropriate one is not defined, you can create it by selecting the \<New Data Source\> item in the Choose Data Source dialog box and clicking OK. Excel will display the Create New Data Source dialog box, shown in Figure 2-11.

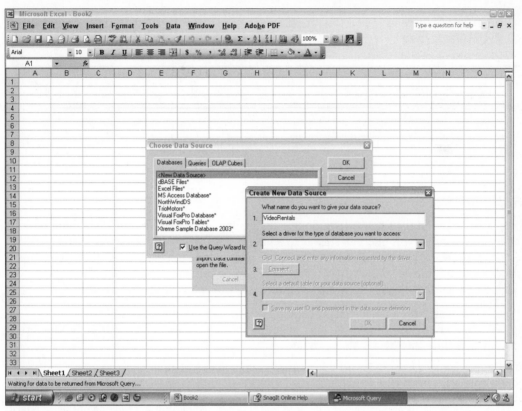

Figure 2-11: The first step in defining a new data source.

In broad outline the procedure is as follows:

1. Enter a name for the data source.

2. Select the driver to use, according to the type of database to which you will be connecting.

3. Click the Connect button to create the connection. (The details of this step will depend on the type of database and the driver.)

4. When the data source definition is complete, click the OK button in the Create New Data Source dialog box.

At this point you return to the Choose Data Source dialog box. The data source that you just defined will be listed on the Databases tab. You can select it and proceed as described earlier in this part in the section "Existing Data Source."

Data Sources

The term *data source* has a specific meaning in Windows. It is a connection to a database that has been defined and assigned a name. The database may be local or located on the network or Internet. You can connect to the database simply by using the name, which is more convenient than defining a new connection from scratch each time. The term *data source* also has the more general meaning of any source of data, so you must be alert to which meaning is intended in a specific context.

Queries

The Queries tab in the Choose Data Source dialog box lets you base your PivotTable report on an existing query. A query is similar to a data source as described earlier in this part. It goes a bit further, however. While data sources and queries are both defined and saved connections to a database, a query adds data-selection definitions. In other words, a query combines a database connection with criteria as to which specific data to retrieve.

When you display the Queries tab in the Choose Data Source dialog box, it will list any queries that are defined and available. Select the desired query and click OK and then proceed to complete the PivotTable as usual.

The Options and Browse buttons on the Queries tab are used as follows:

- **Browse** — If you believe the desired query is defined but not kept in one of the standard locations, click this button to browse for it.

- **Options** — Use this button to specify the folders in which Excel looks for defined queries. By default, Excel looks in the standard Windows locations, but if you have queries saved in another location, you can add that location here so they will automatically appear in the list.

The term *query* has a more general meaning as well. You can use a query as the basis of a PivotTable report even if it is not an officially defined query that shows up on the Query tab. For example, a Microsoft Access database can contain queries. If you connect to the database for your PivotTable, as described earlier in this part, these queries will be available for you to use.

OLAP Cubes

OLAP stands for On-line Analytical Processing, and an *OLAP cube* simply refers to a defined OLAP data source. An OLAP cube is like a data source or a query, just a different way of defining a connection to the data. If there are any cubes defined and available on your system, they will be listed on the OLAP Cube tab of the Choose Data Source dialog box. Select the one you want to use and proceed as usual. Using OLAP data, which are sometimes called *multidimensional data*, is covered in detail in Part 7.

Creating a PivotTable Report from Data in an Access Database

One of the beauties of Excel's PivotTable reports is that they are not limited to using data located in a workbook. In fact, it is fairly common to have your data in a database instead. Depending on the configuration of your system and the database drivers installed, you can access data in a wide variety of database formats. In this tip I will show you how to create a PivotTable report based on data in a Microsoft Access database. While some of the details will be different for other database formats, the general principles will be the same.

For this tip I will use the Northwind database. This is a sample database that is installed as part of most Microsoft Office installations. Its file name is Northwind.mdb and it is typically located in the `Samples` folder under the Microsoft Office installation in `\Program Files`. If you are not able to find it, you can use the Windows search feature to determine its location. (If you cannot find the file, it may not have been installed. You can get it from your Office installation CD and copy it to your hard disk.)

Before creating a PivotTable based on external data, be sure that you know which element in the external database you need. Typically the external database will contain a variety of tables and queries and all of these will be available to you. For this demonstration I will use a query named Product Sales for 1997 that is defined in the Northwind database. This query is shown in Access in Figure 2-12. Note that you do not have to have Access open to create the PivotTable.

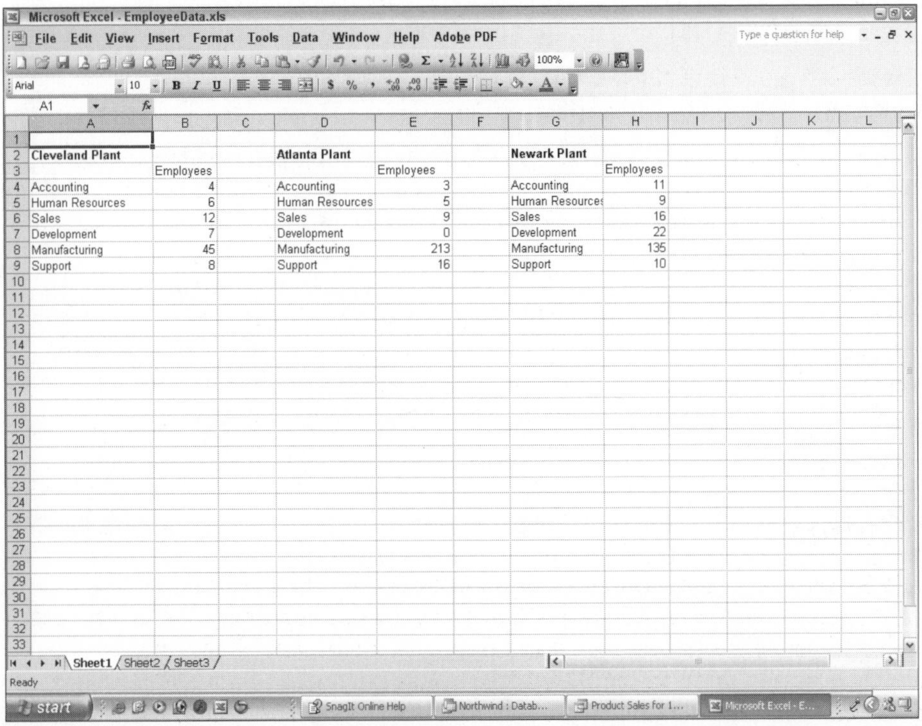

Figure 2-12: The PivotTable will be based on the Northwind database query named Product Sales for 1997.

Part II

After you have Excel open with a blank worksheet displayed, here are the steps to follow:

1. Select Data ➪ PivotTable and PivotChart Report

2. Select External Data Source.

3. Click Next.

4. In the next dialog box click the Get Data button to display the Choose Data Source dialog box.

5. On the Databases tab, be sure the Use the Query Wizard option is checked. Then click the MS Access Database entry. (See Figure 2-13.)

6. Click OK to display the Select Database dialog box. (See Figure 2-14.)

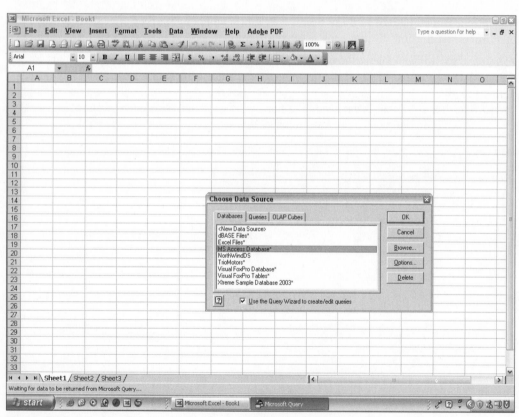

Figure 2-13: Selecting MS Access Database in the Databases tab.

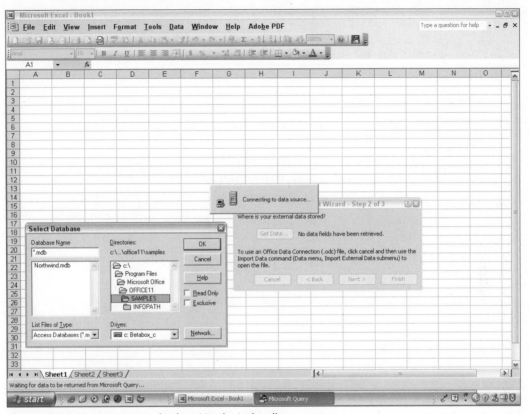

Figure 2-14: Navigate to and select Northwind.mdb.

7. Locate and select the file `Northwind.mdb`; then click OK to display the Query Wizard — Choose Columns dialog box. (See Figure 2-15.)

8. In the Available Tables and Columns list, scroll down until you find Product Sales for 1997.

9. Click the + sign next to Product Sales for 1997 to expand the list to show the available columns. There will be four of them: CategoryName, ProductName, ProductSales, ShippedQuarter.

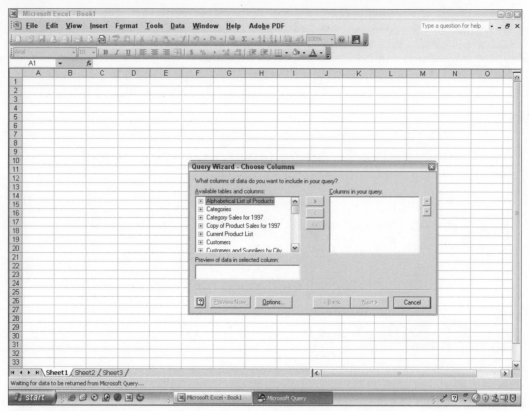

Figure 2-15: The Query Wizard displays the items available in the database.

10. Click CategoryName and then click the > button to move the column name to the field labeled Columns in your query.

11. Repeat to move the other three columns to Columns in your query. At this point the Query Wizard will look as shown in Figure 2-16.

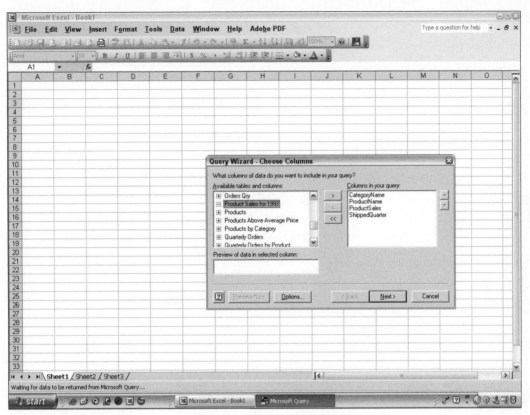

Figure 2-16: After selecting the columns for the PivotTable report.

12. Click Next three times to move through the other wizard steps (you do not need to make changes in these steps so you can accept the defaults). On the final wizard step be sure that the Return Data to Microsoft Office Excel option is selected (Figure 2-17) and then click Finish to return to Step 2 of the Wizard.

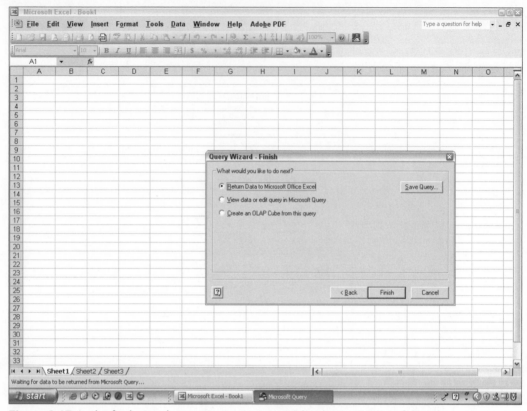

Figure 2-17: In the final wizard step you want to return the data to Microsoft Excel.

13. Click the Next button to proceed to Step 3 of the Wizard.

14. Specify that the PivotTable be placed in cell A1 of the current worksheet.

15. Click Finish to create the blank PivotTable report

The blank report that you created is shown in Figure 2-18.

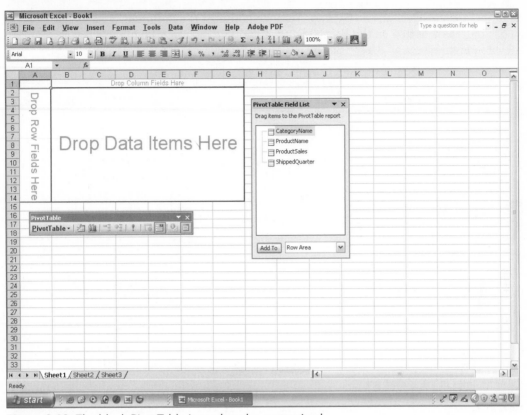

Figure 2-18: The blank PivotTable is ready to be customized.

The four columns that were present in the Access query are listed in the Field List. Next you will drag these field names to the blank PivotTable to achieve the data display you want. Because there are four columns, you have several ways to display these data. Follow these steps to create a PivotTable that displays total sales by category for each quarter:

1. Drag the CategoryName field name and drop it on the field marked Drop Row Fields Here.

2. Drag the ShippedQuarter field name and drop it on the field marked Drop Column Fields Here.

3. Drag the ProductSales field name and drop it on the field marked Drop Data Items Here.

Save Your Files!

When you complete this and other exercises be sure to save all your files. Some of them will be used in later exercises.

As a final touch, select all the data and total cells (B3:F11) and format them as currency by clicking the $ button on the Formatting toolbar. The resulting PivotTable report is shown in Figure 2-19.

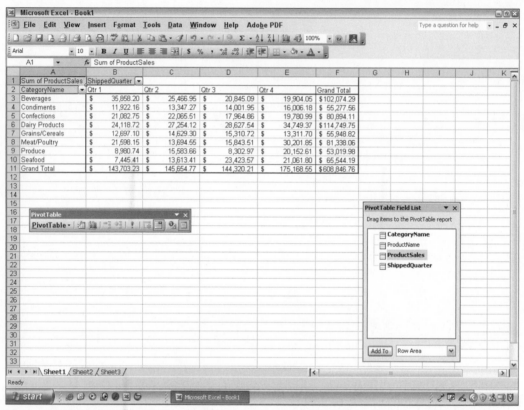

Figure 2-19: The final PivotTable after you have dropped fields and applied basic formatting.

Accessing External Data

Many kinds of external data are protected against unauthorized access. You may need a user name and a password to access the data. If this is the case, you will be prompted for this information during the process.

Using Other External Data Sources

Excel provides you with tremendous power when it comes to accessing data. In some situations the data you want to use in your PivotTable report are located outside Excel but must be imported before you can use them. A detailed explanation of all the ways Excel can import data is beyond the scope of this book. Briefly, some of the options are:

- Define a Web Query that imports data from a Web page (Select Data ➪ Import External Data ➪ New Web Query).

- Define a query that imports data from a database (Select Data ➪ Import External Data ➪ New Web Query).

- Office Data Connection and Query files (Select Data ➪ Import External Data ➪ Import Data).

- Open an XML data file.

While the details of these various data-importing methods vary, the end result is the same: the data will be present in your workbook as a list. For the purposes of creating a PivotTable report you can treat the data like any other Excel list, as was covered earlier. The fact that the data were imported is not relevant at this point.

Using Multiple Consolidation Ranges

The third option in Step 1 of the PivotTable Wizard for the location of the data is Multiple Consolidation Ranges. This is a fancy-sounding name for a simple idea — that your data are located in two or more separate lists in Excel. The lists can be in the same workbook or different workbooks. Each list must have the same format, meaning that the column labels in the first row and the row labels in the first column must be the same in all lists. If the individual lists contain total rows and/or columns, these must not be included when you build the PivotTable report. Figure 2-20 shows an example of data in multiple ranges that can be consolidated into a PivotTable report.

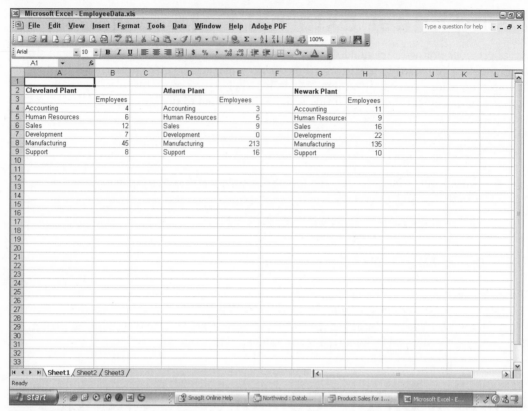

Figure 2-20: Data in multiple ranges.

When you select Multiple Consolidation Ranges in Step 1 of the PivotTable Wizard and click Next, you are presented with two options in the next step, as shown in Figure 2-21.

You have the following options:

- **Create a single page field for me** — Creates one page field with an item for each source range plus an item that consolidates all the ranges.

- **I will create the page field** — Enables you to create your own page fields, up to a maximum of four, with each page consolidating different aspects of the data.

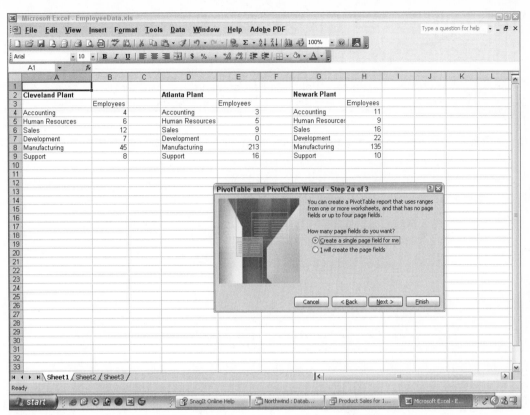

Figure 2-21: Creating a PivotTable report based on multiple consolidation ranges.

Basically, creating multiple page fields gives you greater data-filtering capabilities. (The differences between these two options will become apparent when you learn more.) In the following two sections I will explain the procedures for creating single- and multiple-page field PivotTable reports from multiple consolidation ranges. The details of using this kind of PivotTable will be covered in later parts.

Using Page Fields

Page fields are available in any PivotTable report, not just those based on multiple consolidation ranges. They serve the same purpose: permitting you to filter the entire report based on data values in the page fields. You must create page fields manually in other situations by dragging them from the field list to the Drop Page Fields Here area of the PivotTable.

Letting Excel Create a Single Page Field

When you opt to create a single page field, the next step of the wizard looks like Figure 2-22. You use this dialog box to select the multiple ranges that will be used for the PivotTable report.

To specify the ranges to use, follow these procedures:

- To specify each range, enter its address or assigned range name in the Range box, then click Add. You can also use the Select button to specify a range in any open workbook.

- To specify a range in a workbook that is not open, click the Browse button to locate the workbook file and then follow the on-screen prompts.

- To remove a range, select it in the list and click Delete.

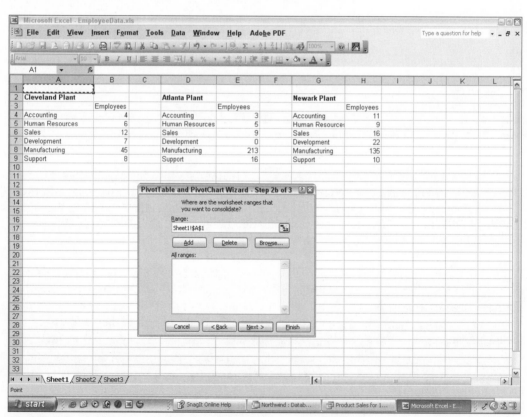

Figure 2-22: Specifying the ranges to be used in a single-page-field PivotTable report.

When you have specified all the ranges, click the Next button to go to the final wizard step, in which you specify where to place the PivotTable report. When you finish the wizard, the report is created, as shown in Figure 2-23. (This PivotTable is based on the data shown earlier in Figure 2-22.)

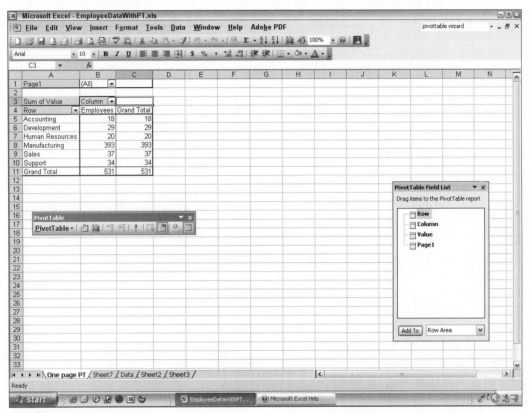

Figure 2-23: A PivotTable report created from the multiple consolidation ranges shown in Figure 2-22.

You should notice a couple of differences between this PivotTable report and those created on the basis of a single data range. First of all, the report is created automatically; you do not have to drag items from the field list to the report to define it. Second, there is a drop-down arrow next to the Page1 label that enables you to select which of the data ranges to include in the report. (You'll see how this works later in the tip.)

You may also wonder about the Grand Total column in the report. Is it really necessary? In this example it is not because the data have only one column, but Excel includes such totals in PivotTable reports by default. In Part 3 you will learn how to remove unneeded report elements such as this.

Creating Your Own Page Fields

Creating a PivotTable report with multiple pages is a source of confusion for some Excel users. To be honest, it *is* a bit confusing! This is partly because of what I consider a bad choice of terminology by Microsoft. When people hear the word *page* they naturally think that a PivotTable report with more than one page field will display multiple pages, but that's not how it works. A page field is a way to filter the PivotTable — in other words, to specify which of the consolidation ranges are summarized in the report. In the process of defining a PivotTable with multiple page fields, you will specify the following:

- How many page fields there will be (zero to four).
- Which data range(s) are associated with each page field.
- Descriptive names for the fields.

If you select zero page fields, the resulting PivotTable report will lack any page-field filtering abilities. This type of report is actually simpler than the standard single-page field report that you learned how to create in the previous section. It's appropriate, however, when you do not need or want an extra level of filtering capability in the PivotTable.

If you select one page field, the resulting PivotTable will be almost identical to the standard single-page field report. You will have a few more customization options, such as the option to assign names to fields, but the filtering capabilities of the final PivotTable will be essentially the same.

It's when you create two or more page fields that things get interesting. This will become clearer as you gain experience and after you go through the tip later in this part. The following steps are involved:

1. When you specify, in Step 2a of the wizard, that you will create the page fields, the next wizard step looks like Figure 2-24.

    The top part of this dialog box is used to select the data ranges, as you learned before. You can perform one of the following actions:

    - Type a range address or range name in the Range field.
    - Use the Select button to select a range with the mouse.
    - Click the Browse button to locate another workbook that contains a data range.
    - Click the Add button to add the defined range to the All Ranges list.

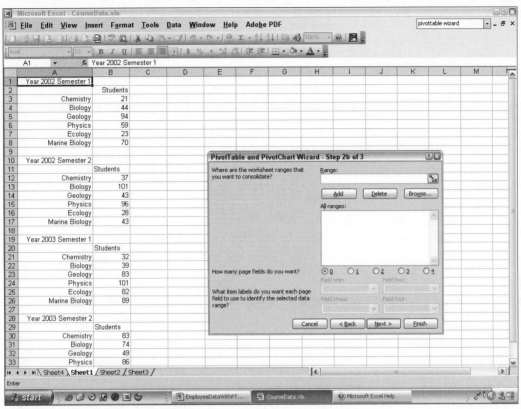

Figure 2-24: Creating a PivotTable and creating your own page fields.

2. So far this is pretty much the same process as defining the ranges when you are letting Excel create a single-page field, as described in the previous section. It's in the lower part of the dialog box that things get more interesting. First of all, you must select how many page fields you want. If you select 0, there is nothing more to do and you can click Next to proceed to the next step of the wizard.

3. If you select another value, the corresponding number of text boxes become active. For example, if you click the 2 option, the text boxes Field one and Field two become active, as shown in Figure 2-25.

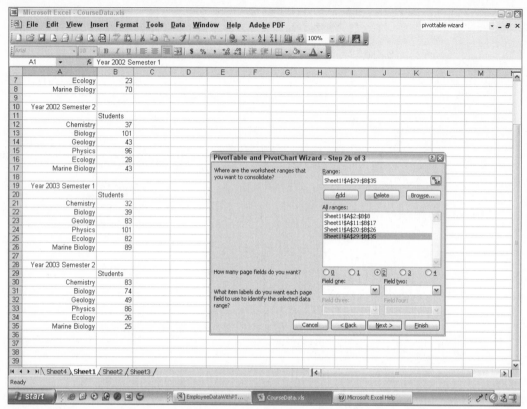

Figure 2-25: One Field box will become available for each page field you are creating.

4. Your next steps will depend on the kind of filtering you want to make available in the PivotTable. Your objective is to associate specific data ranges with specific fields and assign descriptive names to them. Here's how:

   a. In the All Fields list, select a range to be included in a filter.

   b. In the Field one box, type a descriptive name for this filter. If a name has already been assigned to a range and you want to assign it to this range as well, you can select it from the drop-down list.

   c. If you are using more than one field, enter a name for this filter in the Field two, Field three, and Field four boxes.

   d. Return to Step 1 to add another range.

   e. Repeat until all desired filters have been defined.

   f. Click Next to go to the final step of the wizard.

When the final PivotTable report is created, you will see that there is one page field item at the top of the report for each page field that you specified in the wizard (Figure 2-26). Each of these has a drop-down list that enables you to access the filters associated with that field. The judicious use of page fields can be a big help in filtering large data sets to make the PivotTable more understandable.

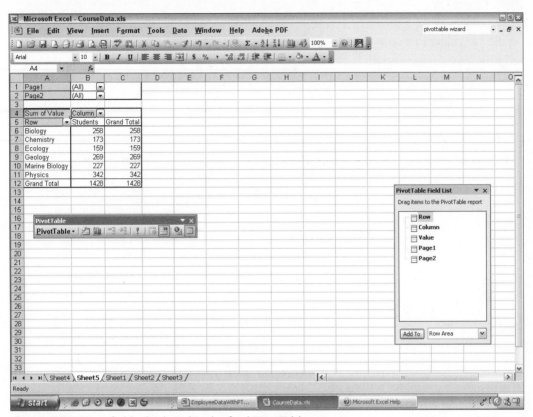

Figure 2-26: Page fields displayed in the final PivotTable report.

Creating a Single-Page Field PivotTable Report from Multiple Consolidation Ranges

To work through this project, you need to open the workbook EmployeeData.xls, which contains the raw data. (These data were shown in Figure 2-12.) You can see that there are three lists, each containing data from a specific plant. Each list contains the number of employees in each of several departments. To create a PivotTable based on these three data ranges, follow these steps:

1. Select Data ⇨ PivotTable and Pivot Chart Report to start the PivotTable and Pivot Chart Wizard.

2. In Step 1 of the wizard, select the Multiple Consolidation Ranges option.

3. Click Next to display Step 2a of the Wizard.

4. In this dialog box, make sure the Create a Single-Page Field option is selected.

5. Click Next to display Step 2b of the wizard.

6. Click the Select button at the right end of the Range field.

7. Drag over cells A3:B9 in the worksheet.

8. Click the Select button again.

9. Click the Add button to add the range to the All ranges list.

10. Repeat Steps 5 though 8 to select and add the ranges D3:D9 and G3:G9 to the All ranges list. At this point the dialog box should look like Figure 2-27.

11. Click Next to go to the final wizard step.

12. Select the New Worksheet option.

13. Click Finish.

The completed PivotTable is shown in Figure 2-28.

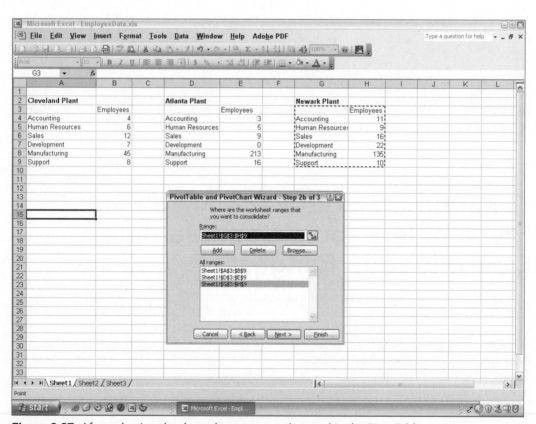

Figure 2-27: After selecting the three data ranges to be used in the PivotTable.

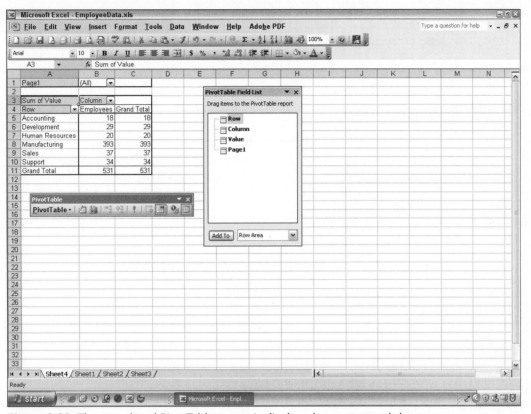

Figure 2-28: The completed PivotTable report is displayed on a new worksheet.

The Column label has an adjacent drop-down arrow that you can use to select which column(s) to display. Since the data used in this PivotTable have only one column, this feature isn't useful, but in reports that contain multiple columns, it would be. Note also that the Row label has a drop-down arrow that lets you select which rows to include. These are features that you have seen in other PivotTable reports.

What's new is the drop-down arrow next to the Page1 label. This enables you to select which of the data ranges to include, as shown in Figure 2-29. The entries Item1, Item2, and Item3 refer to the three data ranges on which the PivotTable is based. You can select all the ranges or any single range to specify which data are summarized in the PivotTable report.

I suggest that you experiment with the filters in this PivotTable report to get a feel for how they work. Filters are an important aspect of PivotTables and you need to understand them to get the most out of PivotTables.

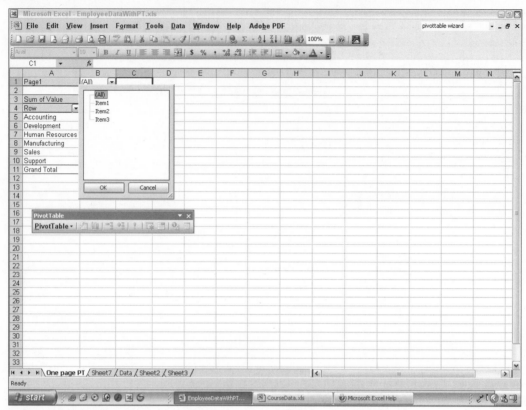

Figure 2-29: Selecting which data ranges to include in the PivotTable report.

Creating a Multiple-Page Field PivotTable Report from Multiple Consolidation Ranges

This tip demonstrates the steps involved in creating a PivotTable from multiple consolidation ranges using multiple page fields. As I discussed earlier in this part, the concept of page fields is difficult for most Excel users to grasp. Seeing them in action is the best way to get a handle on them.

The data for this tip are shown in Figure 2-30. There are four lists, each showing the number of students enrolled in a particular course for a specific year and semester. You'll find this data in CourseData.xls, which you will need to open to follow along.

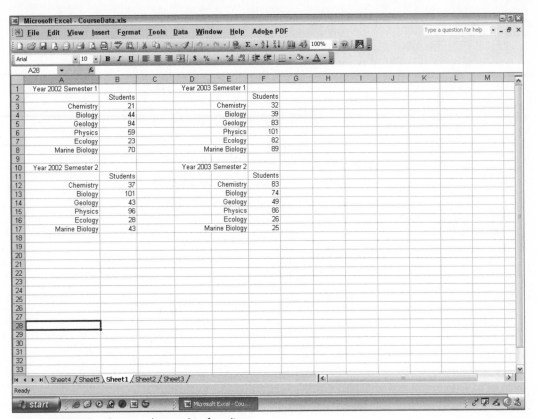

Figure 2-30: The data are located in four lists.

1. To begin, select Data ⇨ PivotTable and Pivot Chart Wizard.

2. In the first wizard step, select the Multiple Consolidation Ranges option.

3. Click Next.

4. In the next dialog box, select the I Will Create the Page Fields option.

5. Click Next to display the next step.

6. In the Range box enter the range address A2:B8, or use the Select button to select the range.

7. Click the Add button to add the range to the All ranges list.

8. Repeat Steps 6 and 7 three times to add the other three data ranges to the All ranges list. At this point the dialog box should look like the one in Figure 2-31.

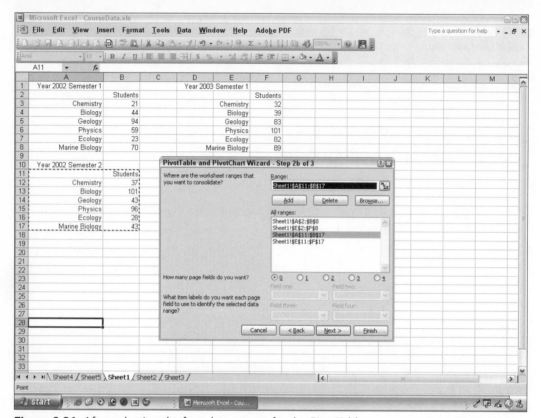

Figure 2-31: After selecting the four data ranges for the PivotTable.

9. Click the 2 option to specify two page fields. You'll see that the Field One and Field Two boxes become available.

At this point it will be wise to pause and do a little planning. How do you want the page fields to work? In other words, how do you want to be able to filter the data? Look at the data and you will see that two years are represented, 2002 and 2003, and two semesters, Semester 1 and Semester 2. It would be ideal to be able to filter on year to show data either from both years or from only one year, and also to filter on semester to show data either from both semesters or from a single one. That's the plan you will follow in the remaining steps.

1. In the All Ranges list select the first range, A2:B8. This range contains data from Year 2002, Semester 1.

2. Enter **Year 2002** in the Field one box.

3. Enter **Semester 1** in the Field two box.

4. Select E2:F8 in the All ranges list. This range contains data from Year 2003, Semester 1.

5. Enter **Year 2003** in the Field one box.

6. Because you already used it, you can simply select Semester 1 from the drop-down list under Field two.

7. Select the range A11:B17. This contains data for Year 2002 and Semester 2.

8. Select Year 2002 from the drop-down list under Field one.

9. Enter **Semester 2** in the Field two box.

10. Select E11:F17 as the final range.

11. Select Year 2003 in the Field one box.

12. Select Semester 2 in the Field two box.

Now you can click Next and complete the wizard, placing the PivotTable on a new worksheet. The result is shown in Figure 2-32.

When you examine this PivotTable report you will see that the design does just what you wanted. If you drop down Page1 you have three choices: All, Year 2002, and Year 2003. Likewise, if you drop down Page2 you have the choices All, Semester 1, and Semester 2. Make your selections to filter the PivotTable as needed.

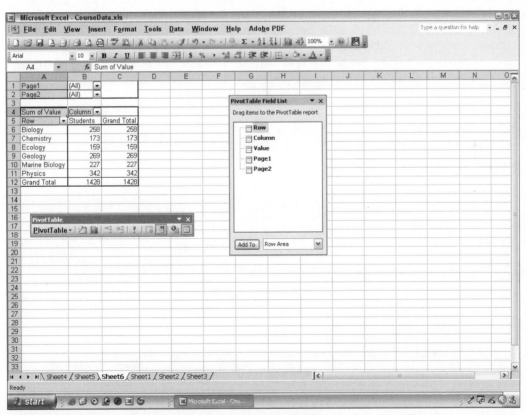

Figure 2-32: The completed PivotTable has two page fields with drop-down lists.

As a final task, get rid of the Grand Total column, which is really not needed. All you need to do is right-click the column heading and select Hide from the pop-up menu. The column vanishes and your PivotTable report is complete.

Basing a PivotTable on Another PivotTable Report

A final option for creating a PivotTable report is to base it on an existing PivotTable or PivotChart. In other words, the summary data in the existing PivotTable report become the raw data for the second report.

To create a PivotTable based on another PivotTable, select the Another PivotTable or PivotChart Report option in Step 1 of the PivotTable and PivotChart Wizard. (This option will be available only if the workbook contains another PivotTable.) When you click Next, the second wizard step displays a list of all available PivotTables and PivotCharts. Simply select the desired source and proceed as usual.

Why base one PivotTable on another? In many cases the second PivotTable will, at least initially, look exactly like the source PivotTable. But by customizing the second PivotTable you can create two different views of the same data, which is useful in some situations. For example, the first PivotTable may summarize the original data but still be a rather complex table. By creating a second PivotTable that uses the first one for its data you could create a more condensed summary that is easier to read.

Creating a PivotTable with Inner and Outer Row Fields

A PivotTable is not limited to having only a single row field. You can have two or more row fields, permitting the report to display details on different levels of data in the various fields. When you have more than one row field, the one at the top level is called the *outer field* and is displayed at the far left of the PivotTable. Other fields at lower levels are called *inner fields* and are displayed to the right. This tip shows you how to create a PivotTable report with two row fields.

Multiple Column Fields?

You can have inner and outer column fields as well. They work in essentially the same way as the inner and outer row fields described in this section. You cannot have inner and outer page fields.

This tip uses the data in `Clothing Stock.xls`, shown in Figure 2-33. This data gives inventory for various clothing items, organized by size and color.

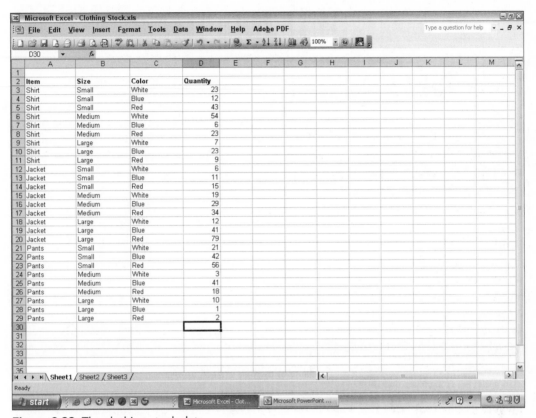

Figure 2-33: The clothing stock data.

Because by now you have a lot of experience using the PivotTable Wizard, I will not detail the steps required to create the initial PivotTable from these data. Go ahead now and create the report, placing it on a new worksheet. The new report is shown in Figure 2-34.

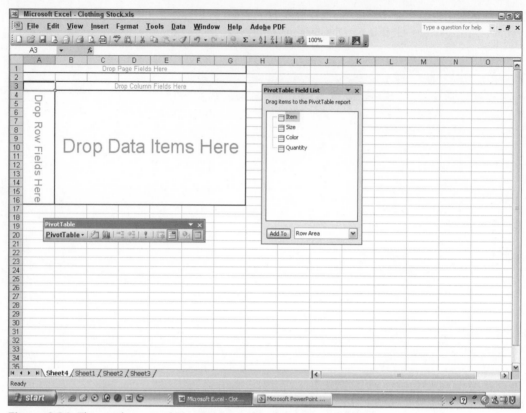

Figure 2-34: The newly created PivotTable waiting for you to add fields.

The next steps are to drag fields to the report as usual. It is here that you will create two row fields.

1. Drag the Color field to the Column area.

2. Drag the Item field to the Row area.

3. Drag the Quantity field to the Data area. At this point the report looks like Figure 2-35, as you would expect.

4. This step creates the multiple row fields. Drag the Size field and drop it in the Row area, being sure to drop it on the right side of this area and not on the left side.

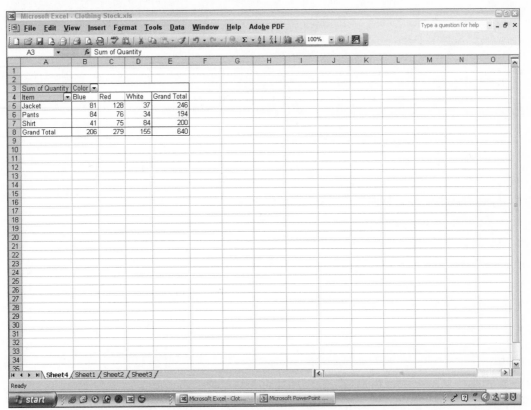

Figure 2-35: The PivotTable after you have added three fields to it.

After you drop the second row field your report will look like Figure 2-36. You can see that there are two row fields, the outer Item field and the inner Size field. With this second row field the data are broken down into more detail, which may be more useful for the kind of analysis you are performing.

There's one more thing that this PivotTable report can illustrate — *pivoting*. As I mentioned in Part 1, the name PivotTables comes from the ability they give you to easily rearrange the fields in the report to provide the data display you need, and from the way they enable you to look at the data from different perspectives. The most common kind of pivoting involves moving a field from one area of the report to another, for example from the Row to the Column area. To do this with the report shown in Figure 2-36, point at the Size button in the report and drag it to the Column area, dropping it directly under the color labels. The result is shown in Figure 2-37. The table has been pivoted and the Size field is now a column field instead of a row field. You can experiment further with this PivotTable, for example by dragging the Color field to the Row area or even to the Page area.

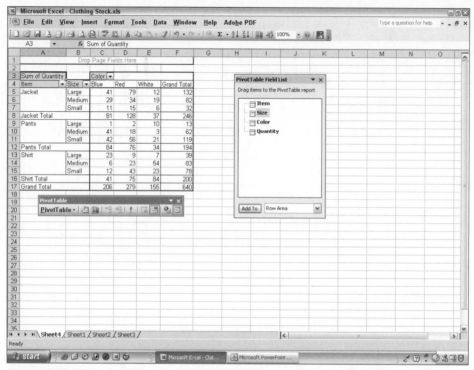

Figure 2-36: After you drop a second field in the Row area the report has inner and outer row fields.

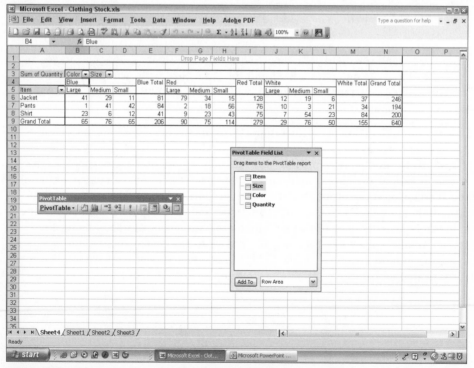

Figure 2-37: After you pivot the report, Size becomes a row field.

Part III

Using PivotTable Tools and Formatting

Excel has some tools — the PivotTable toolbar and the PivotTable menu — that are designed specifically for working with PivotTable reports. You need to understand how to use these tools if you want to use PivotTables efficiently. This chapter also explains some of the options that you can set for PivotTables and the various techniques you can use to format PivotTable reports.

Tips and Where to Find Them

Using the Layout Dialog Box in the PivotTable and PivotChart Wizard

The PivotTable Wizard (officially called the PivotTable and PivotChart Wizard) is used for the creation of all PivotTables. (You learned how to use it in previous parts, and I will not be repeating that basic information here.) However, this wizard has some more advanced features that I have not touched on. You can always create a PivotTable without using these features, but as you gain more experience, you may want to use them to give you additional control over the layout and appearance of the report. You can get to these features in Step 3 of the wizard by clicking the Layout or Options button, as shown in Figure 3-1.

Layout and Option buttons

Figure 3-1: The third step of the PivotTable Wizard lets you access Layout and Option settings.

When you click the Layout button in Step 3 of the wizard, the Layout dialog box will be displayed. (See Figure 3-2.) You have already selected your data range at this point, so the contents of this dialog box will reflect the structure and headings of your data.

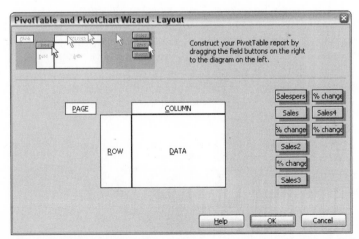

Figure 3-2: You use the Layout dialog box to define the structure of your PivotTable report.

Part III

The example shown in the figure is based on the sporting-goods store data you used in Part I. A diagram of the blank PivotTable is shown on the left and the data-column headings are shown on the right. You have probably noticed that this layout is similar to what you see when you create a PivotTable without using the Layout dialog box; you drag field names to the blank PivotTable in the worksheet from the Field List to define the PivotTable. The Layout dialog box is just another means of defining the structure of the PivotTable.

To define the PivotTable layout in the Layout dialog box, complete these steps:

1. To define one or more row fields, drag the field name(s) and drop them on the Row area.

2. To define one or more column fields, drag the field name(s) and drop them on the Column area.

3. To specify the data that will be summarized, drop the corresponding field in the Data area.

4. To define one or more page fields for filtering the report, drop the field name(s) on the Page box.

If you make an error, remove a field from the PivotTable by dragging it off the PivotTable diagram.

When you finish the PivotTable layout, click the OK button to return to Step 3 of the wizard. Complete the PivotTable by specifying where it should be placed, then click Finish.

In some situations, using the Layout dialog box is equivalent to laying out the PivotTable report in the worksheet after you finish the wizard. If your PivotTable is based on a large amount of external data, however, using the Layout dialog box is preferable, as on-sheet layout can be slow and time-consuming.

PivotTable Options

When you click the Options button in Step 3 of the PivotTable Wizard, Excel displays the PivotTable Options dialog box. You can also display this dialog box after the PivotTable has been created by selecting Table Options from the PivotTable menu. Some of the option settings do not make sense if the PivotTable has not been created. You can set some options at this point, while using the wizard to create the PivotTable, but you'll often set or change them later, after the PivotTable exists. I cover PivotTable options later in this part.

Note, however, that at the top of the Options dialog box is a box in which you can enter a name for the PivotTable. Excel suggests a default name such as PivotTable1, but it's always a good idea to assign a more meaningful name. (This is particularly true when your workbook contains more than one PivotTable.) As you'll learn in Part X, you use this name to refer to the PivotTable in VBA code.

Understanding the PivotTable Toolbar

The PivotTable toolbar, shown in Figure 3-3, provides you with quick access to the most important PivotTable-related commands. It is displayed automatically when you create a PivotTable, and by default floats in the worksheet. It works like any other Excel toolbar, so you can:

- Move it to any desired location by dragging the title bar.

- Dock it at the top of the Excel screen with the other toolbars by dragging it there.

- Grab its border with the mouse and drag it into a different shape.

- Hover the mouse over a button to see a ToolTip describing the button's function.

- Hide it or display it by selecting View ⇨ Toolbars and clicking the toolbar name.

Figure 3-3: The PivotTable toolbar provides easy access to frequently used commands.

I will not describe the function of each toolbar button here; you'll learn about them throughout the book. Most of the commands on the toolbar are also available on the PivotTable menu or on the context menus. Some buttons on this toolbar are disabled at times, depending on the state of the PivotTable and what you are doing.

Customizing the PivotTable Toolbar

You can also customize the PivotTable toolbar by specifying which buttons to display. You can display only those buttons you use frequently to keep the toolbar size small. Or you can display all the buttons so they are available whenever you need them. To customize the PivotTable toolbar, do the following:

1. Click the down arrow near the right end of the toolbar's title bar.

2. Click Add or Remove Buttons.

3. Click PivotTable. Excel will display a list of the available buttons, as shown in Figure 3-4.

4. Check or uncheck individual buttons by clicking their names.

5. When finished, click anywhere outside the button list.

To return the toolbar to its initial default assortment of buttons, click the Reset Toolbar item.

Selected buttons are checked

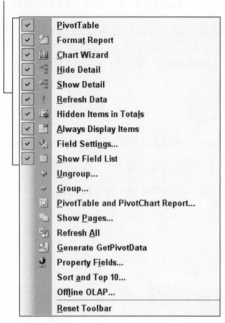

Figure 3-4: You can customize the PivotTable toolbar by adding and removing buttons.

Using the PivotTable Menu

An important element on the PivotTable toolbar is the PivotTable menu. You display this menu by clicking the toolbar button labeled PivotTable, as shown in Figure 3-5.

Figure 3-5: Accessing the PivotTable menu from the PivotTable toolbar.

Use the Context Menus

In PivotTable reports — and PivotCharts as well — many elements in Excel display *context* (also known as *pop-up*) menus when right-clicked. The context menu provides quick access to some frequently used commands. These commands duplicate some of those found on the PivotTable toolbar and the PivotTable menu. The context menu is just another way to get at them that some people prefer.

Some commands on this menu may be grayed out at certain times. Excel does a good job of enabling only those commands that make sense at the moment. You'll learn about these commands as you explore PivotTables and PivotCharts in more detail. Some of the commands duplicate buttons on the toolbar.

Setting PivotTable Options

The PivotTable Options dialog box (shown in Figure 3-6) gives you control over various aspects of a PivotTable.

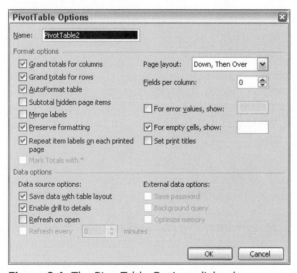

Figure 3-6: The PivotTable Options dialog box.

You can display this dialog box in two ways:

- Before the PivotTable is created, by clicking the Options button in Step 3 of the PivotTable Wizard.
- After the PivotTable is created, by selecting Table Options from the PivotTable menu.

NOTE

The dialog box is divided into two sections, Format Options and Data Options. Some of the options may not make sense right now because I have not yet covered the aspect of PivotTables to which they apply. Don't worry. I will mention option settings again as needed in later chapters.

In the next sections you look at the two parts of the dialog box in turn.

Format Options

The Format Options section is located in the top part of the dialog box. The settings available here enable you to control certain aspects of the PivotTable formatting and layout.

GRAND TOTALS

These two options control whether a total is displayed at the right of each row and at the bottom of each column. Excel's default is to include both, but for some kinds of data, totals are not appropriate in either or both of these locations.

AUTOFORMAT TABLE

If you have applied an autoformat to the PivotTable (covered elsewhere in this part), deselecting this option removes the autoformat from the table and returns the table to its original default formatting. You can also return a PivotTable to its default formatting by clicking the Format Report button on the PivotTable toolbar and then selecting PivotTable Classic.

SUBTOTAL HIDDEN PAGE ITEMS

Depending on your source data and the PivotTable layout, you may have the option to temporarily hide certain items in the report. When you have hidden one or more page fields, this option determines whether the data for the hidden fields are included in the calculation of subtotals. You'll learn more about hiding PivotTable elements in Part V.

MERGE LABELS

In some PivotTables, the same label, such as Quarter or Month, is repeated in the outer row or column cells. If you select this option, the repeated labels will be merged into a single label that spans the columns or months. In my experience this option does not work as it should. It is probably an Excel bug and if you cannot get it to work, you should not spend a lot of time trying.

Removing All Formatting from a PivotTable Report

You can remove all formatting from a PivotTable report by clicking the Format Report button on the PivotTable toolbar and then selecting None.

Cell Borders and Conditional Formatting

You can apply cell borders and conditional formatting to a PivotTable report, but they will not be preserved when the table is refreshed or the layout is changed, regardless of the setting of the Preserve Formatting Option.

PRESERVE FORMATTING

If this option is selected, the PivotTable formatting will be preserved if the table is refreshed or its layout is modified. This applies to cell formatting such as font and color; formats that are part of an autoformat are controlled by the AutoFormat Table option.

REPEAT ITEM LABELS ON EACH PRINTED PAGE

If a PivotTable has more than one row field, selecting this option tells Excel to repeat the outer row labels on the second and subsequent pages when the report is printed. This is not the same as printing regular row and column labels on each page, which you can do with the Set Print Titles option (explained later in this part).

MARK TOTALS WITH *

This option does not do what you expect, mark totals in the PivotTable with an asterisk. Rather it tells Excel that subtotals and grand totals should include hidden items as well as visible items.

PAGE LAYOUT

For reports more than one page wide and more than one page tall, this option controls how the individual pages are printed. Your options are:

- **Down then over** — Pages in column 1 are printed top to bottom, then pages in column 2, and so on.

- **Over then down** — Pages in row 1 are printed left to right, then pages in row 2, and so on.

These two options are illustrated in Figure 3-7.

FIELDS PER COLUMN

When a PivotTable report has multiple page fields, this option determines how many fields are shown in each column of the report.

FOR ERROR VALUES SHOW

If you want PivotTable cells that contain errors to display something other than Excel's usual error messages, select this option and enter the desired display text in the adjacent box. To have error cells display blank, select this option and leave the adjacent box empty.

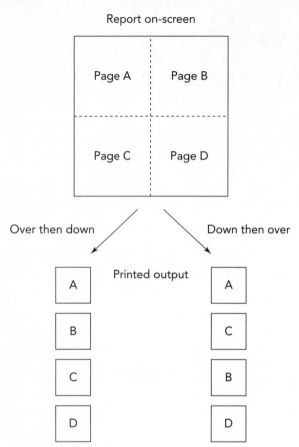

Figure 3-7: The difference between the Over then down and Down then over options for page layout.

For Empty Cells Show
If you want empty cells to display specific text rather than simply displaying as empty, select this option and enter the text in the adjacent box.

Set Print Titles
When this option is selected, row and column labels are repeated on each page of a multipage printed report.

Data Options

The data options are grouped in the lower section of the PivotTable Options dialog box. The External Data options and the Refresh Every option will not be available unless the PivotTable is linked to an external data source.

SAVE DATA WITH TABLE LAYOUT

If this option is selected, Excel will save a PivotTable's data (not the source data) as part of the table. Otherwise, the data are not saved and the table will have to be regenerated the next time the file is opened.

ENABLE DRILL TO DETAILS

Drilling for details is a PivotTable feature that lets you double-click a data cell to display the details that underlie that number in a new worksheet. The Enable Drill to Details option (covered in greater depth in Part IV) enables you to turn this feature on or off for a PivotTable report.

REFRESH ON OPEN

If this option is selected, the PivotTable refreshes automatically when the workbook is opened.

REFRESH EVERY ... MINUTES

You can set this option to automatically refresh external data periodically whenever the workbook is open.

SAVE PASSWORD

If the external data source requires a password, select this option to save the password with the workbook so you do not have to enter it repeatedly.

BACKGROUND QUERY

When this option is selected, the process of refreshing the PivotTable from external data is done in the background so you can continue working in Excel while the query is in progress.

OPTIMIZE MEMORY

Selecting this option causes Excel to make the best use of available memory when retrieving external data. It reduces speed somewhat but is a possible fix if you are working with large amounts of external data and are receiving "Out of Memory" error messages.

Formatting PivotTables

In most ways, a PivotTable is like any other data in Excel and you can use the same formatting techniques to get your report looking the way you want it. Formatting PivotTables does involve some special considerations, however.

Autoformatting a PivotTable

Excel has a terrific autoformat command for applying predefined formats to tables. Because a PivotTable report is in fact a table, you can use this feature to format your reports. It's a simple matter of clicking the Format Report button on the PivotTable toolbar or selecting Format Report from the PivotTable menu. Excel displays the AutoFormat dialog box, shown in Figure 3-8. Scroll through the list of sample formats and click the desired one, then click OK.

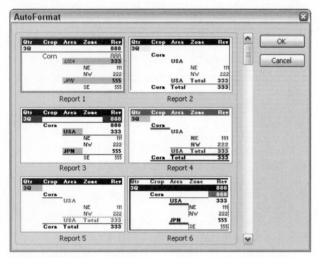

Figure 3-8: Applying an AutoFormat to a PivotTable report.

When using autoformats it's important to understand the difference between an indented format and a non-indented format. In the AutoFormat dialog box the sample formats labeled Report 1 through Report 10 are indented, while those labeled Table 1 through Table 10, as well as PivotTable Classic, are not indented.

The indented formats change the layout of the report so that column fields are moved to the row area. In contrast, the non-indented formats retain the original layout style, in which columns remain as separate columns. Of course, each individual autoformat style applies its own fonts, colors, and backgrounds as well.

The following figures illustrate the difference between indented and non-indented formats. Figure 3-9 shows a PivotTable report with the default PivotTable Classic formatting, a non-indented style.

3	Sum of Titles	Category						
4	Store	Action	Childrens	Classics	Comedy	Drama	Sci-Fi	Grand Total
5	Clarkville	22	203	251	345	172	324	1317
6	Main Street	374	63	203	145	180	324	1289
7	Northgate	45	320	79	225	287	36	992
8	West End	310	220	145	296	369	236	1576
9	Grand Total	751	806	678	1011	1008	920	5174

Figure 3-9: A PivotTable report with the default formatting.

Figure 3-10 shows the same PivotTable with Table 1 style applied. This is another non-indented style.

	A	B	C	D	E	F	G	H
1								
2								
3	Titles	Category ▼						
4	Store ▼	Action	Childrens	Classics	Comedy	Drama	Sci-Fi	Grand Total
5	Clarkville	22	203	251	345	172	324	1317
6	Main Street	374	63	203	145	180	324	1289
7	Northgate	45	320	79	225	287	36	992
8	West End	310	220	145	296	369	236	1576
9	Grand Total	751	806	678	1011	1008	920	5174

Figure 3-10: A PivotTable report with a non-indented style applied.

Finally, Figure 3-11 shows the report with the indented style Report 1 applied.

	A	B	C
3	Category ▼	Store ▼	Titles
4	Action		751
5		Clarkville	22
6		Main Street	374
7		Northgate	45
8		West End	310
9			
10	Childrens		806
11		Clarkville	203
12		Main Street	63
13		Northgate	320
14		West End	220
15			
16	Classics		678
17		Clarkville	251
18		Main Street	203
19		Northgate	79
20		West End	145
21			
22	Comedy		1011
23		Clarkville	345
24		Main Street	145
25		Northgate	225
26		West End	296
27			
28	Drama		1008
29		Clarkville	172
30		Main Street	180
31		Northgate	287
32		West End	369
33			
34	Sci-Fi		920
35		Clarkville	324
36		Main Street	324
37		Northgate	36
38		West End	236
39			
40	Grand Total		5174

Figure 3-11: A PivotTable report with an indented style applied.

Part III

Both indented and non-indented styles display the same information. Which one is better for your report depends on the data and your preferences. The indented style can be useful for a report that is too wide for the page when formatted with a non-indented style.

You can apply a different autostyle to a PivotTable as many times as you like. Note that if you have applied an indented style and then apply the PivotTable Classic style, the report will remain indented, although other aspects of formatting, such as lines between the cells, will change to the Classic style. To remove all formatting, select the None autoformat option.

Remember that the AutoFormat Table option in the PivotTable Options dialog box affects auto-formatting as well (select Table Options from the PivotTable menu to display this dialog box). If this option is selected, the table will retain any applied autoformatting when it is refreshed or its layout is changed. If this option is not selected, the autoformatting will be lost. When you apply an autoformat to a PivotTable report, this option is automatically turned on.

Changing the Number Format

Excel offers a wide variety of number formats suitable for any imaginable data, such as currency formats, percent formats, time-and-date formats, and so on. The normal proce-dure for assigning these formats is to select the cell(s) you want to format, display the Format Cells dialog box, and then select the desired format on the Number tab.

Though you can use this method with PivotTable reports, it is not advisable. For some reports it is likely to be very inconvenient. In more complex reports, the data area will con-tain different kinds of data — for example, money amounts and percentages. An example of such a report, with appropriate number formats already applied, is shown in Figure 3-12. You would not be able to select the entire data area of the PivotTable report and apply a single number format.

3	Salesperson ▼	Data ▼	Total
4	A. Kawasaki	Sum of Sales	$ 158,833
5		Average of % change	-23%
6	A. Smith	Sum of Sales	$ 125,502
7		Average of % change	-18%
8	D. Chen	Sum of Sales	$ 199,551
9		Average of % change	23%
10	F. Baxter	Sum of Sales	$ 165,228
11		Average of % change	-22%
12	G. Rubenstein	Sum of Sales	$ 107,299
13		Average of % change	4%
14	J.W. Alexander	Sum of Sales	$ 191,078
15		Average of % change	-35%
16	L. Price	Sum of Sales	$ 167,714
17		Average of % change	-46%
18	W. Gomez	Sum of Sales	$ 198,454
19		Average of % change	11%
20	Total Sum of Sales		$1,313,659
21	Total Average of % change		-13%

Dollar amounts

Percentage values

Figure 3-12: A PivotTable report can contain different kinds of data in the data area.

Tables with Multiple Data Items

We have not yet covered how to create PivotTable reports that contain multiple data items, as shown in Figure 3-12. You get to that in Part IV. For the present, it is enough for you to know that they are possible and how to format them.

Other Field Settings

You can see that the Field Settings dialog box has a lot more to it than just options for changing the number format. I will cover these other field settings as needed in this and other parts.

Fortunately, Excel has a better way. In the data area of a PivotTable, each cell is linked to a field. This will, of course, be one of the fields that you dragged to the data area when you were laying out the PivotTable. When you apply a number format to one cell in the PivotTable data area, that format will automatically be applied to all cells linked to the same field. In effect you are formatting the field, not the cell. Here's how:

1. Click any cell that is linked to the field you want to format.

2. Select Field Settings from the PivotTable menu. Excel will display the Field Settings dialog box.

3. Click the Number button. Excel will display the Format Cells dialog box.

4. Select the desired format. If necessary, specify the number of decimal places and any other format options.

5. Click OK twice.

Changing Other Formats

The other formatting elements you can change in a PivotTable include font, background color, cell borders — in essence anything you can change for other parts of a worksheet. There are a few things you should keep in mind when formatting a PivotTable.

First of all, you want to make sure that the formatting you apply is preserved when the PivotTable is refreshed or its layout changes. This requires selecting the Preserve Formatting option in the PivotTable Options dialog box. To display this dialog box, select Table Options from the PivotTable menu.

A second concern is ensuring that the formatting is applied to parts of the PivotTable that are not visible. For example, you may have used a page field to filter the PivotTable to display a subset of the data. Before applying the formatting changes, select (All) in the page-field drop-down list to display all the data.

Finally, you need to use the correct technique to select the part of the PivotTable you want to format. As I have mentioned before, cells in the PivotTable that are linked to the same field are connected, and you can select linked cells simultaneously. To do this, ensure that the mouse cursor changes to a right- or down-pointing arrow before clicking to select a table element.

Once you have selected the desired element(s), use the usual formatting commands on the Formatting toolbar or the Format menu to apply the desired formatting.

Part III

Applying Formatting to a PivotTable Report

This tip takes you through the process of formatting a PivotTable report with an autoformat and with cell formats. I will use a PivotTable that you created in Part II from data in an Access database. This PivotTable is shown in Figure 3-13 with the default formatting. You need to open the workbook containing this PivotTable before proceeding.

	A	B	C	D	E	F
1	Sum of ProductSale	ShippedQuarter				
2	CategoryName	Qtr 1	Qtr 2	Qtr 3	Qtr 4	Grand Total
3	Beverages	$ 35,858.20	$ 25,466.95	$ 20,845.09	$ 19,904.05	$102,074.29
4	Condiments	$ 11,922.16	$ 13,347.27	$ 14,001.95	$ 16,006.18	$ 55,277.56
5	Confections	$ 21,082.75	$ 22,065.51	$ 17,964.86	$ 19,780.99	$ 80,894.11
6	Dairy Products	$ 24,118.72	$ 27,254.12	$ 28,627.54	$ 34,749.37	$114,749.75
7	Grains/Cereals	$ 12,697.10	$ 14,629.30	$ 15,310.72	$ 13,311.70	$ 55,948.82
8	Meat/Poultry	$ 21,598.15	$ 13,694.55	$ 15,843.51	$ 30,201.85	$ 81,338.06
9	Produce	$ 8,980.74	$ 15,583.66	$ 8,302.97	$ 20,152.61	$ 53,019.98
10	Seafood	$ 7,445.41	$ 13,613.41	$ 23,423.57	$ 21,061.80	$ 65,544.19
11	Grand Total	$ 143,703.23	$ 145,654.77	$ 144,320.21	$ 175,168.55	$608,846.76

Figure 3-13: The PivotTable report with its default formatting.

The first step is to ensure that the PivotTable options are set so that the formatting you will apply is preserved. While these options are on by default, is it always a good idea to make sure.

1. Click any cell in the PivotTable to make it active.

2. Open the PivotTable menu and select Table Options to display the PivotTable Options dialog box.

3. Make sure that the AutoFormat Table and Preserve Formatting options are checked.

4. Click OK.

The next step is to apply the autoformatting to the PivotTable:

1. With the PivotTable still active, click the Format Table button on the PivotTable toolbar. Excel will display the AutoFormat dialog box.

2. Scroll down and select the Table 1 format.

3. Click OK.

4. Click anywhere outside the PivotTable to deselect it.

Your PivotTable will now look like Figure 3-14.

	A	B		C		D		E	F
1	ProductSales	ShippedQuarter ▾							
2	CategoryName ▾	Qtr 1		Qtr 2		Qtr 3		Qtr 4	Grand Total
3	Beverages	$ 35,858.20	$	25,466.95	$	20,845.09	$	19,904.05	$102,074.29
4	Condiments	$ 11,922.16	$	13,347.27	$	14,001.95	$	16,006.18	$ 55,277.56
5	Confections	$ 21,082.75	$	22,065.51	$	17,964.86	$	19,780.99	$ 80,894.11
6	Dairy Products	$ 24,118.72	$	27,254.12	$	28,627.54	$	34,749.37	$114,749.75
7	Grains/Cereals	$ 12,697.10	$	14,629.30	$	15,310.72	$	13,311.70	$ 55,948.82
8	Meat/Poultry	$ 21,598.15	$	13,694.55	$	15,843.51	$	30,201.85	$ 81,338.06
9	Produce	$ 8,980.74	$	15,583.66	$	8,302.97	$	20,152.61	$ 53,019.98
10	Seafood	$ 7,445.41	$	13,613.41	$	23,423.57	$	21,061.80	$ 65,544.19
11	Grand Total	$ 143,703.23	$	145,654.77	$	144,320.21	$	175,168.55	$608,846.76

Figure 3-14: The PivotTable after you have applied the autoformat.

So far so good, but suppose you want to emphasize certain parts of the report. For example, you might want to emphasize the Dairy Products row because it has shown a lot of improvement, and you might also want to emphasize the Qtr 4 column because the total sales figure was so good. Here's how:

1. Point the mouse at the left end of the Dairy Products row, right about where the *D* in *Dairy* is. The mouse cursor will change to a right-pointing arrow (Figure 3-15).

Selection arrow

	A	B	
1	ProductSales	ShippedQuarter ▾	
2	CategoryName ▾	Qtr 1	
3	Beverages	$ 35,858.20	$
4	Condiments	$ 11,922.16	$
5	Confections	$ 21,082.75	$
6	Dairy Products	$ 24,118.72	$
7	Grains/Cereals	$ 12,697.10	$
8	Meat/Poultry	$ 21,598.15	$
9	Produce	$ 8,980.74	$
10	Seafood	$ 7,445.41	$
11	Grand Total	$ 143,703.23	$

Figure 3-15: When enabling you to select an entire PivotTable element, the cursor changes to an arrow.

2. Click once. The entire row will be selected.

3. Click the Bold button on the Formatting Toolbar. The entire selected row becomes boldfaced.

4. Point the mouse at the top of the Qtr 4 column, just above the label. The cursor will change to a downward-pointing arrow.

5. Click to select the entire column.

6. Click the Italics button on the Formatting Toolbar. The entire selected column will become italicized.

7. Click anywhere outside the PivotTable to deselect it.

At this point your PivotTable will look like Figure 3-16. The combination of the autoformatting and the custom cell formatting results in an attractive, easy-to-read table with the important information emphasized.

	A	B	C	D	E	F
1	ProductSales	ShippedQuarter ▼				
2	CategoryName ▼	Qtr 1	Qtr 2	Qtr 3	Qtr 4	Grand Total
3	Beverages	$ 35,858.20	$ 25,466.95	$ 20,845.09	$ 19,904.05	$102,074.29
4	Condiments	$ 11,922.16	$ 13,347.27	$ 14,001.95	$ 16,006.18	$ 55,277.56
5	Confections	$ 21,082.75	$ 22,065.51	$ 17,964.86	$ 19,780.99	$ 80,894.11
6	**Dairy Products**	**$ 24,118.72**	**$ 27,254.12**	**$ 28,627.54**	**$ 34,749.37**	**$114,749.75**
7	Grains/Cereals	$ 12,697.10	$ 14,629.30	$ 15,310.72	$ 13,311.70	$ 55,948.82
8	Meat/Poultry	$ 21,598.15	$ 13,694.55	$ 15,843.51	$ 30,201.85	$ 81,338.06
9	Produce	$ 8,980.74	$ 15,583.66	$ 8,302.97	$ 20,152.61	$ 53,019.98
10	Seafood	$ 7,445.41	$ 13,613.41	$ 23,423.57	$ 21,061.80	$ 65,544.19
11	**Grand Total**	**$ 143,703.23**	**$ 145,654.77**	**$ 144,320.21**	**$ 175,168.55**	**$608,846.76**

Figure 3-16: The final PivotTable after all formatting has been applied.

Part  IV

Working with PivotTable Components

PivotTables have a lot of power hidden within them. The PivotTable components discussed in this part may not be visible on the surface in all cases, but they are waiting for you to use them to organize and display your PivotTable data in the precise way you need. This is the first of two parts that delve into the use of these tools. With these techniques under your belt, you will be able to go beyond the simple creation of a PivotTable and learn how to customize it to suit your data and your needs.

Tips and Where to Find Them

Using Drop Areas

Every PivotTable report starts out as a group of empty drop areas, and you create the report by dropping fields onto these areas (either in the Layout dialog box or in the worksheet after completing the PivotTable Wizard). Perhaps the most important part of designing the PivotTable to display the data you want in the way you want is the way you use these drop areas. In previous chapters you saw only relatively simple uses of the drop areas with at most one field being dropped per area. This is perfectly legitimate for some needs, but PivotTables have much more power when you drop two or more fields in one area. To do this correctly, you need an understanding of how the Field List and the various drop areas work.

The Field List

The Field List contains the names of all the fields in your source data. Figure 4-1 shows an example (you'll see the raw data on which it is based in the next section). If a field has already been added to the PivotTable, its name is displayed in boldface in the Field List.

Figure 4-1: The Field List displays the names of all the data fields.

Can't See the Field List?

The Field List will be visible only when the PivotTable is active. To make a PivotTable active click any cell in it. If the Field List is still not visible, click the Show Field List button on the PivotTable toolbar. If the toolbar is not visible, right-click any cell in the PivotTable and select Show PivotTable Toolbar from the pop-up menu.

The most common way to add fields to a PivotTable is to drag them from the Field List and drop them on the appropriate area — Row, Column, Data, or Page — of the PivotTable. You can also add them as follows:

1. In the Field List, click the field name.
2. Select the desired destination area from the list at the bottom of the Field List: Row, Column, Data, or Page.
3. Click the Add To button.

Each field name in the Field list displays an icon. This icon indicates where you can place the field in the PivotTable, as described in the following table.

Icon	The field can be placed
	Only in Row, Column, or Page areas.
	Only in the Data area.
	Anywhere (Row, Column, Data, or Page area).

The second and third icons will be displayed only if you are using an OLAP data source. Because of the way OLAP data sources work, there are some restrictions on where fields can be dropped. You will learn the details of using OLAP data sources in Part VII.

Dragging a Field Off a PivotTable

If you make a mistake when dropping a field on a PivotTable, you can correct it by dragging it off. Just point at the field name label and drag; the mouse pointer will display as a four-headed arrow when you are pointed at a field name. You can drag it to another drop area if desired, or you can drop it outside the PivotTable to remove it completely. You can always drag and drop it onto the report again from the Field List.

Using the Row Drop Area

You drop a field on the Row drop area when you want the PivotTable to display data organized based on the values in that field. This is illustrated by the test score data in Figure 4-2. This figure shows only the first few rows of the data.

	A	B	C	D	E	F
1						
2	Subject #	Gender	Age Group	Region	Political Affiliation	Score
3	1	Male	20-29	NorthEast	Dem	92
4	2	Female	40-49	Midwest	Ind	94
5	3	Male	30-39	South	Dem	84
6	4	Male	20-29	NorthEast	Ind	94
7	5	Female	50-59	NorthEast	Rep	95
8	6	Female	30-39	SouthWest	Rep	88
9	7	Male	40-49	Midwest	Rep	80
10	8	Female	50-59	Midwest	Ind	83
11	9	Male	30-39	South	Dem	87
12	10	Male	20-29	NorthWest	Rep	81
13	11	Male	40-49	NorthEast	Dem	97
14	12	Female	50-59	NorthWest	Dem	88
15	13	Male	30-39	Midwest	Rep	88
16	14	Female	60-69	South	Rep	96
17	15	Female	50-59	SouthWest	Dem	80
18	16	Female	50-59	NorthEast	Rep	83
19	17	Male	40-49	NorthWest	Rep	100
20	18	Male	40-49	NorthWest	Ind	83
21	19	Female	50-59	Midwest	Ind	86
22	20	Female	20-29	SouthWest	Rep	93
23	21	Male	30-39	Midwest	Dem	87
24	22	Male	20-29	NorthWest	Dem	90
25	23	Female	40-49	SouthWest	Rep	96
26	24	Female	30-39	South	Ind	98
27	25	Male	30-39	NorthWest	Dem	91
28	26	Female	50-59	NorthWest	Dem	82
29	27	Female	20-29	South	Rep	98
30	28	Male	40-49	NorthEast	Dem	83
31	29	Male	30-39	SouthWest	Rep	84
32	30	Female	30-39	SouthWest	Dem	87

Figure 4-2: The sample test score data.

Suppose you created a PivotTable based on these data and dragged the Gender field and dropped it in the Row area (before dropping any other fields). Your still-incomplete PivotTable would look like Figure 4-3.

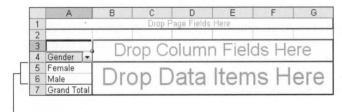

Two rows

Figure 4-3: After you drop the Gender field on the Row area, the table has two rows.

The PivotTable now has two rows (not counting the default Grand Total row): Male and Female. This is because the Gender field contains either the value "Male" or the value "Female" for every subject. There are two possible values for Gender, hence there are two rows in the PivotTable. A label at the top displays the name of the field. The drop-down button next to the field name is used to filter the PivotTable, but that's a topic for another section.

Part IV

Suppose that instead of dragging the Gender field to the Row area you instead dragged the Age Group field. What do you think would happen? Looking at the raw data you can see that the Age Group column contains these five possible values:

- 20–29
- 30–39
- 40–49
- 50–59
- 60–69

You would therefore expect the resulting PivotTable to have five rows, one for each of these data values, and that's exactly what you get, as shown in Figure 4-4.

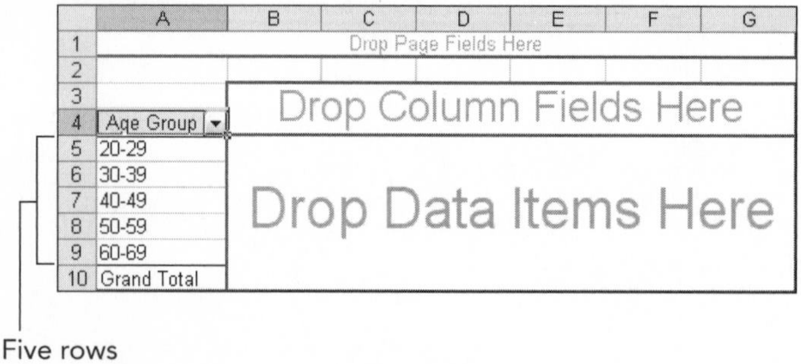

Five rows

Figure 4-4: After you drop the Age Group field on the Row area the table has five rows.

Using Multiple Row Fields

So far you have looked at PivotTables in which only one field has been dropped on the Row area. PivotTables can accommodate more complex scenarios in which you have multiple row fields. If you drop two fields on a Row area, one will become the inner row field and the other will become the outer row field. Data are organized first according to the values in the outer row field; then within each group of outer row fields, they are organized by the values in the inner row field.

To create inner and outer row fields, drop one of the fields in the Row area; it does not matter which field you drop first. When you drop the second one, where you drop it determines which field becomes inner and which becomes outer:

- If you drop the second field at the left side of the Row area, it will become the outer field and the first field that was dropped will become the inner field.

- If you drop the second field at the right side of the Row area, it will become the inner field and the first field that was dropped will become the outer field.

As you drag the field over the Row area, the position it will occupy is indicated by a vertical marker that shows at the right or left border of the Row area. Don't worry about making a mistake; you can always drag the field to a different location.

Suppose you are creating a PivotTable from the score data shown in Figure 4-2. If you drop Age Group as the inner field in the Row area and Gender field as the outer field, the resulting PivotTable will look like Figure 4-5.

3			
4	Gender ▾	Age Group ▾	Drop Column Fields Here
5	Female	20-29	
6		30-39	
7		40-49	
8		50-59	
9		60-69	
10	Female Total		Drop Data Items Here
11	Male	20-29	
12		30-39	
13		40-49	
14		50-59	
15		60-69	
16	Male Total		
17	Grand Total		

Figure 4-5: In this PivotTable, Age Group is the inner row field and Gender is the outer row field.

If you reverse the field positions, however, you will get Gender as the inner row field and Age Group as the outer row field, as shown in Figure 4-6.

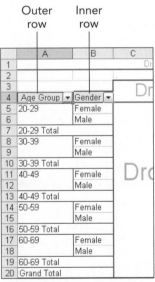

Outer row   Inner row

	A	B	C
1			Dr
2			
3			Dr
4	Age Group ▾	Gender ▾	
5	20-29	Female	
6		Male	
7	20-29 Total		
8	30-39	Female	
9		Male	
10	30-39 Total		
11	40-49	Female	Dr
12		Male	
13	40-49 Total		
14	50-59	Female	
15		Male	
16	50-59 Total		
17	60-69	Female	
18		Male	
19	60-69 Total		
20	Grand Total		

Figure 4-6: Age Group as the outer row field and Gender as the inner row field.

Why would you select one field for the inner and another for the outer? The answer lies in the subtotals. Excel automatically creates subtotals for each outer row field. For example, in Figure 4-5 there is a row labeled Male Total and another labeled Female Total. Likewise,

Figure 4-6 shows a total row for each age group. Therefore, you choose your inner and outer row fields based on which you need subtotals for.

Using the Column Drop Area

The Column drop area works the same way as the Row drop area except that you get a separate column, rather than a row, for each data value.

A PivotTable can use multiple column fields as well. They work much like multiple row fields. Even though you might think that column fields would be called *upper* and *lower* they are still referred to as *inner* and *outer*, just like multiple row fields. In summary, it works like this:

1. After dropping the first column field, drop the second one at the upper edge of the Column area to make it the outer field, and drop it at the lower edge of the Column area to make it the inner field.

2. Excel creates a subtotal column for each outer field group.

Figure 4-7 shows a portion of a PivotTable in which the Gender and Age Group fields have been placed in the Column area.

Outer column

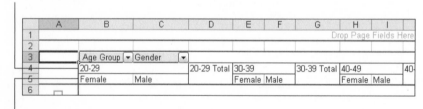

Inner column

Figure 4-7: You can define inner and outer column fields as well.

You can have multiple column fields and multiple row fields in the same PivotTable. The resulting table is likely to be rather complex, but this may be necessary for certain kinds of data presentation.

More Than Two Row/Column Fields?

There's nothing preventing you from creating a PivotTable with more than two fields in the Column or Row area. The only problem is that the resulting PivotTable is usually too complex to understand easily. It is usually better to use filtering or multiple PivotTables in situations where you might consider three or more row/column fields.

Creating a PivotTable with Two Column Fields and Two Row Fields

By actually creating a PivotTable with multiple column and row fields you will gain a better understanding of how this works. For this walkthrough you need the data in the workbook TestScores.xls. (You saw these data earlier in Figure 4-2.) After opening the workbook the first steps are to create a blank PivotTable:

1. Select the data range A2:F122.

2. Select Data ⇨ PivotTable ⇨ and PivotChart Report.

3. In the first wizard step, leave the default options selected and click Next.

4. In the second wizard step, the range you selected will already be specified. Click Next.

5. In the third wizard step, select the New Workbook option and click Finish.

The resulting blank PivotTable is shown in Figure 4-8.

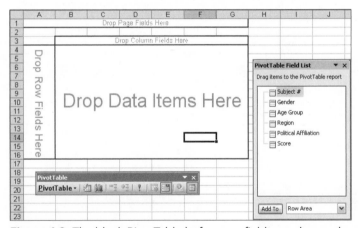

Figure 4-8: The blank PivotTable before any fields are dropped on it.

Before continuing, it is a good idea to do some planning. You want your PivotTable to be set up as follows:

- Gender is the outer row field because you want subtotals for this variable.

- Age Group is the inner row field.

- Political Affiliation will be the outer column field. You do not actually want subtotals for this variable. Although Excel will automatically create them, you can get rid of them after the PivotTable is created.

- Region is the inner column field.
- Score is the data field.

With your plan in place, you can create the PivotTable:

1. Drag the Age Group field to the Row area.
2. Drag the Gender field to the left side of the Row area.
3. Drag the Political Affiliation field to the Column area.
4. Drag the Region field to the bottom section of the Column area.
5. Drag the Score field to the Data area.

At this point your PivotTable will look like the one in Figure 4-9. (The figure shows only part of the PivotTable.) Note that I adjusted the column widths to show more columns. If you want column widths to be preserved through refreshes and layout changes, you must turn on the Preserve Formatting option and turn off the Autoformat Table option in the PivotTable Options dialog box. As you learned in Part III, you access this dialog box by selecting Table Options from the PivotTable menu.

		Dem					Dem Total	Ind					Ind Total	Rep	
Sum of Score	Politic ▾	Region ▾													
Gender ▾	Age Group ▾	Midwest	NorthEast	NorthWest	South	SouthWest		Midwest	NorthEast	NorthWest	South	SouthWest		Midwest	Nort
Female	20-29	88		100	83	189	460			82			82	97	
	30-39			434		252	686			94	98	83	275	84	
	40-49		81	98		99	278	94		278			372	100	
	50-59	94		333		80	507	169					169		
	60-69		99			195	294			279			279	100	
Female Total		182	180	965	83	815	2225	263		733	98	83	1177	381	
Male	20-29		92	177		179	448		94				94	98	
	30-39	177	94	363	171	86	891					92	92	88	
	40-49	95	180	89	91	91	546	93	94	83	81		351	171	
	50-59	96		96			192	94					94	84	
	60-69			95			95							84	
Male Total		368	366	820	262	356	2172	187	188	83	81	92	631	525	
Grand Total		550	546	1785	345	1171	4397	450	188	816	179	175	1808	906	

Figure 4-9: The completed PivotTable.

The final step in this walkthrough is to remove the column subtotals. Although subtotals are useful for some kinds of data, they are not in this situation. The simplest way to get rid of these columns is to hide them:

1. Right-click any one of the subtotal column headings (Dem Total, Rep Total, or Ind Total).
2. Select Hide from the pop-up menu.

Before you leave this PivotTable, note the following: First, some of the cells in the Data area are blank. This is not an error but the result of the data. For example, cell D6 is blank because there were no test scores from females in the 20–29 age group who were in the NorthEast region and reported a Dem political affiliation.

Second, you can see that each row and column field features a label and drop-down list. You use these, as you saw in earlier parts, to filter the data in the PivotTable based on values in that field. For example, Figure 4-10 shows the filter-selection list for the Region field.

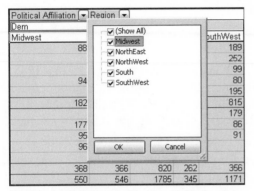

Figure 4-10: Filtering the PivotTable based on the Region field.

When a Row or Column area has more than one field, you can change their order, for example by moving the outer field to the inner position. One way to do this is by dragging — pointing at the Field button and dragging it to the new position within the Row or Column area. You can also use the Field button's pop-up menu. Right-click the Field button, select Order, then select one of the following commands:

- **Move to Beginning** — Makes the field the outer field.
- **Move Left** — Moves the field one position outward.
- **Move Right** — Moves the field one position inward.
- **Move to End** — Makes the field the inner field.

Some of these commands will not be available, depending on the current position of the field. For instance, if the field is already the outer field, the Move to Beginning and Move Left commands will not be available.

Using the Data Drop Area

The Data drop area is where you drop the field that contains the data to be summarized by the PivotTable. Each cell in the Data area summarizes a subset of the data based on the row and column the cell is in. For an example, look at the data and PivotTable in Figure 4-11. In this PivotTable the data field is Sold.

Part IV

18	Drop Page Fields Here			
19				
20	Sum of Sold	Size ▼		
21	Flavor ▼	Large	Small	Grand Total
22	Chocolate	109	44	153
23	Vanilla	67	107	174
24	Grand Total	176	151	327

Figure 4-11: A simple PivotTable report.

Look at the value 109 in the cell. Where did this number come from? You can see that this cell is in the Large column and the Chocolate row. This tells you that the value 109 is the sum of the Sold field values for all data records where Flavor=Chocolate and Size=Large. In other words, it is the sum of the Sold values. The other cells in the PivotTable work the same way.

What if you do not want to sum the data but rather display some other calculation such as the average or count? You can do this using the field settings, which are covered later in this part in Tip 35, "Working with Field Settings."

Using Multiple Data Fields

There's no reason that the Data area of the PivotTable has to be limited to a single data field, although this is often all you need. Sometimes you want to summarize two or more data items in the table. Look, for instance, at the data in Figure 4-12, which show the total sales for both 2003 and 2004 for several salespeople over four quarters. Can you include both the 2003 and 2004 sales amounts in your PivotTable? You bet.

	A	B	C	D
1				
2	**Sales Person**	**Quarter**	**2003 Sales**	**2004 Sales**
3	J. Smith	Qtr 1	$ 240,868	$ 300,381
4	L. Anderson	Qtr 1	$ 207,010	$ 290,473
5	J. Gomez	Qtr 1	$ 351,364	$ 238,898
6	F. Chang	Qtr 1	$ 186,858	$ 369,874
7	A. Zimmer	Qtr 1	$ 142,802	$ 316,046
8	J. Smith	Qtr 2	$ 124,985	$ 302,352
9	L. Anderson	Qtr 2	$ 265,816	$ 325,814
10	J. Gomez	Qtr 2	$ 287,292	$ 221,950
11	F. Chang	Qtr 2	$ 361,827	$ 209,041
12	A. Zimmer	Qtr 2	$ 389,893	$ 222,731
13	J. Smith	Qtr 3	$ 363,411	$ 389,028
14	L. Anderson	Qtr 3	$ 215,785	$ 404,197
15	J. Gomez	Qtr 3	$ 365,308	$ 421,544
16	F. Chang	Qtr 3	$ 197,629	$ 164,248
17	A. Zimmer	Qtr 3	$ 112,210	$ 252,738
18	J. Smith	Qtr 4	$ 216,253	$ 348,974
19	L. Anderson	Qtr 4	$ 153,260	$ 219,914
20	J. Gomez	Qtr 4	$ 231,852	$ 294,411
21	F. Chang	Qtr 4	$ 350,327	$ 429,986
22	A. Zimmer	Qtr 4	$ 353,689	$ 236,775

Figure 4-12: This raw data contains two data items, 2003 Sales and 2004 Sales, both of which can be included in the same PivotTable report.

To create a PivotTable with more than one data field, you drag each data field to the Data area. The resulting PivotTable created from the data in Figure 4-12 (after the application of numeric formatting) is shown in Figure 4-13. You can see that for each salesperson there is a row for each of the data fields, 2003 Sales and 2004 Sales.

	A	B	C	D	E	F	G
1							
2							
3			Quarter ▾				
4	Sales Person ▾	Data ▾	Qtr 1	Qtr 2	Qtr 3	Qtr 4	Grand Total
5	A. Zimmer	Sum of 2003 Sales	$142,802	$389,893	$112,210	$353,689	$998,594
6		Sum of 2004 Sales	$437,804	$160,424	$402,910	$436,750	$1,437,888
7	F. Chang	Sum of 2003 Sales	$186,858	$361,827	$197,629	$350,327	$1,096,641
8		Sum of 2004 Sales	$216,693	$157,235	$366,924	$430,323	$1,171,175
9	J. Gomez	Sum of 2003 Sales	$351,364	$287,292	$365,308	$231,852	$1,235,816
10		Sum of 2004 Sales	$164,087	$448,265	$341,163	$374,844	$1,328,359
11	J. Smith	Sum of 2003 Sales	$240,868	$124,985	$363,411	$216,253	$945,517
12		Sum of 2004 Sales	$208,823	$308,976	$440,003	$442,275	$1,400,077
13	L. Anderson	Sum of 2003 Sales	$207,010	$265,816	$215,785	$153,260	$841,871
14		Sum of 2004 Sales	$228,383	$335,481	$150,529	$202,546	$916,939
15	Total Sum of 2003 Sales		$1,128,902	$1,429,813	$1,254,343	$1,305,381	$5,118,439
16	Total Sum of 2004 Sales		$1,255,790	$1,410,381	$1,701,529	$1,886,738	$6,254,438

Figure 4-13: A PivotTable created with two data fields.

When you place more than one data field in a PivotTable report, the report includes a Data button. In Figure 4-13, this button is in cell B4 of the PivotTable report. You can use the drop-down arrow on this button to filter the report, display all the data fields, or display only selected ones.

You may be thinking that the labels in column B of this PivotTable report aren't right; after all, the values in the cells are not actually sums but single values brought over from the raw data. Can you change this? Yes, it's another action you can take with field settings, covered later in this chapter in Tip 35, "Working with Field Settings."

Part IV

Drop a Data Field Twice?

You can drop the same field twice or more on the Data area. What's the point of this? Initially both instances of the data field display the sum of the data, which is not at all useful. You can, however, change the way one of the fields summarizes the data. For example, you can set it to display the average or count of the data rather than the sum. For an Amount field you can display the sum, the average, and the maximum — three different summaries based on the same raw data. You'll learn how to do this later in this part in Tip 35.

Using the Page Drop Area

Though some PivotTable reports do not use them, page fields are powerful tools, essential for advanced tasks. A page field enables you to filter the entire report based on the data in the field. This is similar in concept to the kind of filtering you can do with row and column fields, but the results are somewhat different. A given field cannot be both a page field and a row or column field at the same time. If you add to the Page area a field that is already a row or column field, it is removed from its original location.

For each page field that you add, the PivotTable displays a page button with the name of the field. To the right of this button a cell displays the current filter setting. By default this is (All), indicating that data from all page field values are included in the PivotTable. See Figure 4-14 for an example of a page field named Quarter.

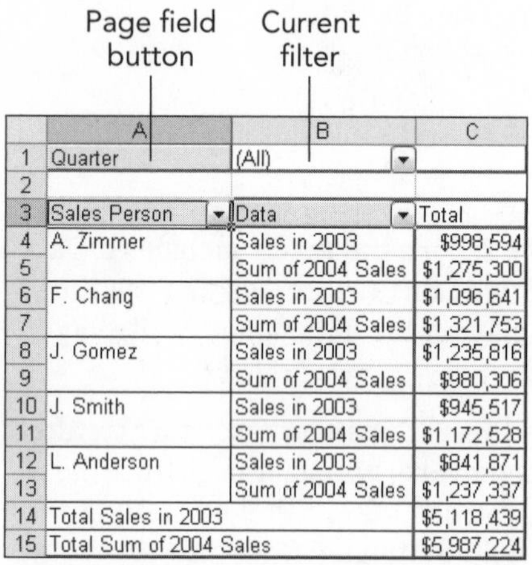

	A	B	C
1	Quarter	(All)	
2			
3	Sales Person	Data	Total
4	A. Zimmer	Sales in 2003	$998,594
5		Sum of 2004 Sales	$1,275,300
6	F. Chang	Sales in 2003	$1,096,641
7		Sum of 2004 Sales	$1,321,753
8	J. Gomez	Sales in 2003	$1,235,816
9		Sum of 2004 Sales	$980,306
10	J. Smith	Sales in 2003	$945,517
11		Sum of 2004 Sales	$1,172,528
12	L. Anderson	Sales in 2003	$841,871
13		Sum of 2004 Sales	$1,237,337
14	Total Sales in 2003		$5,118,439
15	Total Sum of 2004 Sales		$5,987,224

Figure 4-14: A page field displays as a button with the field name, and an adjacent cell indicates the current filter setting.

If you click the down arrow next to the field button, Excel displays a list of the data values for the field. In Figure 4-15, the Quarter field has four possible values: Qtr 1, Qtr 2, Qtr 3, and Qtr 4. You can select one or more values to filter, or select (All) to display all data. As soon as you click OK to close the filter selection box, the PivotTable updates to reflect the new filter.

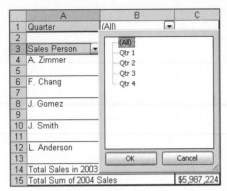

Figure 4-15: You can select which page field value or values to include in the PivotTable.

Creating a PivotTable with Three Page Fields

This tip takes you through the steps involved in creating a PivotTable with three page fields. The data, part of which is shown in Figure 4-16, are sales of items with five variables: Store, Month, Item, Color, and Size. The goal is to create a PivotTable that shows total sales for each store for each month, and that gives you the ability to filter on the Item, Color, and Size variables. To start you should open the workbook `ThreePageFields.xls`.

1. Select the range that contains the data (A2:F162).

2. Select PivotTable and PivotChart Report from the Data menu.

3. In the first wizard step, be sure that the PivotTable option and either the Microsoft Office Excel List option or the Database option are selected; then click Next.

4. In the second wizard step, the data range that you selected is already entered, so just click Next.

5. In the third wizard step select the New Worksheet option; then click Finish. The blank PivotTable will look like Figure 4-17.

Part IV

	A	B	C	D	E	F
1						
2	**Store**	**Month**	**Item**	**Color**	**Size**	**Amount**
3	Downtown	Jan	4	Red	Large	$ 1.67
4	Northside	Feb	4	Blue	Small	$ 12.90
5	East End	Feb	1	Red	Medium	$ 17.03
6	Downtown	Mar	1	Green	Small	$ 6.11
7	South Plaza	Jan	4	White	Large	$ 11.85
8	East End	Feb	5	Blue	Medium	$ 1.55
9	Downtown	Mar	1	Green	Small	$ 13.98
10	Downtown	Mar	5	White	Large	$ 13.37
11	Northside	Mar	2	Red	Large	$ 16.02
12	South Plaza	Jan	5	Red	Medium	$ 5.31
13	Downtown	Feb	4	Blue	Large	$ 17.21
14	Northside	Feb	5	Red	Medium	$ 14.75
15	East End	Jan	5	Green	Small	$ 14.61
16	South Plaza	Jan	1	White	Medium	$ 13.98
17	Downtown	Jan	1	Blue	Medium	$ 12.63
18	East End	Mar	2	White	Medium	$ 17.31
19	Downtown	Mar	3	White	Small	$ 6.29
20	Downtown	Jan	3	Red	Large	$ 2.21
21	Northside	Mar	3	Red	Small	$ 5.46
22	South Plaza	Jan	5	Blue	Medium	$ 19.59
23	Downtown	Mar	4	Red	Large	$ 2.96
24	Northside	Feb	1	Green	Small	$ 16.68
25	East End	Feb	5	White	Medium	$ 18.71
26	Downtown	Mar	4	Blue	Small	$ 2.83
27	South Plaza	Mar	1	Green	Large	$ 8.17
28	East End	Jan	2	White	Large	$ 10.47
29	Downtown	Jan	5	Blue	Medium	$ 18.09
30	Downtown	Feb	2	Red	Large	$ 4.63
31	Northside	Mar	3	Blue	Medium	$ 8.27
32	South Plaza	Jan	1	Red	Medium	$ 13.98
33	Downtown	Mar	5	Green	Small	$ 2.44

Figure 4-16: The sample sales data.

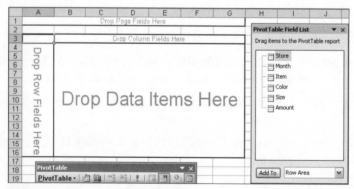

Figure 4-17: The blank PivotTable before any fields have been added.

6. Drag the Store field to the Row drop area.

7. Drag the Month field to the Column drop area.

8. Drag the Amount field to the Data drop area.

9. Drag the Item, Color, and Size fields to the Page drop area.

10. Right-click any of the number cells in the PivotTable and select Field Settings from the pop-up menu to display the Field Settings dialog box.

11. Click the Number button to display the Format Cells dialog box.

12. In the Category list, click Currency.

13. Click OK twice.

At this point, your PivotTable should look like Figure 4-18. You can see that there is a button for each of the three page fields. The drop-down arrow next to each button enables you to select how the data in the table are filtered. By default, the setting is (All) for each page field, meaning that all data for the field are displayed.

	A	B	C	D	E
1	Color	(All)			
2	Item	(All)			
3	Size	(All)			
4					
5	Sum of Amount	Month			
6	Store	Jan	Feb	Mar	Grand Total
7	Downtown	$245.62	$102.72	$226.06	$574.40
8	East End	$114.06	$131.24	$100.56	$345.86
9	Northside	$16.68	$203.12	$126.28	$346.08
10	South Plaza	$273.80	$13.98	$56.64	$344.42
11	Grand Total	$650.16	$451.06	$509.54	$1,610.76

Figure 4-18: The complete PivotTable report displays three page buttons.

Try some filtering. Click the arrow next to the Size field to see the list shown in Figure 4-19. You can select any one of the three Size values — Large, Medium, and Small — and the PivotTable report will change to include only data that pass the filter. You can also select (All) to remove any filtering based on this field.

Figure 4-19: The Size filter options.

Follow these steps to experiment with filtering:

1. Pull down the Color filter list and select Red, then click OK.

2. Pull down the Item filter list and select 2, then click OK.

3. Pull down the Size filter list and select Large, then click OK.

After you have applied these filters, your PivotTable will look like Figure 4-20.

	A	B	C	D
1	Color	Red ▼		
2	Item	2 ▼		
3	Size	Large ▼		
4				
5	Sum of Amount	Month ▼		
6	Store ▼	Feb	Mar	Grand Total
7	Downtown	$9.26		$9.26
8	Northside		$32.04	$32.04
9	Grand Total	$9.26	$32.04	$41.30

Figure 4-20: The PivotTable report after the application of three filters.

Please note the following:

- Each page field button displays the current filter setting: Red for Color, 2 for Item, and Large for Size.

- The PivotTable no longer has a column for Jan because the filtered data did not include any results where Month=Jan. This is also why only two stores are listed; the other stores did not have any matching data.

- The cell for the Downtown store in Mar is blank, as is the cell for the Northside store in Feb. This means no data passed the filter and matched these criteria.

This walkthrough is an example of how page fields can be used to add flexibility to a PivotTable. As you gain experience with PivotTables, you will develop a feeling for whether it is better to drop a field on the Page area or on the Row or Column area. There is no right way to do things; it all depends on your data and what you want to get out of them.

Working with Field Settings

A PivotTable report is made up of fields, and each field has a group of settings associated with it. These settings control how (and whether) the field displays, its number format, the summary calculation used, and a few other things. It's essential that you understand these settings.

To change field settings you must display the PivotTable Field dialog box using one of these methods:

- Right-click a field cell and select Field Settings from the pop-up menu.

- Select the cell and click the Field Settings button on the PivotTable toolbar.

- Double-click the Field button.

Field settings are different depending on the type of field you are working with: data, row/column, or page. These are covered in the following tips.

Using Settings for Data Fields

The PivotTable Field dialog box for a data field is shown in Figure 4-21.

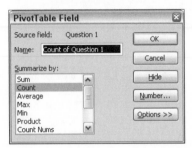

Figure 4-21: The PivotTable Field dialog box for a data field.

In this dialog box are the following elements:

- **Source field** — Lists the name of the data field on which this PivotTable field is based.

- **Name** — The name of the PivotTable field. Edit this name to change the way it is displayed in the PivotTable report.

- **Hide** — Hides the field. This command is poorly named because it does not simply hide the field; rather, it removes the field from the PivotTable report. To display the field again you must drag it from the Field List to the Data area of the PivotTable.

- **Number** — Displays the Format Cells dialog box, in which you can select a number format for the field. (This was covered in detail in Part III.)

- **Options** — enables you to set advanced data field options. These options are covered later in this part in Tip 41, "Setting Advanced Data Field Options."

- **Summarize by** — Enables you to select how the field summarizes the data.

The Summarize by setting gives you great flexibility in the way the PivotTable presents the data. By default, a data field is set to sum: The numbers displayed in the PivotTable will be the sums of the corresponding data items. The other summary options available are:

- **Count** — The number of data items.

- **Average** — The average of the data values.

- **Max** — The largest data value.

- **Min** — The smallest data value.

- **Product** — The result of multiplying all the data values together.

- **Count nums** — The number of data items that are numeric.

Count Versus Count Nums

What is the difference between the Count summary option and the Count Nums option? Count counts all data items regardless of whether they are a number, text, or a blank. In contrast, Count Nums counts only those items that are numbers.

Using Different Summary Functions

This tip shows you how to use field settings to summarize data in different ways. It uses the test score data shown in Figure 4-22. These data are located in `TestScores2.xls`. After you open that file you can proceed.

	A	B	C
1			
2	Student #	Gender	Score
3	1	Male	81
4	2	Male	79
5	3	Female	86
6	4	Male	92
7	5	Female	87
8	6	Female	99
9	7	Male	70
10	8	Male	98
11	9	Female	85
12	10	Male	87
13	11	Female	71
14	12	Female	97
15	13	Male	98
16	14	Male	78
17	15	Female	72
18	16	Male	77
19	17	Female	97
20	18	Female	87
21	19	Male	74
22	20	Male	93
23	21	Female	78
24	22	Male	70
25	23	Female	83
26	24	Female	81
27	25	Male	70
28	26	Male	85
29	27	Female	71
30	28	Male	82
31	29	Female	70
32	30	Female	75
33	31	Male	86

Sheet1 / Sheet2 / Sheet3 /

Figure 4-22: The sample test score data.

The first steps are to create the basic PivotTable report:

1. Select the cells that contain the data (A2:C45).

2. Select PivotTable and PivotChart Report from the Data menu.

3. Accept the default options in all three steps of the wizard.

4. When the blank PivotTable is displayed in the worksheet, drag the Gender field to the Row drop area.

5. Drag the Score field to the Data drop area.

6. Repeat Step 5 two more times, dragging the Score field to the Data drop area a second and third time.

At this point the PivotTable will look like the one shown in Figure 4-23. It has three Score fields, Sum of Score, Sum of Score2, and Sum of Score3. Each displays the same result, but this is not what you want. In fact you don't want a sum at all; rather, you want the average, the maximum, and the minimum for each group.

	A	B	C
1	Drop Page Fields Here		
2			
3	Gender ▼	Data ▼	Total
4	Female	Sum of Score	1792
5		Sum of Score2	1792
6		Sum of Score3	1792
7	Male	Sum of Score	1856
8		Sum of Score2	1856
9		Sum of Score3	1856
10	Total Sum of Score		3648
11	Total Sum of Score2		3648
12	Total Sum of Score3		3648

Figure 4-23: The PivotTable report with three copies of the Score field.

To continue follow these steps:

1. Click one of the Sum of Score field cells — one of the cells that contain the field name Sum of Score or one of the adjacent cells that contain the sum itself.

2. Click the Field Settings button on the PivotTable toolbar to display the Field Settings dialog box (shown in Figure 4-24).

3. Select Average in the Summarize by list. The Name box changes to `Average of Score`.

4. Edit the Name box so it says Average.

5. Click OK.

Figure 4-24: Changing the field settings for the Sum of Score field.

Part IV

At this point the PivotTable looks like the one in Figure 4-25. You successfully changed one data field to display the average, but you really do not need so many decimal places.

2			
3	Gender ▾	Data ▾	Total
4	Female	Average	85.33333333
5		Sum of Score2	1792
6		Sum of Score3	1792
7	Male	Average	84.36363636
8		Sum of Score2	1856
9		Sum of Score3	1856
10	Total Average		84.8372093
11	Total Sum of Score2		3648
12	Total Sum of Score3		3648

Figure 4-25: The PivotTable after the Sum of Score field has been changed to summarize by average.

Changing the number of decimal places displayed requires another visit to the Field Settings dialog box:

1. Click the Field Settings button on the PivotTable toolbar to display the Field Settings dialog box again.

2. Click the Number button to display the Format Cells dialog box.

3. Select Number in the Category list and enter 1 in the Decimal Places box.

4. Click OK twice.

The remaining steps in this tip change the summary for the other two fields:

1. Click one of the Sum of Score2 field cells.

2. Click the Field Settings button on the PivotTable toolbar to display the Field Settings dialog box.

3. Select Max in the Summarize by list and change the name to Maximum.

4. Click OK.

5. Click one of the Sum of Score3 field cells.

6. Click the Field Settings button on the PivotTable toolbar to display the Field Settings dialog box.

7. Select Min in the Summarize by list and change the Name to Minimum.

8. Click OK.

There's one more thing to do. The three total rows at the bottom of the table are not needed. Here's how to get rid of them:

1. Select PivotTable Options from the PivotTable menu to display the PivotTable Options dialog box.

2. Turn off the Grand Totals for Columns option.

3. Click OK.

Now the PivotTable report look like Figure 4-26. It's just what you wanted, providing three different summaries for the Score field.

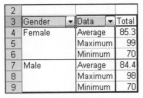

Figure 4-26: The PivotTable after the three data fields have been changed to summarize by average, maximum, and minimum.

Working with Settings for Row and Column Fields

Field settings for row and column fields are somewhat different from those for data fields. The PivotTable Field dialog box for a row or column field is shown in Figure 4-27.

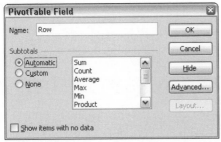

Figure 4-27: The PivotTable Field dialog box for row and column fields.

This dialog box offers the following fields:

- **Name** — The display name for the row or column.

- **Hide** — Removes the field from the PivotTable. To add it back you must drag it from the Field List again.

- **Advanced** — Sets advanced row or column field options.

- **Layout** — This button is available only if the PivotTable has two or more row fields. See below for more details.

- **Subtotals** — Determines how the row/column field is summarized.

- **Show items with no data** — Determines whether row/column entries without data are displayed. (The default is for such items not to be displayed.)

By default, rows and columns are subtotaled automatically as a sum of data items. This is what you get if the Automatic option is selected under Subtotals. You can also select None to have no subtotals or Custom to use the subtotal calculation selected in the list. (Of course, most of these subtotal options don't really provide totals, but that's the term Excel uses for all of them.) You can click more than one custom subtotal and the PivotTable will display a separate row/column for each one. Click again to deselect. The following custom subtotal options are available:

- **Sum** — The sum of the data items.

- **Count** — The number of data items.

- **Average** — The average of the data items.

- **Max** — The largest data item.

- **Min** — The smallest data item.

- **Product** — The result of multiplying the data items together.

- **Count Nums** — The number of data items with a numeric value.

- **StdDev** — The sample standard deviation.

- **StdDevp** — The population standard deviation.

- **Var** — The sample variance.

- **Varp** — The population variance.

Advanced Row and Column Field Settings

When the PivotTable Field dialog box is open for a row or column field, you can click the Advanced button to set advanced options for the field. Because these settings are the same as for page fields, they are covered later in the section "Understanding Advanced Field Settings."

Field Layout Settings

Certain layout options for row fields are relevant only for the outer field in the Row area. These settings do not apply to column fields under any circumstances. The button to access these options, located in the PivotTable Field dialog box, is available only if the PivotTable has more than one row field and the selected field is the outer row field. Clicking this button opens the PivotTable Field Layout dialog box, shown in Figure 4-28.

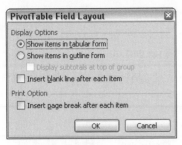

Figure 4-28: The PivotTable Field Layout dialog box enables you to set certain layout options for outer row fields.

The first option in this dialog box gives you a choice between tabular and outline form. Tabular form, which is the default, displays the row fields in a row-and-column format, as shown on the left in Figure 4-29. Outline form dispenses with some cell borders and organizes field entries more like a typical outline, as shown on the right in Figure 4-29. Both forms display the same data; it's just the appearance that changes.

	A	B	C	D
1	Sum of ProductSales		ShippedQuarter	
2	CategoryName	ProductName	Qtr 1	Qtr 2
3	Beverages	Chai	$ 705.60	$ 878.40
4		Chang	$ 2,720.80	$ 228.00
5		Chartreuse verte	$ 590.40	$ 360.00
6		Côte de Blaye	$ 25,127.36	$ 12,806.10
7		Guaraná Fantástica	$ 529.20	$ 467.55
8		Ipoh Coffee	$ 1,398.40	$ 4,496.50
9		Lakkalikööri	$ 1,141.92	$ 1,774.08
10		Laughing Lumberjack Lager		$ 518.00
11		Outback Lager	$ 1,508.40	$ 384.00
12		Rhönbräu Klosterbier	$ 214.52	$ 1,508.92
13		Sasquatch Ale	$ 179.20	$ 1,037.40
14		Steeleye Stout	$ 1,742.40	$ 1,008.00
15	Beverages Total		$ 35,858.20	$ 25,466.95
16	Condiments	Aniseed Syrup	$ 544.00	$ 600.00
17		Chef Anton's Cajun Seasoning	$ 225.28	$ 2,970.00

	A	B	C	D
1	Sum of ProductSales		ShippedQuarter	
2	CategoryName	ProductName	Qtr 1	Qtr 2
3	Beverages			
4		Chai	$ 705.60	$ 878.40
5		Chang	$ 2,720.80	$ 228.00
6		Chartreuse verte	$ 590.40	$ 360.00
7		Côte de Blaye	$ 25,127.36	$ 12,806.10
8		Guaraná Fantástica	$ 529.20	$ 467.55
9		Ipoh Coffee	$ 1,398.40	$ 4,496.50
10		Lakkalikööri	$ 1,141.92	$ 1,774.08
11		Laughing Lumberjack Lager		$ 518.00
12		Outback Lager	$ 1,508.40	$ 384.00
13		Rhönbräu Klosterbier	$ 214.52	$ 1,508.92
14		Sasquatch Ale	$ 179.20	$ 1,037.40
15		Steeleye Stout	$ 1,742.40	$ 1,008.00
16	Beverages Total		$ 35,858.20	$ 25,466.95
17	Condiments			
18		Aniseed Syrup	$ 544.00	$ 600.00
19		Chef Anton's Cajun Seasoning	$ 225.28	$ 2,970.00

Figure 4-29: Tabular form (left) and outline form (right) are two layout options.

If you select the outline form, you can also select the option Display subtotals at top of group, which moves the subtotal from the bottom to the top of each outer field group. You can see the difference in Figure 4-30.

	A	B	C	D
1	Sum of ProductSales		ShippedQuarter	
2	CategoryName	ProductName	Qtr 1	Qtr 2
3	Beverages			
4		Chai	$ 705.60	$ 878.40
5		Chang	$ 2,720.80	$ 228.00
6		Chartreuse verte	$ 590.40	$ 360.00
7		Côte de Blaye	$ 25,127.36	$ 12,806.10
8		Guaraná Fantástica	$ 529.20	$ 467.55
9		Ipoh Coffee	$ 1,398.40	$ 4,496.50
10		Lakkalikööri	$ 1,141.92	$ 1,774.08
11		Laughing Lumberjack Lager		$ 518.00
12		Outback Lager	$ 1,508.40	$ 384.00
13		Rhönbräu Klosterbier	$ 214.52	$ 1,508.92
14		Sasquatch Ale	$ 179.20	$ 1,037.40
15		Steeleye Stout	$ 1,742.40	$ 1,008.00
16	Beverages Total		$ 35,858.20	$ 25,466.95
17	Condiments			
18		Aniseed Syrup	$ 544.00	$ 600.00
19		Chef Anton's Cajun Seasoning	$ 225.28	$ 2,970.00

	A	B	C	D
1	Sum of ProductSales		ShippedQuarter	
2	CategoryName	ProductName	Qtr 1	Qtr 2
3	Beverages		$ 35,858.20	$ 25,466.95
4		Chai	$ 705.60	$ 878.40
5		Chang	$ 2,720.80	$ 228.00
6		Chartreuse verte	$ 590.40	$ 360.00
7		Côte de Blaye	$ 25,127.36	$ 12,806.10
8		Guaraná Fantástica	$ 529.20	$ 467.55
9		Ipoh Coffee	$ 1,398.40	$ 4,496.50
10		Lakkalikööri	$ 1,141.92	$ 1,774.08
11		Laughing Lumberjack Lager		$ 518.00
12		Outback Lager	$ 1,508.40	$ 384.00
13		Rhönbräu Klosterbier	$ 214.52	$ 1,508.92
14		Sasquatch Ale	$ 179.20	$ 1,037.40
15		Steeleye Stout	$ 1,742.40	$ 1,008.00
16	Condiments		$ 11,922.16	$ 13,347.27
17		Aniseed Syrup	$ 544.00	$ 600.00
18		Chef Anton's Cajun Seasoning	$ 225.28	$ 2,970.00

Figure 4-30: A PivotTable in outline form with subtotals displayed at the bottom (left) and top (right) of each outer field item.

The final two options in this dialog box are:

- **Insert blank line after each item** — Inserts a blank line between outer field items.

- **Insert page break after each item** — When printing the PivotTable report, starts each outer field item on a new page.

Working with Settings for Page Fields

When you open the PivotTable Field dialog box for a page field (see Figure 4-31), it looks like the PivotTable Field dialog box for a row or column field. Most of the dialog box elements are in fact the same as for row and column fields:

- The Name box enables you to specify the display name of the page field.

- The Subtotals section enables you to specify how page field subtotals are calculated.

- The option labeled Show items with no data determines whether fields that don't contain data are displayed.

- The Hide button removes the page field from the report.

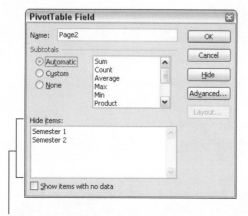

The Hide Items list

Figure 4-31: The PivotTable Field dialog box for a page field contains a Hide Items list.

Subtotals Option Has No Effect?

When you change the Subtotals option for a page field you may wonder why the PivotTable report does not change. This setting takes effect only for row and column fields. If you pivot the table by dragging the page field to the Row or Column area, you'll see the effect of the Subtotals option you selected.

The one new item in this dialog box is the Hide items list. This list contains the values for the field; in the figure, for example, they are Semester 1 and Semester 2. You can click one or more items in this list to hide them. This means that their data will not be displayed in the PivotTable report and they will not be available in the drop-down list for the page field. However, they are really just hidden, not removed. You can always display the PivotTable Field dialog box for the page field again and unselect the items in the Hide Items list and they will again be part of the PivotTable report.

Understanding Advanced Field Settings

If you click the Advanced button in the Field Settings dialog box for a row, column, or page field, Excel will display the PivotTable Field Advanced Options dialog box, shown in Figure 4-32. These options work the same for all three kinds of fields but are not relevant for data fields.

Figure 4-32: You use the PivotTable Field Advanced Options dialog box to set advanced row/column/page field options.

Page Field Options

The options in the top section of this dialog box will be available for page fields only if the PivotTable is based on external data that are not another Excel workbook, such as an Access database. These options have to do with how the external data is retrieved and are usually relevant only when there is a large amount of data.

- **Retrieve external data for all page field items** — This default tells Excel to retrieve all page field data at the same time, even for pages that are not currently displayed, for example when you refresh the report. It results in a faster response when you are working with the PivotTable, but when there are a lot of data, it can place severe demands on memory resources.

When Using an OLAP Data Source

The Query external data source as you select each page field item option is not available if your PivotTable is based on an OLAP data source because, by default, OLAP retrieves data as needed. This option also may not be available for certain third-party ODBC drivers that do not support parameter queries.

- **Query external data source as you select each page field item** — Tells Excel to retrieve data for a page field item only when that item is actually selected. Response is slower because you have to wait for data to be retrieved each time the page field selection is changed, but this option places fewer demands on system memory. Note that the (All) selection won't be available in the page field drop-down list when this option is selected; you are limited to viewing data a page at a time.

- **Disable pivoting of this field** — Prevents the field from being dragged to another section of the PivotTable (for example, from the Row area to the Column area), which would cause all the data to be retrieved.

My advice is to leave these options at their default settings unless you are using external data and start to get Out of Memory or similar error messages when working with the PivotTable.

Sort Options

The remaining options in this dialog box have to do with the way data are sorted in the PivotTable and are applicable to page, row, and column fields. Under AutoSort you have these options:

- **Manual** — You can change the order of items by dragging them.

- **Ascending** — Items are sorted in ascending alphabetical order (A–Z).

- **Descending** — Items are sorted in descending alphabetical order (Z–A).

- **Data source order** — When you are using an external data source and the source permits it, this option lets the external source perform the sorting based on the field selected in the Using field drop-down list.

Top 10 AutoShow is an option for displaying the top or bottom ten items for the field (or another number). For example, suppose your PivotTable report is displaying a list of your 35 sales reps and their total sales for last year. Using this option you can filter the report to display only the ten sales reps with the highest sales totals. To use this option:

1. Click the On option.

2. Select Top or Bottom from the Show drop-down menu.

3. In the adjacent menu, specify the number of items to show.

4. In the Using field drop-down list, select the PivotTable field that will be used to rank the items.

When a field has the AutoShow option turned on, its button appears in blue boldfaced text to indicate this. To show all field items, simply display the Advanced Field Settings dialog box and click Off.

Using the Sort and AutoShow Options

This tip shows you how to use the Sort and AutoShow options to change the way a PivotTable report is displayed. It uses the raw data shown in Figure 4-33. The data are a list of individual sales, with each record giving the sales rep's name, the item sold, the cost per item, the quantity, and the total cost. These data are in the workbook SalesBySalesRep.xls.

	A	B	C	D	E	F
1						
2	Date	Sales Rep	Item	Cost each	Quantity	Sale total
3	7/1/2005	F. Rosenstein	Q00345B	$ 39.00	5	$ 195.00
4	7/1/2005	W. Carver	Q00345B	$ 39.00	17	$ 663.00
5	7/1/2005	O. McBride	C55440D	$ 16.75	5	$ 83.75
6	7/2/2005	J.T. Baker	Q00345B	$ 39.00	13	$ 507.00
7	7/2/2005	Q. Ackerman	Q00345B	$ 39.00	20	$ 780.00
8	7/2/2005	L. Sanchez	C55440D	$ 16.75	8	$ 134.00
9	7/3/2005	O. McBride	J21344A	$ 19.50	9	$ 175.50
10	7/3/2005	A. Yamamoto	J21344A	$ 19.50	7	$ 136.50
11	7/3/2005	L. Sanchez	C55440D	$ 16.75	5	$ 83.75
12	7/3/2005	S. Muller	L98700F	$ 8.25	6	$ 49.50
13	7/3/2005	A. Yamamoto	L98700F	$ 8.25	14	$ 115.50
14	7/4/2005	J. Wilson	C55440D	$ 16.75	4	$ 67.00
15	7/4/2005	J. Wilson	Q00345B	$ 39.00	11	$ 429.00
16	7/5/2005	A. Yamamoto	J21344A	$ 19.50	4	$ 78.00
17	7/5/2005	Q. Ackerman	B20011A	$ 22.15	16	$ 354.40
18	7/5/2005	J. Wilson	C55440D	$ 16.75	16	$ 268.00
19	7/5/2005	J.T. Baker	L98700F	$ 8.25	5	$ 41.25
20	7/5/2005	L. Sanchez	C55440D	$ 16.75	16	$ 268.00
21	7/5/2005	F. Rosenstein	B20011A	$ 22.15	12	$ 265.80
22	7/6/2005	Q. Ackerman	Q00345B	$ 39.00	19	$ 741.00
23	7/6/2005	J. Wilson	Q00345B	$ 39.00	18	$ 702.00
24	7/6/2005	O. McBride	J21344A	$ 19.50	9	$ 175.50
25	7/6/2005	D.F. Chang	C55440D	$ 16.75	7	$ 117.25
26	7/6/2005	L. Sanchez	B20011A	$ 22.15	8	$ 177.20
27	7/7/2005	W. Carver	B20011A	$ 22.15	3	$ 66.45
28	7/7/2005	O. McBride	B20011A	$ 22.15	16	$ 354.40
29	7/7/2005	Q. Ackerman	J21344A	$ 19.50	6	$ 117.00
30	7/8/2005	F. Rosenstein	J21344A	$ 19.50	3	$ 58.50
31	7/8/2005	F. Rosenstein	Q00345B	$ 39.00	10	$ 390.00
32	7/8/2005	A. Yamamoto	J21344A	$ 19.50	7	$ 136.50
33	7/8/2005	L. Sanchez	B20011A	$ 22.15	11	$ 243.65

Sheet1 / Sheet2 / Sheet3 /

Figure 4-33: The raw sales data.

Part IV

First, create the basic PivotTable:

1. Select the range A2:F120.

2. Select PivotTable and PivotChart Report from the Data menu to start the PivotTable Wizard.

3. Complete the wizard steps, accepting the default settings at each stage.

4. When the blank PivotTable is created, drop the Sales Rep field in the Row area.

5. Drop the Sale Total field in the Data area.

6. Double-click the Sum of Sale Total button to open the Field Settings dialog box.

7. Click the Number button to display the Format Cells dialog box.

8. Select the Currency format.

9. Click OK twice to return to the worksheet.

At this point your PivotTable will display the data — the names of the sales reps — in a seemingly random order. To sort them in ascending order:

1. Double-click the Sales Rep button to open the Field Settings dialog box.

2. Click the Advanced button to open the PivotTable Field Advanced Options dialog box.

3. Under Sort, click the Ascending option.

4. Click OK twice to return to the worksheet.

Now the PivotTable report looks like the one in Figure 4-34. You can see that the data are sorted alphabetically by name.

2		
3	Sum of Sale total	
4	Sales Rep	Total
5	Ackerman, Q.	$3,928.90
6	Baker, J.T.	$1,815.95
7	Carver, W.	$4,137.55
8	D.F. Chang	$1,072.25
9	McBride, O.	$1,542.55
10	Muller, S.	$1,384.25
11	Rosenstein, F.	$5,575.20
12	Sanchez, L.	$2,817.65
13	Wilson, J.	$2,738.25
14	Yamamoto, A.	$3,099.75
15	Grand Total	$28,112.30

Figure 4-34: After the Sales Rep field has been sorted in ascending alphabetical order.

Now try the AutoShow option. In a small PivotTable report such as this one, it's easy to pick out the top (or bottom) few items, but if there are dozens or even hundreds of rows, you will be glad to have this tool.

1. Double-click the Sales Rep button to open the Field Settings dialog box.

2. Click the Advanced button to open the PivotTable Field Advanced Options dialog box.

3. Under AutoSort select the On option.

4. Select Top in the Show drop-down menu.

5. Select 3 from the adjacent menu.

6. Click OK twice to return to the worksheet.

Now the PivotTable report looks like the one in Figure 4-35. Only three sales reps are displayed — the three with the highest sales totals. Note also that the text on the Sales Rep button appears in blue boldfaced text to indicate that the field has an AutoShow option applied.

3	Sum of Sale total	
4	Sales Rep ▼	Total
5	Ackerman, Q.	$3,928.90
6	Carver, W.	$4,137.55
7	Rosenstein, F.	$5,575.20
8	Grand Total	$13,641.65

Figure 4-35: Using AutoShow to display only the top three sales reps.

Setting Advanced Data Field Options

When you display the PivotTable Field dialog box for a data field, an Options button is available. Clicking this button toggles the display of an extra section of the dialog box, shown in Figure 4-36. The options that you can set here control some of the most sophisticated capabilities of PivotTable reports.

The default setting in this part of the dialog box is Normal in the Show data as drop-down list. With this option, which you'll probably use most of the time, the field is summarized by means of the calculation you selected in the Summarize by list — for example, a straightforward sum, count, or average. If you pull down the Show data as list, however, you'll see several different ways in which the field data can be summarized. Just to give one example, a data item could be displayed as the percentage of the total of all data items in that row.

Watch Where You Click

Double-clicking a field button brings up the PivotTable Field dialog box for that field, but double-clicking a data cell activates drill-down, which displays the underlying data for the cell in a new worksheet. If you do this by mistake you'll have to delete the drill-down worksheet and return to the sheet where the PivotTable is located.

Part IV

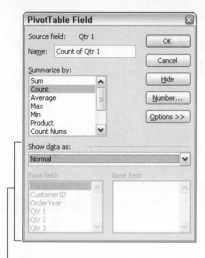

Advanced options

Figure 4-36: The Options button toggles the display of part of the dialog box when you are changing field settings for a data field.

The following table shows some raw data that give the number of each of three items that were sold, plus the overall total.

	Widgets	Doohickeys	Dinguses	Total
Number sold	55	24	66	145

Suppose you are not interested in the actual number but in percentages. For example, you want to know what percentage of items sold were widgets, what percentage were doohickeys, and so on. You can do this in a PivotTable report. The result is that, instead of displaying the value 55 in the Widgets column, Excel divides that number by 145 (the value in the Total column) and then multiplies by 100 to get the percentage value. The resulting PivotTable will look like this:

	Widgets	Doohickeys	Dinguses	Total
Number sold	38%	17%	46%	100%

When you set up a field to show data as something other than the default Normal, the first choice you must make is from the Show data as list. Then, for some of these selections, you must also make a selection in the Base field and/or Base item lists. It's essential that you understand what these choices mean because it's not that uncommon for Excel users to set up a summary that displays something different from what they intended!

The simplest options in the Show data as list — simple because they do not require Base field or Base item selections — are as follows:

- **% of Row** — The data value as a percentage of the total for that row.
- **% of Column** — The data value as a percentage of the total for that column.
- **% of Total** — The data value as a percentage of the total for the entire report.

When you select Running Total in the Show data as list you must also select a base field. The resulting display will be a running total of the base field — in other words, the display for the current item will be the actual data value for the current item added to the total values for all preceding data items.

For an example, look at these raw data:

Month	Totals
Jan	123
Feb	95
Mar	141
Apr	77
May	90
Jun	122

If these data were displayed as a running total you would see the following:

Month	Running Totals
Jan	123
Feb	218
Mar	359
Apr	436
May	526
Jun	648

Part IV

The value displayed for Jan is the same as the raw data because there is no previous item. The value displayed for Feb is Feb's value plus Jan's value: (123+95)=218. The value displayed for Mar is Mar's raw value plus the value displayed for Feb: (141+218)=359. And so on.

The remaining Show data as options require you to specify a base field and a base item:

- The base field is one of the fields in the PivotTable. This includes fields that have been dragged to the PivotTable as well as those that have not (that is, those that are in the Field List but not the PivotTable itself).

- The base item is a value for the column field. It can also be either of the special values (previous) or (next), which use the previous or next item, respectively, for the calculation.

The calculations are:

- **Difference From** — Displays the difference between the raw value and the value of the base field/base item data.

- **% Of** — Displays the raw value as a percentage of the value of the base field/base item data.

- **% Difference From** — Displays, as a percentage, the difference between the raw value and the value of the base field/base item data.

The final option available in the Show data as list is Index. It calculates the display value as follows:

```
((value in cell) x (Grand Table Total)) / ((Grand Row Total) x (Grand Column
Total))
```

Part V

More About PivotTable Components

You saw in the previous chapter how PivotTable components provide you with a lot of flexibility and power in designing your PivotTable reports. This chapter continues the exploration of PivotTable components, showing you how to create calculated items and fields, show and hide detail, and group data.

Tips and Where to Find Them

Working with Calculated Fields and Items

Calculated fields and calculated items are often confused with each other, and for good reason. Not only are the names similar, they are similar in concept. You need to understand the differences to use them effectively.

Calculated Fields

A calculated field acts like any other field in your PivotTable. Its name appears in the Field List and you can drag it to the PivotTable just as you would any other field. It exists only in the PivotTable, however, and only for the duration of the PivotTable.

Suppose your data source contains the total annual sales for each of your company's sales reps. The annual bonus for each rep is calculated as 2% of his or her total annual sales, but the data source doesn't contain the bonus amount. You can create a calculated field in your PivotTable to do this. It calculates total annual sales times 2% for each rep and lets you use this field in your PivotTable.

To create a calculated field, follow these steps:

1. Click anywhere in the PivotTable report to make sure it is active.

2. Select Formulas from the PivotTable menu; then select Calculated Field. Excel will display the Insert Calculated Field dialog box, as shown in Figure 5-1.

3. Enter the name for the calculated field in the Name box.

4. Enter the formula for the calculation in the Formula box:

   - The formula must start with an equal sign.

   - It can contain numbers, parentheses in pairs, and the operators + (addition), - (subtraction), * (multiplication), / (division), and ^ (exponentiation).

   - To add an existing field to the formula, click the field name in the Fields list and then click Add.

5. When the formula is complete, click the Add button to add the field to the Fields list.

6. Click OK to close the dialog box. The field will now be included in the Field List and also automatically added to the PivotTable's Data area.

OLAP? Sorry, No Formulas for You

If your PivotTable is based on an external Online Analytical Processing (OLAP) data source, you will not be able to create calculated fields or items.

Part V

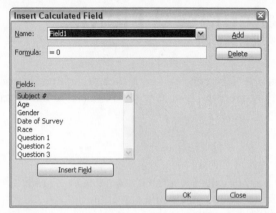

Figure 5-1: You use the Insert Calculated Field dialog box to define a calculated field.

A calculated field can be based on any fields in the data source as well as on other calculated fields that have already been defined. For example, look at this formula for a calculated field:

```
=(ProductTotal+ServiceTotal)*.1
```

The formula adds the values in the ProductTotal and ServiceTotal fields and multiplies the sum by 0.1. ProductTotal and ServiceTotal can each be a field in the data source or another calculated field.

You also use the Insert Calculated Field dialog box to add and delete calculated fields. Display the dialog box as described previously; then select an existing calculated field in the Name box. Then perform one of these actions:

- To delete the calculated field, click the Delete button.
- To modify the calculated field, edit the formula and then click the Add button.

Creating and Using a Calculated Field

For this tip you will use the data shown in Figure 5-2. These data contain the measurements of the maximum and minimum heights of a river over a week, as measured at two locations. These data are in the workbook `RiverHeights.xls`. The first step in creating a calculated field is to create a basic PivotTable report.

	A	B	C	D
1				
2	Date	Location	Max Height	Min Height
3	7/1/2005	West Bridge	22	19
4	7/2/2005	West Bridge	21	19
5	7/3/2005	West Bridge	20	18
6	7/4/2005	West Bridge	24	21
7	7/5/2005	West Bridge	23	22
8	7/6/2005	West Bridge	22	21
9	7/7/2005	West Bridge	17	16
10	7/1/2005	Power Plant	19	17
11	7/2/2005	Power Plant	23	21
12	7/3/2005	Power Plant	24	23
13	7/4/2005	Power Plant	22	21
14	7/5/2005	Power Plant	20	17
15	7/6/2005	Power Plant	17	16
16	7/7/2005	Power Plant	19	17

Figure 5-2: The sample river height data.

1. Select the range A2:D16.

2. Select Data ⇨ PivotTable and PivotChart Report to start the wizard.

3. Complete the wizard, accepting the defaults at each step.

4. When the blank PivotTable is displayed, drag the Date field from the Field List to the Row area.

5. Drag the Location field to the Column area.

6. Drag both the Max Height and Min Height fields to the Data area.

At this point the PivotTable report will look like the one shown in Figure 5-3. You can probably see that some changes are needed, but you should create and add the calculated fields first.

	A	B	C	D	E
1		Drop Page Fields Here			
2					
3			Location ▾		
4	Date ▾	Data ▾	Power Plant	West Bridge	Grand Total
5	7/1/2005	Sum of Max Height	19	22	41
6		Sum of Min Height	17	19	36
7	7/2/2005	Sum of Max Height	23	21	44
8		Sum of Min Height	21	19	40
9	7/3/2005	Sum of Max Height	24	20	44
10		Sum of Min Height	23	18	41
11	7/4/2005	Sum of Max Height	22	24	46
12		Sum of Min Height	21	21	42
13	7/5/2005	Sum of Max Height	20	23	43
14		Sum of Min Height	17	22	39
15	7/6/2005	Sum of Max Height	17	22	39
16		Sum of Min Height	16	21	37
17	7/7/2005	Sum of Max Height	19	17	36
18		Sum of Min Height	17	16	33
19	Total Sum of Max Height		144	149	293
20	Total Sum of Min Height		132	136	268

Figure 5-3: The initial PivotTable report.

Now you discover that the client wants the heights expressed in meters, and the data you have are in feet. This is a perfect place to use calculated fields. Here are the steps to follow:

1. Make sure the PivotTable is active by clicking anywhere in it.

2. Select Formulas from the PivotTable menu; then select Calculated Field. Excel will display the Insert Calculated Field dialog box, as shown in Figure 5-4.

3. Type **Max Height (M)** in the Name box.

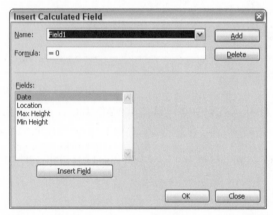

Figure 5-4: The Insert Calculated Field dialog box lists the PivotTable's fields.

4. Click in the Formula box and press Backspace to delete the 0, being sure to leave the equals sign.

5. Enter **0.3048***.

6. Click the Max Height field in the Fields list.

7. Click the Insert Field button. The Max Height field name will be entered, enclosed in single quotes, in the formula. At this point the Insert Calculated Field dialog box will look like the one shown in Figure 5-5.

8. Click OK to close the dialog box and add the newly defined field to the Data area.

9. Repeat Steps 2–8 to create a calculated field for minimum height in meters. The name will be Min Height (M) and you will use the same formula to create it, using the Min Height field in place of the Max Height field.

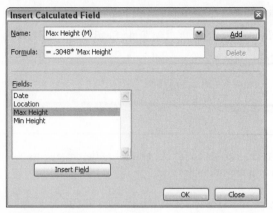

Figure 5-5: The Insert Calculated Field dialog box after a calculated field has been defined for maximum height in meters.

At this point your PivotTable will look like Figure 5-6. The Data area includes the two calculated fields you just created as well as the two original data fields. You can treat these calculated fields like any others. In fact, next you do just that, changing the number display to show only a single decimal place and also changing the field display name:

	A	B	C	D	E	
1						
2						
3			Location ▾			
4	Date ▾	Data ▾	Power Plant	West Bridge	Grand Total	
5	7/1/2005	Sum of Max Height	19	22	41	⎫ Regular Fields
6		Sum of Min Height	17	19	36	⎭
7		Sum of Max Height (M)	5.7912	6.7056	12.4968	⎫ Calculated Fields
8		Sum of Min Height (M)	5.1816	5.7912	10.9728	⎭
9	7/2/2005	Sum of Max Height	23	21	44	
10		Sum of Min Height	21	19	40	
11		Sum of Max Height (M)	7.0104	6.4008	13.4112	
12		Sum of Min Height (M)	6.4008	5.7912	12.192	
13	7/3/2005	Sum of Max Height	24	20	44	
14		Sum of Min Height	23	18	41	
15		Sum of Max Height (M)	7.3152	6.096	13.4112	
16		Sum of Min Height (M)	7.0104	5.4864	12.4968	
17	7/4/2005	Sum of Max Height	22	24	46	
18		Sum of Min Height	21	21	42	
19		Sum of Max Height (M)	6.7056	7.3152	14.0208	
20		Sum of Min Height (M)	6.4008	6.4008	12.8016	
21	7/5/2005	Sum of Max Height	20	23	43	
22		Sum of Min Height	17	22	39	
23		Sum of Max Height (M)	6.096	7.0104	13.1064	
24		Sum of Min Height (M)	5.1816	6.7056	11.8872	
25	7/6/2005	Sum of Max Height	17	22	39	
26		Sum of Min Height	16	21	37	
27		Sum of Max Height (M)	5.1816	6.7056	11.8872	
28		Sum of Min Height (M)	4.8768	6.4008	11.2776	
29	7/7/2005	Sum of Max Height	19	17	36	
30		Sum of Min Height	17	16	33	
31		Sum of Max Height (M)	5.7912	5.1816	10.9728	
32		Sum of Min Height (M)	5.1816	4.8768	10.0584	

Figure 5-6: The PivotTable after the two calculated fields have been defined.

Part V

1. Click one of the label cells that says Sum of Max Height (M).

2. Select Field Settings from the PivotTable menu to display the Field Settings dialog box.

3. Change the field name to Maximum Height (M).

4. Click the Number button to display the Format Cells dialog box.

5. Select the Number format with one decimal place.

6. Click OK twice to return to the worksheet.

7. Repeat these steps with the Sum of Min Height (M) field, changing the field name to Minimum Height (M) and assigning the same number format.

The final steps involve hiding unneeded parts of the table. You no longer need the original data (in feet). Also, there is no need for the Grand Total calculations in column E or for the various total rows at the bottom of the PivotTable. Here are the required steps:

1. Select PivotTable Options from the PivotTable menu.

2. Turn off the Grand Totals for Rows and Grand Totals for Columns options.

3. Click OK.

4. Click any cell for the Sum of Max Height field.

5. Select Field Settings from the PivotTable menu.

6. Click the Hide button.

7. Repeat steps 4–6 for the Sum of Min Height field.

Your final PivotTable report is shown in Figure 5-7. It displays only the two calculated fields, which is just what you want. The original fields still exist, of course, but they are not displayed. If the raw data are changed, the calculated fields will update to reflect this.

	A	B	C	D
1		Drop Page Fields Here		
2				
3			Location	
4	Date	Data	Power Plant	West Bridge
5	7/1/2005	Maximum Height (M)	5.8	6.7
6		Minimum Height (M)	5.2	5.8
7	7/2/2005	Maximum Height (M)	7.0	6.4
8		Minimum Height (M)	6.4	5.8
9	7/3/2005	Maximum Height (M)	7.3	6.1
10		Minimum Height (M)	7.0	5.5
11	7/4/2005	Maximum Height (M)	6.7	7.3
12		Minimum Height (M)	6.4	6.4
13	7/5/2005	Maximum Height (M)	6.1	7.0
14		Minimum Height (M)	5.2	6.7
15	7/6/2005	Maximum Height (M)	5.2	6.7
16		Minimum Height (M)	4.9	6.4
17	7/7/2005	Maximum Height (M)	5.8	5.2
18		Minimum Height (M)	5.2	4.9

Figure 5-7: The final PivotTable displays only the two calculated fields.

Working with Calculated Items

As you have seen, a calculated field performs a calculation on the data in an existing field. A calculated item, on the other hand, performs a calculation on one or more items within a field. So what's the difference? An item is an individual data value in a field. In your data source, you might have a field named Department and within that field you might have the items Accounting, Design, Maintenance, and so on.

To create a calculated item, make sure the PivotTable is active. Click a cell that belongs to the field that the calculated item will be based on. The calculated item will be inserted in the row below where you click. Then open the PivotTable menu and select Formulas ➪ Calculated Item. Excel will display the Insert Calculated Item dialog box, shown in Figure 5-8. Note that the title of the dialog box indicates the field you are using, Month in this case.

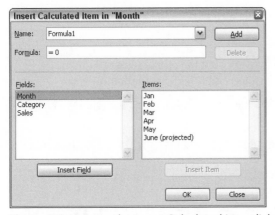

Figure 5-8: You use the Insert Calculated Item dialog box to define a calculated item.

Ungroup First

If the items in a field are grouped (grouping is covered later in this part), you should ungroup them before creating a calculated item:

1. Right-click the group.

2. Select Group and Outline from the pop-up menu.

3. Click Ungroup.

You can regroup the items after the calculated item has been created, if you wish.

The Fields list in the lower part of the dialog box lists the PivotTable's fields. When you select a field in this list, the Items list displays the names of the items for that field. This can be confusing because the dialog box lets you insert (or try to insert) things in the formula that cannot be used. For example, you will never use the Insert Field button because calculated items are not based on fields but on items. Likewise, you cannot insert items from fields other than the selected one (the one you clicked in the PivotTable before displaying this dialog box). Fortunately Excel prevents you from entering incorrect items in the formula by displaying an error message, either when you try to add the item or when you try to close the dialog box.

To complete the calculated item, follow these steps. They are similar in many ways to the procedure for creating a calculated field.

1. In the Name box, enter the name for the calculated item. This is the name that will be displayed in the PivotTable.

2. Enter the formula for the item in the Formula box:

   - The formula must start with an equals sign.

   - It can contain numbers, parentheses in pairs, and the operators + (addition), - (subtraction), * (multiplication), / (division), and ^ (exponentiation).

   - To add an item to the formula, click the item name in the Items list and then click Insert Item.

3. When the formula is complete, click the Add button and then the OK button to add the calculated item to the PivotTable.

Creating and Using a Calculated Item

This tip uses the data shown in Figure 5-9. These data, found in the workbook SalesProjections.xls, contain sales totals for different categories over five months. The first step is to create the basic PivotTable report.

1. Open the workbook.

2. Select the range A2:C27.

3. Select PivotTable and PivotChart Report from the Data menu to start the PivotTable Wizard.

4. Complete the wizard, accepting the default settings at each step.

5. When the PivotTable is displayed, drop the Month field on the Row area.

6. Drop the Sales field on the Data area.

	A	B	C
1			
2	**Month**	**Category**	**Sales**
3	Jan	Shoes	$ 1,769
4	Jan	Shirts	$ 2,397
5	Jan	Pants	$ 2,150
6	Jan	Outerwear	$ 2,820
7	Jan	Accessories	$ 1,845
8	Feb	Shoes	$ 2,192
9	Feb	Shirts	$ 2,846
10	Feb	Pants	$ 2,814
11	Feb	Outerwear	$ 2,606
12	Feb	Accessories	$ 2,718
13	Mar	Shoes	$ 1,055
14	Mar	Shirts	$ 2,319
15	Mar	Pants	$ 1,187
16	Mar	Outerwear	$ 1,606
17	Mar	Accessories	$ 2,078
18	Apr	Shoes	$ 2,919
19	Apr	Shirts	$ 2,648
20	Apr	Pants	$ 1,873
21	Apr	Outerwear	$ 2,255
22	Apr	Accessories	$ 2,195
23	May	Shoes	$ 2,742
24	May	Shirts	$ 2,798
25	May	Pants	$ 1,880
26	May	Outerwear	$ 1,714
27	May	Accessories	$ 1,590

Figure 5-9: The sample sales data.

7. Double-click the Sum of Sales button to open the Field Settings dialog box for that field.

8. Click the Number button to display the Format Cells dialog box.

9. Select the Currency format and specify no decimal places.

10. Click OK twice.

At this point the PivotTable will look like the one shown in Figure 5-10.

	A	B
1		
2		
3	Sum of Sales	
4	Month ▼	Total
5	Jan	$10,981
6	Feb	$13,176
7	Mar	$8,245
8	Apr	$11,890
9	May	$10,724
10	Grand Total	$55,016

Figure 5-10: The basic PivotTable report displays the sum of sales for each month.

The next step is to define a calculated item to display projected sales for June. In past years you have found that sales in June tend to be 120% of the average sales for the previous two months, April and May. Here's how to define that calculated item:

1. Click the May cell in the PivotTable. Excel will insert the calculated item below this row.

2. Select Formulas ➪ Calculate Item from the PivotTable menu to display the Insert Calculated Item dialog box.

3. Enter **June (projected)** in the Name box.

4. Click in the Formula field and erase the 0 (leaving the equals sign in place).

5. Enter **.5*(** after the equals sign.

6. Click Month in the Fields list.

7. Click May in the Items list.

8. Click Insert Item to insert "May" into the formula.

9. Enter a plus sign.

10. Click Apr in the Items list.

11. Click Insert Item to insert "Apr" in the formula.

12. Enter **)*1.2**. The dialog box should now appear as shown in Figure 5-11.

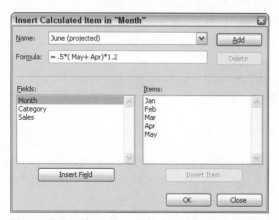

Figure 5-11: The Insert Calculated Item dialog box after you define a calculated item for projected June sales.

13. Click Add, then click OK.

Excel adds the calculated item to the PivotTable report, as shown in Figure 5-12.

	A	B
1	Drop Page Fields Here	
2		
3	Sum of Sales	
4	Month　▼	Total
5	Jan	$10,981
6	Feb	$13,176
7	Mar	$8,245
8	Apr	$11,890
9	May	$10,724
10	June (projected)	$13,568
11	Grand Total	$68,584

— Calculated item

Figure 5-12: The calculated item displayed in the PivotTable report.

Before you finish with this tip, look at some additional features of calculated items. In the PivotTable report used in the previous example, the Category field was not used and the PivotTable simply summed all values across categories for each month. What happens when you add the Category field to the PivotTable? Go ahead. All you need to do is drag the Category field from the Field List and drop it in the Row area. Now the PivotTable looks like what you see in Figure 5-13. The calculated item is automatically extended across all rows.

	A	B	C	D	E	F	G
1				Drop Page Fields Here			
2							
3	Sum of Sales	Category　▼					
4	Month　▼	Accessories	Outerwear	Pants	Shirts	Shoes	Grand Total
5	Jan	$1,845	$2,820	$2,150	$2,397	$1,769	$10,981
6	Feb	$2,718	$2,606	$2,814	$2,846	$2,192	$13,176
7	Mar	$2,078	$1,606	$1,187	$2,319	$1,055	$8,245
8	Apr	$2,195	$2,255	$1,873	$2,648	$2,919	$11,890
9	May	$1,590	$1,714	$1,880	$2,798	$2,742	$10,724
10	June (projected)	$2,271	$2,381	$2,252	$3,268	$3,397	$13,568
11	Grand Total	$12,697	$13,382	$12,156	$16,276	$14,074	$68,584

Calculated item

Figure 5-13: When you add the Category field to the Row area, the calculated item is automatically entered in each column.

In a situation like this, where a calculated item is displayed in more than one cell, you can modify the calculated item for individual cells. Move the Excel pointer onto calculated item cells in the PivotTable, cells B10 to F10. The Formula bar shows that each cell contains the formula you specified for the calculated item:

```
=.5*(May+Apr)*1.2
```

Suppose you know that while this projection formula is accurate overall, you would get a more accurate projection for the Pants category if you were to use a factor of 1.4 instead of 1.2. All you need to do is move the pointer to cell D10, where the calculated projection for Pants is located, press F2 to edit the formula, and make the desired change.

Showing and Hiding Detail

PivotTable reports give you the ability to view a greater or lesser amount of detail depending on your current needs.

Viewing Detail for Data Items

Viewing detail for data items is sometimes referred to as *drilling down*. When you drill down, Excel displays the raw data records that underlie the selected data item. To use this feature, you must ensure that the Enable Drill to Details option is turned on in the PivotTable Options dialog box (select Table Options from the PivotTable menu to display this dialog box).

To drill down, simply double-click the data cell of interest. Excel places the underlying raw data in a new worksheet and displays them. Figure 5-14 shows an example from the PivotTable you created earlier in this part from the data in SalesBySalesRep.xls. Double-clicking the data cell for Baker, J.T. creates the detail worksheet shown on the right. You can see that this contains all the raw data for Baker, J.T.

Double-click...

...to view details

2	
3	Sum of Sale total
4	Sales Rep ▾	Total
5	Ackerman, Q.	$3,928.90
6	Baker, J.T.	$1,815.95
7	Carver, W.	$4,137.55
8	D.F. Chang	$1,072.25
9	McBride, O.	$1,542.55
10	Muller, S.	$1,384.25
11	Rosenstein, F.	$5,575.20
12	Sanchez, L.	$2,817.65
13	Wilson, J.	$2,738.25
14	Yamamoto, A.	$3,099.75
15	Grand Total	$28,112.30
16	

	A	B	C	D	E	F
1	Date	Sales Rep	Item	Cost each	Quantity	Sale total
2	7/31/2005	Baker, J.T.	L98700F	8.25	2	16.5
3	7/27/2005	Baker, J.T.	L98700F	8.25	14	115.5
4	7/25/2005	Baker, J.T.	J21344A	19.5	8	156
5	7/2/2005	Baker, J.T.	Q00345B	39	13	507
6	7/24/2005	Baker, J.T.	L98700F	8.25	15	123.75
7	7/23/2005	Baker, J.T.	B20011A	22.15	18	398.7
8	7/23/2005	Baker, J.T.	C55440D	16.75	11	184.25
9	7/10/2005	Baker, J.T.	J21344A	19.5	14	273
10	7/5/2005	Baker, J.T.	L98700F	8.25	5	41.25

Figure 5-14: Double-clicking a data cell (left) drills down to the underlying raw data (right).

To remove detail data, simply delete the worksheet they are on (Select Delete Sheet from the Edit menu).

Viewing Details for Field Items

To control details for a field, right-click the field button, select the Group and Show Detail command from the pop-up menu, and then select either Hide Detail or Show Detail. You can also use the Show Detail and Hide Detail buttons on the PivotTable toolbar.

Showing and hiding detail for a field item has different effects depending on the field position in the PivotTable. If the PivotTable has two or more row fields and the field of interest is not the inner field, hiding detail for a field works by collapsing any fields that are more "inner." I am speaking here of row fields but it works the same way for column fields.

An example will help clarify this. The top part of Figure 5-15 shows the PivotTable you created earlier from the data in `TestScores.xls`. If you hide the details for the Gender field, the result is that the inner field, Age Group, is collapsed and the PivotTable looks like the lower part of Figure 5-15. Showing the detail for the Gender field returns the PivotTable to its original display.

	A	B	C	D	E	F
1						
2						
3	Sum of Score		Political Affiliation ▼	Region ▼		
4			Dem			
5	Gender ▼	Age Group ▼	Midwest	NorthEast	NorthWest	South
6	Female	20-29	88		100	83
7		30-39			434	
8		40-49		81	98	
9		50-59	94		333	
10		60-69		99		
11	Female Total		182	180	965	83
12	Male	20-29		92	177	
13		30-39	177	94	363	171
14		40-49	95	180	89	91
15		50-59	96		96	
16		60-69			95	
17	Male Total		368	366	820	262
18	Grand Total		550	546	1785	345
19						

	A	B	C	D	E	F
1						
2						
3	Sum of Score		Political Affiliation ▼	Region ▼		
4			Dem			
5	Gender ▼	Age Group ▼	Midwest	NorthEast	NorthWest	South
6	Female		182	180	965	83
7	Male		368	366	820	262
8	Grand Total		550	546	1785	345
9						

Figure 5-15: The PivotTable report before (top) and after (bottom) the detail for the Gender field is hidden.

In Figure 5-15 the details for Age Group are hidden, but the Field button is still displayed. You can still pull down this list and filter the PivotTable based on Age Group.

In other situations the Hide Details command has the following effects:

- If the field is the inner field, hiding its details has the same effect as hiding the details of its parent field (as in the previous example). To show the details again you must execute the Show Details command on the parent field.

- If the field is the only row field, the Hide Details command has no effect.

When you select Show Details for an inner or only field, Excel displays a list of available fields, including those that are already part of the PivotTable and any that have not been added to the PivotTable. It does not, however, list fields that are already added to the region (row or column) where the field of interest is located. This is shown for the TestScores PivotTable in Figure 5-16.

Figure 5-16: Showing detail for an inner or only field means adding a field to the Row or Column area.

When you select a field from this list and click OK, Excel adds the field as an inner field to the Row area:

- If the field was already part of the PivotTable, the effect is the same as that of pivoting the table; the field is moved from its current location (for example, the Column area) to the new location as the inner field in the Row area.

- If the field was not already part of the PivotTable it is simply added as the inner field.

This is shown in Figure 5-17. At the top is the original PivotTable. At the bottom is the PivotTable after you have shown detail for the Age Group field and selected the column Subject #.

Viewing Detail in OLAP Reports

Things work slightly differently for PivotTables based on OLAP data sources. To display or hide lower-level detail, click the field and then click the Show Detail or Hide Detail button on the PivotTable toolbar.

To hide upper-level detail, right-click the field button for the lowest level you want to hide and then select Hide Levels from the pop-up menu. The level you selected and all higher levels in the dimension are hidden. To redisplay upper levels, right-click any field in the dimension and select Show Levels from the pop-up menu.

	A	B	C	D	E
1					
2					
3	Sum of Score		Political Affiliation ▼	Region ▼	
4			Dem		
5	Gender ▼	Age Group ▼	Midwest	NorthEast	NorthWest
6	Female	20-29	88		100
7		30-39			434
8		40-49		81	98
9		50-59	94		333
10		60-69		99	
11	Female Total		182	180	965
12	Male	20-29		92	177
13		30-39	177	94	363
14		40-49	95	180	89
15		50-59	96		96
16		60-69			95
17	Male Total		368	366	820
18	Grand Total		550	546	1785

	A	B	C	D	E
1					
2					
3	Sum of Score			Political Affiliation ▼	Region ▼
4				Dem	
5	Gender ▼	Age Group ▼	Subject # ▼	Midwest	NorthEast
6	Female	20-29	20		
7			27		
8			32		
9			37		
10			51	88	
11			56		
12			67		
13			83		
14			85		
15			90		
16			100		
17		20-29 Total		88	
18		30-39	6		

Figure 5-17: A PivotTable report before (top) and after (bottom) you have shown detail for the Age Group field and selected the column Subject #.

PivotTables based on OLAP data sources also enable you to hide property fields:

1. Click the field for which you want to hide or display property fields.

2. Select Property Fields from the PivotTable menu to display the Property Fields dialog box.

3. In the Choose properties from level list, click each level for which you want to display property fields.

4. Double-click the name of each property field you want displayed.

5. In the Properties to display box, click a property name and use the up and down buttons to arrange the property fields in the order in which you want to display them.

6. Ensure that the Show Fields for this Dimension in Outline Form option is turned on.

7. Click OK.

Part V

Can't See Your Property Fields?

If the property fields you select for display are not visible, it is probably because the level(s) to which they belong are hidden. Click the field and then click the Show Detail button on the PivotTable toolbar.

Grouping PivotTable Items

Excel gives you the ability to group items in a PivotTable report, providing another level of analysis that can be very useful in some situations. Suppose, for instance, that your raw data are about individual people and one of the data items is Age. This value will range from, say, 18 to 65. Using the Group command you can define three groups:

Group 1: 18 to 35

Group 2: 36 to 49

Group 3: 50 to 65

The resulting PivotTable summarizes data according to the groups you define. You can also group non-numeric data. Suppose your sales data include the city of the branch that is reporting, and you want to analyze by region. You can define groups that contain specified cities, such as:

Northeast: Boston, Hartford, New York

South: Atlanta, Miami, Charleston

Midwest: Chicago, Toledo, Omaha

The details for grouping depend on the kind of data being grouped, as explained in the following sections. For any field, you group items by right-clicking the field button, selecting Group and Show Detail from the pop-up menu, and then selecting Group from the next menu. Excel will display the Grouping dialog box. To ungroup a field, follow the preceding steps, but select Ungroup from the final menu.

Grouping Numeric Items

When a field contains numeric data you can group the items by numeric value. The Grouping dialog box for a field that contains numeric data is shown in Figure 5-18. It has Starting at and Ending at options that determine the value at which the grouping starts and ends. By default these options are on and filled in with the lowest and highest values from the actual data. (Normally you will leave these at the default settings.) The By box determines the size of each group.

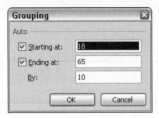

Figure 5-18: The Grouping dialog box for a field that contains numeric data.

An example of this kind of data is shown in Figure 5-19, which lists survey results by the age of the respondent. To make the data easier to read you can create age groups.

Count of Question 1	Question 1	Gender		No Total	Unsure		Unsure Total	Yes		Yes Total
	No				Unsure			Yes		
Age	F	M			F	M		F	M	
18			1	1	1	2	3	1	2	3
19			2	2		1	1	2		2
20	1	1		2	2		2	1	2	3
21	1	2		3						
22	1	1		2	1	1	2		1	1
23	2			2	3		3	3	2	5
24	2	4		6	1	3	4	1	1	2
25					2	1	3		2	2
26	3	1		4		1	1	1		1
27		3		3					1	1
28	5			5	1	1	2	2	1	3
29	1	1		2	1		1	2		2
30					2	2	4		1	1
31		1		1	2		2	2	3	5
32	1			1		1	1	1	2	3
33	1			1	2	1	3		1	1
34	1	2		3		2	2	1	1	2
35	1	2		3		1	1	1	1	2
36	1	1		2		2	2		1	1
37	1	2		3		2	2	3	2	5
38		2		2		1	1	1	3	4
39	1	3		4	1	2	3		2	2
40	2			2		1	1		1	1
41	2	1		3					1	1
42								3		3
43		1		1		1	1	1	1	2
44	3	2		5				2		2

Figure 5-19: Survey data that list respondent ages in the Row area.

If you display the Grouping dialog box for the Age field and accept the defaults — starting at 18, ending at 65, and by 10 — the result is shown in Figure 5-20.

	A	B	C	D	E	F	G	H	I	J
1			Drop Page Fields Here							
2										
3	Count of Question 1	Question 1	Gender							
4		No			No Total	Unsure		Unsure Total	Yes		Yes Total
5	Age	F	M			F	M		F	M	
6	18-27	10	15		25	10	9	19	9	11	20
7	28-37	12	9		21	8	12	20	12	13	25
8	38-47	11	13		24	2	8	10	9	10	19
9	48-57	7	4		11	12	20	32	6	11	17
10	58-67	11	10		21	12	7	19	6	9	15

Figure 5-20: The PivotTable after the Age field is grouped by 10.

Part V

Suppose, however, you want the groups to be by decade — 20–29, 30–39, and so on. Then you set the Starting at and Ending at options manually:

1. Turn both options off.

2. Enter 20 in the Starting at box.

3. Enter 59 in the Ending at box.

The dialog box will look like Figure 5-21.

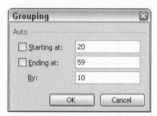

Figure 5-21: Setting numeric field group options manually.

When you click OK the PivotTable changes, as shown in Figure 5-22. The PivotTable now displays six groups:

- One group labeled <20 for all data below the Starting at value.

- Four groups for the age groups 20–29, 30–39, and so on.

- One group labeled >60 for all data above the Ending at value.

	A	B	C	D	E	F	G	H	I	J
1				Drop Page Fields Here						
2										
3	Count of Question 1	Question 1 ▼	Gender ▼							
4		No		No Total	Unsure		Unsure Total	Yes		Yes Total
5	Age ▼	F	M		F	M		F	M	
6	<20		3	3	1	3	4	3	2	5
7	20-29	16	13	29	11	7	18	10	10	20
8	30-39	7	13	20	7	14	21	9	17	26
9	40-49	10	8	18	1	7	8	8	6	14
10	50-59	11	5	16	13	21	34	7	15	22
11	>60		7	9	16	11	4	15	5	4	9

Figure 5-22: The PivotTable after the group options have been set manually.

Grouping Dates

When a field contains dates, you can define groups based on essentially any measurement ranging from seconds up to years. Remember, in Excel the term *date* refers to data that can specify a date, a time, or both. You can create a single grouping, such as by grouping dates by weeks, or you can create more than one level of grouping, such as by grouping dates by years and then within years by quarters.

When a field contains date data, the Grouping dialog box looks as it does in Figure 5-23.

Figure 5-23: Setting grouping options for a field that contains date data.

At the top of this dialog box are Starting at and Ending at options. These options are turned on by default, and the starting and ending dates (or times) are determined automatically by Excel. In most instances you will leave these unchanged.

The By list contains all the intervals by which you can group: seconds through years. Click an interval to select it; click again to deselect. You can select one or more intervals.

Depending on the interval or intervals selected, the Number of option may be available. When it is, you enter a value to determine the size of the grouping. For example, if you select Days as the interval you can enter **5** to create groups of five days.

For an illustration, look at the PivotTable report in Figure 5-24. It shows survey data organized by date in the Row area. The dates fall into two groups: several in early September and several in late September.

	A	B	C	D	E
1		Drop Page Fields Here			
2					
3	Count of Question 1	Question 1 ▾			
4	Date of Survey ▾	No	Unsure	Yes	Grand Total
5	9/1/2005	22	15	10	47
6	9/2/2005	12	18	18	48
7	9/3/2005	16	13	18	47
8	9/25/2005	9	13	6	28
9	9/26/2005	21	20	21	62
10	9/27/2005	22	21	23	66
11	Grand Total	102	100	96	298

Figure 5-24: Survey data organized by date.

To create groups for these data, display the Grouping dialog box for the Date of Survey field, select Days as the interval, and enter **3** in the Number of box. The resulting grouped PivotTable is shown in Figure 5-25.

	A	B	C	D	E
1					
2					
3	Count of Question 1	Question 1 ▾			
4	Date of Survey ▾	No	Unsure	Yes	Grand Total
5	9/1/2005 - 9/3/2005	50	46	46	142
6	9/25/2005 - 9/27/2005	52	54	50	156
7	Grand Total	102	100	96	298

Figure 5-25: The Date of Survey field after being grouped.

You can use the Starting at and Ending at options to change the way groups are formed. They work like these same options for numeric data, as described in the previous section. The defaults give the results, as shown previously. But suppose you turn off the Ending at option and enter **9/4/2005** in the adjacent box? Then the PivotTable will look like Figure 5-26. You can see that all data after 9/4/2005 are lumped into a single group called >9/4/2005.

	A	B	C	D	E
1		Drop Page Fields Here			
2					
3	Count of Question 1	Question 1 ▾			
4	Date of Survey ▾	No	Unsure	Yes	Grand Total
5	9/1/2005 - 9/3/2005	50	46	46	142
6	>9/4/2005	52	54	50	156
7	Grand Total	102	100	96	298

Figure 5-26: Using a manually set Ending at option.

Grouping Other Items

The category "other items" refers to any data that are not numbers or dates. States, department names, product descriptions, colors, and flavors are just a few examples of this kind of data (sometimes called *category data*). To group this kind of data, click each individual item while holding down Ctrl. When all the items to be grouped have been selected, right-click one of the selected items, select Group ⇨ Show Details from the pop-up menu, and then select Group. Repeat for additional groups. You'll see how in the next tip — you will also see how to create subtotals for the groups you define.

Grouping Category Data

This tip shows you how to group category data as well as how to create subtotals for a group, something that Excel does not do automatically. You'll use the data shown in Figure 5-27, which is located in the workbook SurveyResults2.xls.

	A	B	C	D	E	F	G	H
1								
2	Subject #	Age	Gender	Date of Survey	Race	Question 1	Question 2	Question 3
3	1	50	M	9/1/2005	Black	No	Yes	Yes
4	2	19	M	9/3/2005	Hispanic	No	Unsure	Unsure
5	3	31	F	9/2/2005	White	Yes	Yes	No
6	4	51	M	9/2/2005	Asian	Yes	No	Yes
7	5	24	F	9/1/2005	White	No	Unsure	Yes
8	6	58	F	9/3/2005	Other	No	Unsure	Yes
9	7	21	F	9/1/2005	Black	No	No	No
10	8	36	M	9/3/2005	White	Unsure	No	Yes
11	9	49	M	9/2/2005	White	Yes	Unsure	No
12	10	55	F	9/2/2005	Asian	No	Unsure	No
13	11	31	M	9/1/2005	White	No	Yes	Unsure
14	12	18	F	9/3/2005	Other	Unsure	Unsure	Unsure
15	13	44	M	9/1/2005	Black	No	Yes	Unsure
16	14	45	M	9/3/2005	White	Yes	Yes	Yes
17	15	39	M	9/2/2005	Black	Unsure	Unsure	No
18	16	52	F	9/2/2005	Hispanic	No	Yes	Unsure
19	17	65	M	9/1/2005	White	No	Yes	No
20	18	42	F	9/3/2005	Asian	Yes	Unsure	No
21	19	19	F	9/1/2005	White	Yes	No	Unsure
22	20	41	F	9/3/2005	Other	No	Yes	Yes
23	21	18	M	9/2/2005	Black	Yes	No	No
24	22	61	M	9/2/2005	White	Yes	Unsure	No
25	23	23	F	9/1/2005	White	No	Yes	Yes
26	24	58	M	9/3/2005	Asian	Yes	No	Yes
27	25	45	F	9/1/2005	White	No	No	No
28	26	35	M	9/3/2005	Other	No	No	Yes
29	27	56	M	9/2/2005	Black	Yes	Yes	No
30	28	30	M	9/2/2005	White	Unsure	Yes	Unsure
31	29	28	F	9/1/2005	Hispanic	No	Yes	Yes
32	30	62	M	9/3/2005	White	Yes	No	Yes

Figure 5-27: The survey data that will be used for the PivotTable report.

The first task is to create the basic PivotTable:

1. Select the data range A2:H300.

2. Select PivotTable and PivotChart Report from the Data menu to start the PivotTable Wizard.

3. Click Finish to accept all the default settings. Excel creates the blank PivotTable.

4. Drag the Race field to the Row area.

5. Drag the Question 1 field to the Column area.

6. Drag the Question 1 field again, this time to the Data area.

At this point your PivotTable will look like the one in Figure 5-28. Note how putting the Question 1 field in both the Column and Data areas has given you the desired result — a count of the number of people in each category giving answers of Yes, No, and Unsure.

	A	B	C	D	E
1		Drop Page Fields Here			
2					
3	Count of Question 1	Question 1 ▾			
4	Race ▾	No	Unsure	Yes	Grand Total
5	Asian	14	20	16	50
6	Black	15	15	16	46
7	Hispanic	11	4	5	20
8	Other	20	13	15	48
9	White	42	48	44	134
10	Grand Total	102	100	96	298

Figure 5-28: The basic PivotTable report displays count totals.

But now you want to look at the data in a new way; you want to compare the results for the White group to the total results for all other groups. This is an ideal situation for grouping: you create a group that contains the Asian, Black, Hispanic, and Other categories. Here's how:

1. Click the Asian field (the cell with the text "Asian").

2. Hold down the Ctrl key and click the Black, Hispanic, and Other fields.

3. Release the Ctrl key.

4. Right-click any of the selected fields and select Group ⇨ Show Detail from the pop-up menu; then select Group.

Now the PivotTable looks like Figure 5-29. You can see that a group named Group1 has been created, containing the four categories you selected. Note also that another field, called Race2, has in effect been created. This field contains two items: Group1 and White. You can use the Race2 field button to filter the report on these values.

	A	B	C	D	E	F
1						
2						
3	Count of Question 1		Question 1 ▼			
4	Race2 ▼	Race ▼	No	Unsure	Yes	Grand Total
5	Group1	Asian	14	20	16	50
6		Black	15	15	16	46
7		Hispanic	11	4	5	20
8		Other	20	13	15	48
9	White	White	42	48	44	134
10	Grand Total		102	100	96	298

Figure 5-29: The PivotTable report after four of the categories have been grouped.

This is okay as far as it goes, but you also want to display subtotals for Race2. To do so, right-click the field and select Field Settings, and then select Automatic under Subtotals. Now the PivotTable looks like Figure 5-30, with subtotals for each category in the Race2 field.

	A	B	C	D	E	F
1						
2						
3	Count of Question 1		Question 1 ▼			
4	Race2 ▼	Race ▼	No	Unsure	Yes	Grand Total
5	Group1	Asian	14	20	16	50
6		Black	15	15	16	46
7		Hispanic	11	4	5	20
8		Other	20	13	15	48
9	Group1 Total		60	52	52	164
10	White	White	42	48	44	134
11	White Total		42	48	44	134
12	Grand Total		102	100	96	298

Subtotals

Figure 5-30: The PivotTable report with subtotals for the groups.

There's one more thing to do. For this kind of data it is usually better to display percentages. Because the different groups contain different numbers of people, the raw numbers do not tell you much. Each value should show the percentage of people in that category with a particular answer. Here's how to set this up:

1. Right-click a data cell and select Field Settings from the pop-up menu to display the Field Settings dialog box.

2. Click the Options button to expand the dialog box.

3. Pull down the Show data as list and select % of Row.

4. Click OK.

The final PivotTable report is shown in Figure 5-31.

	A	B	C	D	E	F
1			Drop Page Fields Here			
2						
3	Count of Question 1		Question 1 ▼			
4	Race2 ▼	Race ▼	No	Unsure	Yes	Grand Total
5	Group1	Asian	28.00%	40.00%	32.00%	100.00%
6		Black	32.61%	32.61%	34.78%	100.00%
7		Hispanic	55.00%	20.00%	25.00%	100.00%
8		Other	41.67%	27.08%	31.25%	100.00%
9	Group1 Total		36.59%	31.71%	31.71%	100.00%
10	White	White	31.34%	35.82%	32.84%	100.00%
11	White Total		31.34%	35.82%	32.84%	100.00%
12	Grand Total		34.23%	33.56%	32.21%	100.00%

Figure 5-31: The PivotTable report with data displayed as the percentage of the row total.

Part VI

Understanding and Using PivotCharts

One of Excel's strong points is its charting capabilities. If you can chart regular data in Excel, why not the data in a PivotTable? Indeed you can, and the result is called, appropriately enough, a PivotChart. In many respects a PivotChart is like any other Excel chart. In some ways, however, it is special, reflecting its link to PivotTable data. In this chapter you learn to create and use PivotCharts.

Tips and Where to Find Them

Understanding PivotCharts

A PivotChart is a graphical representation of the data in a PivotTable report. Excel has long been known for its excellent charting capabilities. The value of charts is that they let you see trends and relationships that may not be obvious when looking at the data in a tabular form. PivotTables are no different and the data they contain can also benefit from graphical display.

A PivotChart is always based on a PivotTable report. Although you can create a PivotTable without a PivotChart, you cannot do the reverse. They are linked so that changes in the report are always reflected in the chart. In fact, the way to make many changes to a PivotChart is to change the underlying PivotTable report.

Remember that a PivotChart is for the most part just a regular Excel chart that happens to be linked to a PivotTable report. Essentially, anything you can do with a regular chart you can also do with a PivotTable chart, including formatting. This part does not describe all of Excel's charting features, just the ones that apply to PivotCharts.

Creating a PivotChart

There are two ways to create a PivotChart:

- From an existing PivotTable
- From scratch

The results are the same and you can use whichever method suits your situation.

Create a PivotChart from an Existing PivotTable

If you have already created your PivotTable report, creating a PivotChart is a simple matter. All you need to do is make sure the PivotTable is active, then click the PivotChart button on the PivotTable toolbar. (You can also select the PivotChart command from the PivotTable menu.) The PivotChart will be created in a new worksheet.

Create a PivotChart from Scratch

If you have not created the PivotTable yet, you can create the PivotChart from scratch. You use the PivotTable and PivotChart Report Wizard, and the procedure is similar to the one you would use to create a PivotTable report. In fact, the only difference is that in Step 1 of the wizard you select the PivotChart report (with PivotTable report) option, as shown in Figure 6-1. The remaining steps are the same as when you are creating just a PivotTable.

Figure 6-1: Selecting the wizard option to create a PivotChart report.

When the initial blank PivotChart is created it looks like Figure 6-2. Note the following:

- The Field List is displayed.

- The PivotChart toolbar is similar to the PivotTable toolbar. The main difference is that there is a PivotChart menu on the toolbar with commands relevant to PivotCharts (more on these commands later).

- The blank chart has places for you to drop page fields and data items, just like a PivotTable.

- The chart also has places to drop category fields and series fields. These correspond to rows and columns in a PivotTable report.

The remaining steps for completing the PivotChart are just like those for creating a PivotTable report — you drag fields from the Field List and drop them in the appropriate area of the chart.

As you create your chart, something else is going on. Excel is working behind the scenes to create a PivotTable report. Remember, a PivotChart is always based on a PivotTable report, so this is necessary — no PivotTable, no PivotChart! When you are finished, your workbook will contain the new PivotChart and the PivotTable on which it is based.

This parallel creation of the PivotChart and PivotTable offers you another option. After the blank PivotChart and PivotTable have been created, you can work in either, dragging fields to place them in the PivotTable or the PivotChart. Whatever you do with one will be reflected in the other.

Where Is the PivotChart Placed?

A PivotChart is always placed on a new worksheet with the name Chart 1, Chart 2, and so on. The underlying PivotTable can be placed on the new worksheet or on an existing worksheet, as specified in Step 3 of the wizard.

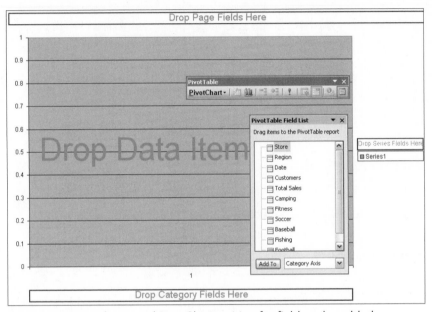

Figure 6-2: A newly created PivotChart waiting for fields to be added.

Creating a PivotChart from Scratch

This section takes you through the steps of creating a PivotChart from scratch, without an existing PivotTable. You use the data in SportingGoodsRawData.xls. You used these data in Part V; they are shown again in Figure 6-3.

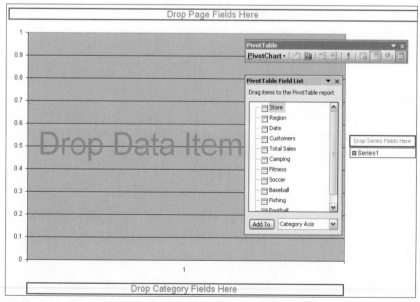

	A	B	C	D	E	F	G	H	I	J	K
1											
2	Store	Region	Date	Customers	Total Sales	Camping	Fitness	Soccer	Baseball	Fishing	Football
3	2134	Northeast	06-Jun-05	207	$ 6,581	$ 326	$ 1,284	$ 970	$ 1,270	$ 1,488	$ 1,243
4	2134	Northeast	07-Jun-05	162	$ 3,584	$ 901	$ 247	$ 765	$ 1,251	$ 228	$ 192
5	2134	Northeast	08-Jun-05	188	$ 4,713	$ 837	$ 1,260	$ 959	$ 765	$ 179	$ 713
6	2134	Northeast	09-Jun-05	171	$ 5,263	$ 553	$ 1,134	$ 236	$ 1,353	$ 1,011	$ 976
7	2134	Northeast	10-Jun-05	64	$ 4,731	$ 775	$ 294	$ 1,480	$ 160	$ 864	$ 1,158
8	2134	Northeast	11-Jun-05	246	$ 3,853	$ 429	$ 853	$ 773	$ 760	$ 739	$ 299
9	2134	Northeast	12-Jun-05	63	$ 6,077	$ 1,075	$ 1,418	$ 659	$ 1,445	$ 1,340	$ 140
10	2298	Midwest	06-Jun-05	86	$ 4,075	$ 866	$ 399	$ 270	$ 690	$ 418	$ 1,432
11	2298	Midwest	07-Jun-05	234	$ 3,933	$ 1,056	$ 266	$ 781	$ 131	$ 1,376	$ 323
12	2298	Midwest	08-Jun-05	286	$ 3,818	$ 1,330	$ 459	$ 314	$ 1,119	$ 149	$ 447
13	2298	Midwest	09-Jun-05	99	$ 4,923	$ 456	$ 426	$ 368	$ 1,045	$ 1,453	$ 1,175
14	2298	Midwest	10-Jun-05	85	$ 5,084	$ 1,061	$ 729	$ 211	$ 939	$ 939	$ 1,205
15	2298	Midwest	11-Jun-05	218	$ 3,517	$ 1,191	$ 341	$ 123	$ 1,293	$ 300	$ 269
16	2298	Midwest	12-Jun-05	124	$ 4,435	$ 998	$ 581	$ 350	$ 1,249	$ 295	$ 962
17	2166	South	06-Jun-05	215	$ 8,625	$ 1,957	$ 1,995	$ 615	$ 1,623	$ 370	$ 2,065
18	2166	South	07-Jun-05	266	$ 5,902	$ 1,829	$ 612	$ 709	$ 878	$ 1,218	$ 656
19	2166	South	08-Jun-05	92	$ 8,032	$ 1,844	$ 1,099	$ 1,804	$ 1,005	$ 1,509	$ 771
20	2166	South	09-Jun-05	237	$ 7,786	$ 911	$ 1,470	$ 1,430	$ 787	$ 2,074	$ 1,114
21	2166	South	10-Jun-05	65	$ 7,669	$ 1,377	$ 2,092	$ 364	$ 1,793	$ 502	$ 1,541
22	2166	South	11-Jun-05	263	$ 5,211	$ 1,201	$ 360	$ 655	$ 522	$ 559	$ 1,914
23	2166	South	12-Jun-05	159	$ 9,388	$ 1,663	$ 1,978	$ 828	$ 1,375	$ 1,747	$ 1,797

Figure 6-3: The raw data on sporting goods sales.

1. Select the data range A2:K23.
2. Select PivotTable and PivotChart Report from the Data menu to start the wizard.
3. In the first step, select the PivotChart report (with PivotTable report) option.
4. Click Finish to complete the wizard with the default settings. Excel creates the blank PivotChart shown in Figure 6-4.

Figure 6-4: The blank PivotChart before any fields are added.

5. Drag the Region field and drop it on Drop Series Fields Here.

6. Drag the Date field and drop it on Drop Category Fields Here.

7. Drag the Camping field and drop it on Drop Data Items Here.

At this point the PivotChart will look like Figure 6-5. I have hidden the Field List to make the entire chart visible. (You can click the Hide/Show Field List button on the PivotChart toolbar.) The PivotChart displays field buttons, just like a PivotTable (see Figure 6-5). You can click the down arrow on these buttons to display a list of values for filtering the chart. The PivotChart in Figure 6-5 has field buttons for the category field (Date) and the series field (Region). If you had added any page fields to the chart it would have a field button for these as well.

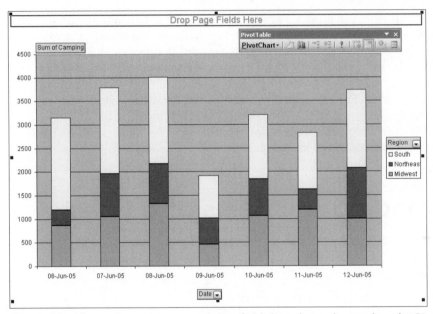

Figure 6-5: After series, category, and data fields have been dropped on the PivotChart.

You should also take a look at the underlying PivotTable that was created. This will be on another worksheet, probably the one named Sheet 4. It is shown in Figure 6-6.

	A	B	C	D	E
1					
2					
3	Sum of Camping	Region			
4	Date	Midwest	Northeast	South	Grand Total
5	06-Jun-05	866	326	1957	3149
6	07-Jun-05	1056	901	1829	3786
7	08-Jun-05	1330	837	1844	4011
8	09-Jun-05	456	553	911	1920
9	10-Jun-05	1061	775	1377	3213
10	11-Jun-05	1191	429	1201	2821
11	12-Jun-05	998	1075	1663	3736
12	Grand Total	6958	4896	10782	22636

Figure 6-6: The PivotTable report that was created when you designed the PivotChart.

Changing a PivotChart to a Static Chart

To change a PivotChart to a static chart, one that is no longer linked to the data source, delete the underlying PivotTable report. You can delete the entire worksheet that the report is on, or you can delete just the PivotTable, as follows:

1. Click anywhere in the PivotTable.

2. From the PivotTable menu choose Select, then choose Entire Table.

3. Press Delete.

After you create a PivotChart, you must always remember that it is linked to the PivotTable report. Changes that you make in one will be reflected in the other. For example, if you change the number display format of a data field in the report, that format change will carry over to the category or series labels in the PivotChart. Likewise, if you use the field buttons in the PivotChart to filter the data, that filtering will be applied to the PivotTable. Not all changes are linked, of course. For example, if you change the PivotChart chart type (say from bar to line), this has no effect on the PivotTable. The PivotChart and the linked PivotTable report have the same name. Select Options from the PivotTable or PivotChart menu and the name is displayed in the Name box.

Understanding the Parts of a Chart

Before I go into more detail about creating and using PivotCharts, you should be sure you understand Excel's chart terminology. Let's look at some frequently used terms with reference to the chart in Figure 6-7.

- **Plot area** — Where the actual data are displayed.
- **Data series** — The chart elements corresponding to one related group of numbers. In a PivotChart, this refers to a column of numbers, although in regular (non-pivot) charts it can also refer to a row.
- **Category axis** — Lists the values of the data categories.
- **Data series axis** — Identifies the individual data series. Relevant only for 3-D charts.
- **Value axis** — Displays a scale of values for the data points.
- **Chart title** — The title of the chart.
- **Axis labels** — Titles for the individual axes.
- **Legend** — Identifies the data series by color and/or pattern.

Some of these chart elements are options: the chart and axis titles and the legend.

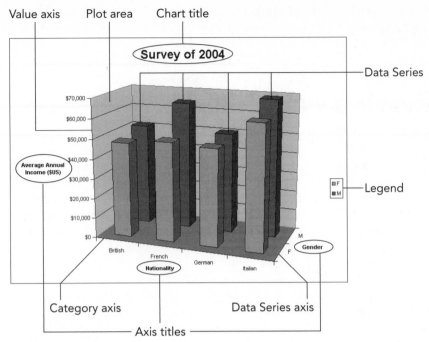

Figure 6-7: Parts of a typical Excel chart.

Working with the PivotChart Menu

When you are working with a PivotChart, the PivotTable toolbar displays on the screen. Instead of a PivotTable menu, it displays the PivotChart menu with its own set of commands. Actually, all but one of the commands on the PivotChart menu also exists on the PivotTable menu. The availability of certain commands on this menu depends on what, if anything, you have selected in the PivotChart.

- **Field Settings** — Displays the Field Settings dialog box for the selected field (covered in Part III). You must first select a data series that corresponds to a field, before selecting this command.

- **Options** — Displays the PivotTable Options dialog box for the underlying PivotTable (covered in Part III).

- **Refresh Data** — Refreshes the PivotTable and PivotChart.

- **Formulas** — Displays commands for working with calculated fields and items (covered in Part V).

- **Hide Field** — Removes the selected field from the PivotTable and PivotChart.

Part VI

One PivotChart menu command is unique to this menu: Hide PivotChart Field Buttons. It hides all the field buttons in the PivotChart so you can display and print the chart without these elements. Select the command again to redisplay the buttons.

Understanding and Changing PivotChart Types

Unless you changed the default settings, Excel's default is to create a new PivotChart as a stacked column chart. After the chart has been created, you can change its type to almost any one of Excel's chart types, and you can also use Excel's capability to define your own custom types. (One restriction is that the XY (Scatter), Bubble, and Stock types cannot be used for PivotCharts.) It's easy to try out the different chart types and see which one best suits your data.

To change the chart type of a PivotChart:

1. Right-click the chart and select Chart Type from the pop-up menu. Excel displays the Chart Type dialog box. (See Figure 6-8.)

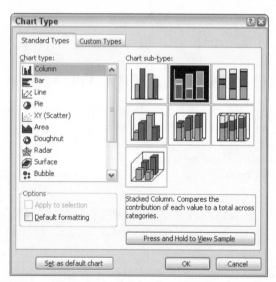

Figure 6-8: Using the Chart Type dialog box to change the type of a PivotChart.

2. Click the desired type in the Chart type list.

3. Click the desired subtype in the Chart subtype list. (Some custom charts do not offer subtypes.)

4. Click the Press and Hold to View Sample button to preview the selected type as applied to your data.

5. Click OK to accept the selected type and apply it to the PivotChart.

For example, Figure 6-9 shows the same PivotChart in Figure 6-5 after its type has been changed to clustered 3-D column. You can change a chart's type as many times as you want without affecting its data or other formatting.

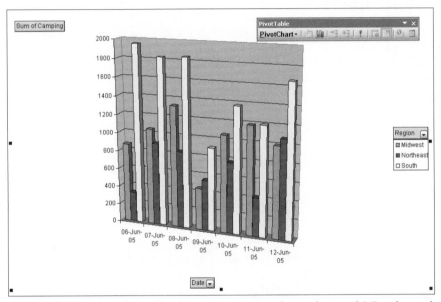

Figure 6-9: The PivotChart from Figure 6-5 changed to a clustered 3-D column chart.

Returning to Default Formatting

Certain aspects of a chart's formatting, such as colors and patterns, can be changed independently of the chart type. Such format changes are normally retained when you change the chart type. If you want to discard any custom formatting and return the chart to the default formatting, select the Default Formatting option in the Chart Type dialog box.

Changing the Default Chart Type

You can change Excel's default chart type from stacked column to another type by displaying the Chart Type dialog box, selecting the chart type and subtype, and clicking the Set as default chart button.

Understanding a PivotChart's Structure

Excel follows certain rules when creating a PivotChart. These rules determine how the PivotTable data are arranged in the chart — which categories are placed on which axis, how data series are defined, and so on. You want to have a good understanding of these rules to create PivotCharts with the structure you want. In this section you look at some examples.

A Simple PivotChart

The PivotTable shown in Figure 6-10 is about as simple as possible. It consists of only one row field and one column of data.

4	Sum of Value	Column ▼
5	Row ▼	Students
6	Biology	258
7	Chemistry	173
8	Ecology	159
9	Geology	269
10	Marine Biology	227
11	Physics	342
12	(blank)	
13	Grand Total	1428

Figure 6-10: A PivotTable that contains one row field and one data field.

When you create a PivotChart from this table you get a chart like the one shown in Figure 6-11. You can see that each data value in the row field becomes an item on the chart's horizontal (category) axis.

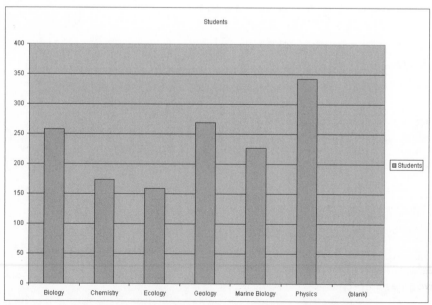

Figure 6-11: A PivotChart created from the PivotTable in Figure 6-10.

Suppose you had created the chart with a column field instead of a row field. The PivotTable would now look like Figure 6-12 and the PivotChart would look like Figure 6-13. Now there is only one item on the horizontal axis and the different column fields are represented by different color portions of the one bar.

4	Sum of Value	Row	▼	Column	▼						
5		Biology		Chemistry		Ecology		Geology		Marine Biology	Physics	(blank)
6		Students		Students		Students		Students		Students	Students	Students
7	Total		258		173		159		269	227	342	

Figure 6-12: The same PivotTable as in Figure 6-10 with a column field instead of a row field.

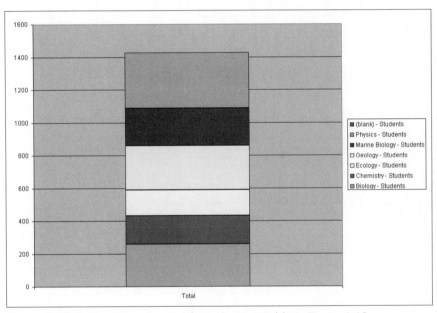

Figure 6-13: A PivotChart created from the PivotTable in Figure 6-12.

A PivotChart with Two Row Fields

The PivotTable shown in Figure 6-14 has some added complexity, with its two row fields. The data themselves are simple, consisting only of a single number for each row.

3	Gender ▼	Data ▼	Total
4	Female	Average	85.3
5		Maximum	99
6		Minimum	70
7	Male	Average	84.4
8		Maximum	98
9		Minimum	70

Figure 6-14: A PivotTable that contains two row fields.

A PivotChart created from this PivotTable is shown in Figure 6-15. Note how the PivotChart handles the two row fields. The outer row field, Gender, has two values, Male and Female. These values are represented on the lower level of the horizontal axis. The inner row field, Data, has three values: Average, Maximum, and Minimum, which are represented on the upper level of the horizontal axis. The result is two groups of three bars, one for males and one for females.

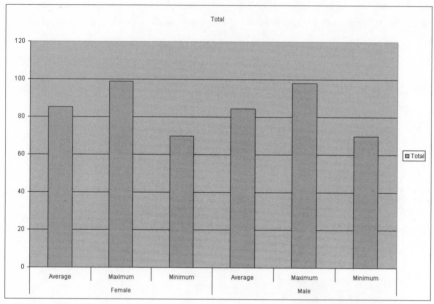

Figure 6-15: A PivotChart created from the PivotTable in Figure 6-14.

Suppose you want to reorganize the chart to make it easier to compare the results for males and females for each of the three measures. You need to go to the underlying PivotTable and drag the Gender field to the inner row position. The PivotTable will then look like Figure 6-16.

3	Data	Gender	Total
4	Average	Female	85.3
5		Male	84.4
6	Maximum	Female	99
7		Male	98
8	Minimum	Female	70
9		Male	70

Figure 6-16: The PivotTable with the Gender field in the inner row position.

Because the PivotChart is linked, it automatically updates to reflect the change and will now appear as in Figure 6-17.

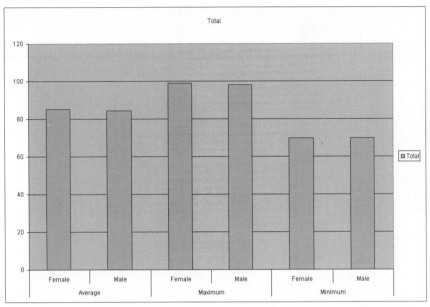

Figure 6-17: The PivotChart that results when you move the Gender field to the inner row position.

Another possibility with this PivotTable report is to make the Gender field a column field and leave Data as the row field. The resulting PivotTable and PivotChart are shown in Figures 6-18 and 6-19 respectively. The PivotChart now lists only the Data field on the horizontal axis and represents the Gender field by separate bars. I do not think that this arrangement is particularly useful for these data, but it does illustrate another way in which a PivotChart changes when you modify the underlying PivotTable.

	Gender ▾	
Data ▾	Female	Male
Average	85.3	84.4
Maximum	99	98
Minimum	70	70

Figure 6-18: The PivotTable with the Gender field in the Column area.

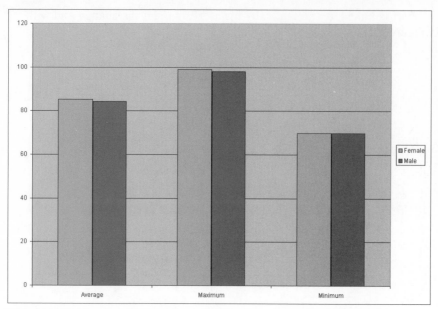

Figure 6-19: The PivotChart that results when you move the Gender field to the Column area.

A PivotChart with Two Column Fields

When a PivotTable has more than one column field, the PivotChart handles it a bit differently from when there are multiple row fields. Whereas row fields become items on the horizontal axis, column fields become data series. When there are two column fields, Excel creates a data series for each combination of field values.

Figure 6-20 shows a PivotTable report with two column fields. One field has two values, M and F. The other field has three values, Yes, No, and Unsure.

3	Count of Question 1	Question 1 ▼	Gender ▼								
4		No			No Total	Unsure		Unsure Total	Yes		Yes Total
5	Age ▼	F	M			F	M		F	M	
6	<20			3	3	1	3	4	3	2	5
7	20-29	16	13		29	11	7	18	10	10	20
8	30-39	7	13		20	7	14	21	9	17	26
9	40-49	10	8		18	1	7	8	8	6	14
10	50-59	11	5		16	13	21	34	7	15	22
11	>60	7	9		16	11	4	15	5	4	9

Figure 6-20: A PivotTable report with two column fields.

When you create a PivotChart from this report, as shown in Figure 6-21, Excel creates six data series: M-Yes, M-No, M-Unsure, and so on. The single row field, Age, is represented by categories on the horizontal axis, as you would expect.

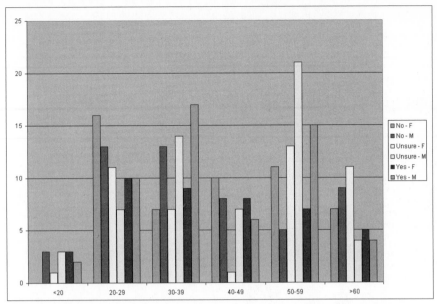

Figure 6-21: The PivotChart based on the PivotTable report in Figure 6-20.

When your PivotTable gets relatively complex, you can take advantage of Excel's three-dimensional chart types, which have features for clearly displaying more fields. The next tip provides a step-by-step example of creating this kind of PivotChart.

Creating a 3-D PivotChart

The extra visual dimension that 3-D charts provide is often just what you need to create a clear graphical presentation of your PivotTable data. In this section you work through an example of creating a 3-D PivotChart. The source data, which are the results of a survey about educational level and income, are shown in Figure 6-22. You'll find them in the workbook SurveyResults3.xls.

1. Select the data range A2:E80.
2. Select PivotTable and PivotChart Report from the Data menu to start the wizard.
3. In Step 1 of the wizard, select the PivotChart report with PivotTable report option.
4. Click Finish to complete the Wizard and display the blank PivotChart.
5. Drag the Gender field to the Drop Category Fields Here area.
6. Drag the Nationality field to the same area.
7. Drag the Annual Income field to the Drop Data Items Here area.

	A	B	C	D	E
1					
2	ID	Gender	Nationality	Years Education	Annual Income
3	1	M	German	9	$ 71,110
4	2	F	British	10	$ 40,783
5	3	M	Italian	16	$ 82,250
6	4	M	German	17	$ 43,558
7	5	F	French	6	$ 80,840
8	6	F	British	16	$ 75,379
9	7	F	French	10	$ 19,324
10	8	M	Italian	20	$ 38,808
11	9	F	German	10	$ 42,081
12	10	F	British	7	$ 94,963
13	11	M	Italian	20	$ 57,887
14	12	M	German	6	$ 45,273
15	13	M	French	19	$ 86,696
16	14	F	British	14	$ 16,977
17	15	M	French	9	$ 62,121
18	16	M	Italian	7	$ 77,721
19	17	F	Italian	19	$ 34,877
20	18	F	German	16	$ 28,164
21	19	F	French	18	$ 96,901
22	20	M	British	19	$ 16,955
23	21	F	French	12	$ 50,611
24	22	M	Italian	7	$ 97,196
25	23	M	German	8	$ 47,697
26	24	F	British	8	$ 79,746
27	25	F	Italian	12	$ 85,501
28	26	F	German	10	$ 62,962
29	27	M	French	18	$ 28,528
30	28	F	British	10	$ 24,800
31	29	F	German	11	$ 75,884
32	30	M	French	15	$ 93,282
33	31	M	British	18	$ 74,606

Figure 6-22: The survey data that will be used for this example.

At this point the PivotChart looks like Figure 6-23. There are two problems with it. First, the data show the sum of Annual Income, not the average, which is what you want. Second, the chart is still in 2-D format. Follow the next set of steps to fix these things.

1. Switch to the worksheet that contains the PivotTable report (shown in Figure 6-24).

2. Right-click the Sum of Annual Income button.

3. Select Field Settings from the pop-up menu to display the Field Settings dialog box.

4. In the Summarize by list, select Average.

5. Click the Number button to display the Format Cells dialog box.

6. Select the Currency format with no decimal places.

7. Click OK to close the Format Cells dialog box.

8. Click OK again to close the Field Settings dialog box.

9. Return to the worksheet that contains the PivotChart.

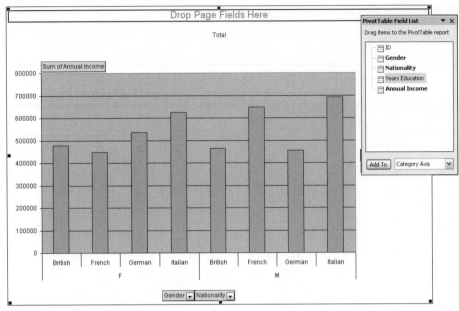

Figure 6-23: The initial PivotChart.

3	Sum of Annual Income		
4	Gender	Nationality	Total
5	F	British	478192
6		French	448835
7		German	535847
8		Italian	625619
9	F Total		2088493
10	M	British	464683
11		French	647656
12		German	455021
13		Italian	692048
14	M Total		2259408
15	Grand Total		4347901

Figure 6-24: The PivotTable that was created along with the PivotChart.

At this point the PivotChart correctly displays the average of Annual Income, and the vertical axis numbers are formatted as currency. The final step is to change the chart to a 3-D style.

1. Right-click anywhere in the central area of the PivotChart and select Chart Type from the pop-up menu. Excel displays the Chart Type dialog box shown in Figure 6-25.

2. On the Standard Types tab, select Column in the Chart Type list and then select 3-D Column in the Chart subtype box.

3. Click OK.

Part VI

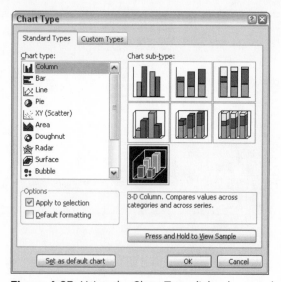

Figure 6-25: Using the Chart Type dialog box to change the type of the PivotChart.

Now the PivotChart will look like Figure 6-26. But wait, this is not what you wanted! The chart has a 3-D look but the data are still displayed in one dimension. What's wrong? The PivotTable needs to be pivoted. A 3-D PivotChart uses the two data dimensions for row and column fields respectively. Here's what to do, including a few extra steps to improve the chart's appearance:

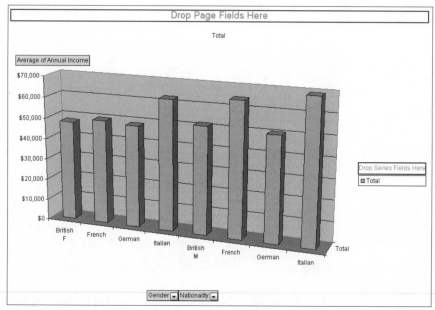

Figure 6-26: The PivotChart after being changed to a 3-D column chart.

1. Go to the worksheet that contains the PivotTable.

2. Drag the Gender field from the Row area to the Column area. The PivotTable appears as shown in Figure 6-27.

3	Average of Annual Income	Gender ▼		
4	Nationality ▼	F	M	Grand Total
5	British	$47,819	$51,631	$49,625
6	French	$49,871	$64,766	$57,710
7	German	$48,713	$50,558	$49,543
8	Italian	$62,562	$69,205	$65,883
9	Grand Total	$52,212	$59,458	$55,742

Figure 6-27: The PivotTable after the Gender field has been pivoted from the Row area to the Column area.

3. Return to the worksheet containing the PivotChart.

4. Pull down the PivotChart menu and select Hide PivotChart Field Buttons.

5. Right-click the chart legend (the small box with M and F in it) and select Clear from the pop-up menu. The legend is not needed because the field values M and F are indicated on the chart.

The final PivotChart is shown in Figure 6-28. You can see that by pivoting the PivotTable report, moving Gender from the Row area to the Column area, you made use of the PivotChart's 3-D capabilities to create a chart that displays the data clearly.

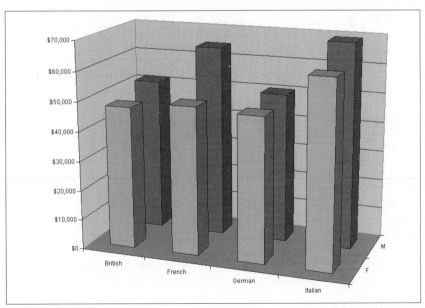

Figure 6-28: The final PivotChart displays the data in a 3-D structure after pivoting the underlying PivotTable report.

Lost Chart Formatting

Some aspects of PivotChart formatting are lost when you make certain changes to the PivotChart or its underlying PivotTable. The lost formatting includes changes you have made to data points, data labels, and data series, including trend lines and error bars. The changes that cause these formatting losses are:

- Adding or removing fields.
- Changing the layout.
- Hiding or redisplaying items.
- Changing page field filtering.
- Grouping or ungrouping items.
- Hiding or displaying details.
- Changing a field's summary function.
- Sorting.
- Modifying subtotal display.
- Changing the source data.
- Refreshing the PivotTable.

Because of these limitations, it's a good idea to complete all changes to the PivotTable before applying your final formatting.

Part VII

Using PivotTables with Multidimensional Data

Excel PivotTables give you the ability to work with multidimensional data. In fact, it is not uncommon to come across analysis tasks that require multidimensional data; there's just no other way to approach them. To truly master PivotTables, you must understand what multidimensional data are and how they are used. These are the topics of this chapter.

Tips and Where to Find Them

Using Multidimensional Data

Before getting to the *what* of multidimensional data, you will find it useful to look at the *why*. So far this book has used small data sources that consisted of a single table in an Excel worksheet (or in some cases an Access database). For clarity of presentation I have deliberately kept these data sources small — consisting of maybe a hundred rows of data at most. Of course real-world data are almost always a lot larger, but Excel can handle it — right? Let's take a look.

Excel is limited to 65,535 rows and 256 columns of data in a single worksheet. It sounds like a lot, but it really isn't. Compared with the data needs of modern businesses and organizations, it's a drop in the bucket. Databases consisting of millions of records are not uncommon, and PivotTables can be a useful tool for analyzing them. Consider sales records for a large online retailer, inventory for a major manufacturing concern, or demographic data kept by an insurance company. These and other data sources are well beyond the capabilities of Excel.

PivotTables and PivotCharts themselves also have some limitations:

- Two hundred and fifty-six page fields.

- Two hundred and fifty-six data fields.

- Two hundred and fifty-six data series in a PivotChart.

- Four thousand data points in a data series in a 3-D PivotChart; thirty-two thousand in a 2-D PivotChart.

- Thirty-two thousand, five hundred unique items in a PivotTable field.

These limitations would seem to put the analysis of large data sets beyond the realm of Excel and PivotTables. The fact is that huge data sets place severe demands on any analysis tool and can result in processing times of several hours or more. To deal with this challenge, programmers have developed a set of tools called *Online Analytical Processing*, or OLAP. OLAP is designed to work with hierarchical raw data, organizing and summarizing them in a multidimensional form. When your analysis program, such as Excel, accesses the data it is actually accessing the OLAP summaries and not the raw data themselves. In other words, OLAP does most of the analysis grunt work so that the final analysis program — Excel or whatever — doesn't have to.

Some Other Terms

Multidimensional data are sometimes referred to as *hierarchical data* or *OLAP data* even though these terms don't mean precisely the same thing. Multidimensional data may or may not actually contain hierarchies and they may or may not reside on an OLAP server or data warehouse. When you come across the other two terms, it's a good idea to determine precisely what they mean.

Understanding Multidimensional Data

Before you can start using Excel PivotTables with multidimensional data, you need to understand exactly what they are. You can best do this by looking at multidimensional data in relation to two other kinds of data, *flat data* and *relational data.* Multidimensional data are the most complex of these types. Let's start with the simplest and work up.

Flat Data

Flat data, sometimes called *non-relational data,* are the kind of data with which most people are accustomed to working. (The raw data used in all the previous parts are flat data.) The defining characteristic of flat data is that all the information is contained in a single table — one set of rows (records) and columns (fields). Figure 7-1 shows an example of a flat parts inventory database. Each record contains full information for a particular part — the part name and number, its wholesale cost, and the name and address of the supplier.

	A	B	C	D	E	F	G	H
1	Part_Num	Description	WholesaleCost	Supplier_Name	Supplier Address	Supplier_City	Supplier_Stat	Supplier_Phone
2	Q123	Cotter pin	$ 0.56	Wilson Mfg.	12 Oak Street	Cleveland	OH	555-666-7777
3	L12-45	Hex nut	$ 0.90	Trumbill Machine	1244 Park Way	Atlanta	GA	111-222-3333
4	ZS-5667	Axle bolt	$ 1.25	Parts Unltd.	15-A West End Ave.	Albany	NY	333-444-5555
5	F-445566	Washer Asst	$ 2.50	Wilson Mfg.	12 Oak Street	Cleveland	OH	555-666-7777
6	LK-13224	Allen bolt	$ 1.78	Parts Unltd.	15-A West End Ave.	Albany	NY	333-444-5555
7	D-990-a	Punch	$ 4.55	Parts Unltd.	15-A West End Ave.	Albany	NY	333-444-5555
8	S-4500	Hinge	$ 0.98	Trumbill Machine	1244 Park Way	Atlanta	GA	111-222-3333
9	DF-555-g	Pulley	$ 3.38	Wilson Mfg.	12 Oak Street	Cleveland	OH	555-666-7777

Figure 7-1: A flat data source contains all the information in one table.

In Figure 7-1 each supplier's information is present more than once. This causes several problems. First it is an inefficient use of storage space to keep the same information in more than one location. Second, updating a supplier's information — for example, if the address changes — will require changes in multiple locations and introduce the possibility of errors. Finally, there is the possibility of completely deleting a supplier from the database when you do not want to, if, for example, all of that supplier's parts are deleted. To avoid these problems, *relational databases* were devised.

Relational Data

A relational database keeps related data in separate tables. Records in the two tables are linked by a *key field* that defines which record(s) in one table are associated with which record(s) in the other table. Figure 7-2 shows the same data from Figure 7-1 in a relational database.

	A	B	C	D	E	F
1	**Part_Num**	**Description**	**WholesaleCost**	**Supplier_ID**		
2	Q123	Cotter pin	$ 0.56	1		
3	L12-45	Hex nut	$ 0.90	2		
4	ZS-5667	Axle bolt	$ 1.25	3		
5	F-445566	Washer Asst	$ 2.50	1		
6	LK-13224	Allen bolt	$ 1.78	3		
7	D-990-a	Punch	$ 4.55	3		
8	S-4500	Hinge	$ 0.98	2		
9	DF-555-g	Pulley	$ 3.38	1		
10						
11						
12						
13						
14						
15	**Supplier_ID**	**Name**	**Address**	**City**	**State**	**Phone**
16	1	Wilson Mfg.	12 Oak Street	Cleveland	OH	555-666-7777
17	2	Trumbill Machin	1244 Park Way	Atlanta	GA	111-222-3333
18	3	Parts Unltd.	15-A West End Ave.	Albany	NY	333-444-5555
19						

Figure 7-2: A relational data source contains two or more tables that are related to one another.

This time there is a table of suppliers with one record for each. Each supplier record is identified by a unique Supplier_ID number. There is also a table of parts with one record for each part. Each part record also has a Supplier_ID field that identifies the supplier for that part in the Suppliers table. For example, in the first record in the Parts table, the Supplier_ID field contains the value 1. If you go to the linked Suppliers table, you can see that this key is associated with Wilson Manufacturing, therefore identifying the supplier for this part. The problems described earlier for a flat database have been solved:

- Each supplier's information is present only once.

- Modifying a supplier's information requires a change in only one location, the single record for that supplier.

- Deleting part records cannot delete supplier information.

Relational databases are the mainstay of almost all modern data storage systems. Despite their great flexibility and power, they do not, however, solve all problems. Particularly when it comes to detailed analysis of large amounts of data, relational databases do not really simplify or speed up the process. Multidimensional data is the preferred solution for these challenges.

But Not in Excel

While I have used Excel in Figures 7-1 and 7-2 to illustrate what relational data look like, you should be aware that Excel does not have the capability to actually work with relational data, at least not directly. You need a dedicated database program such as Microsoft Access for that.

Multidimensional Data

As its name implies, *multidimensional data* have more than one dimension. But what exactly does the word *multidimensional* mean in this context? It is not used in the same sense as in geometry, as, for example, in a three-dimensional Excel chart. It will perhaps be easiest to understand if you work through the same data from flat to relational to multidimensional.

Figure 7-3 shows a sales database that is flat. In other words, each record contains all the relevant information. In this case each record includes a field named Sale_ID that contains a unique numeric ID for each record. This is called the *primary key* and is used in all database tables, although it is not directly relevant to our exploration of multidimensional data. This database also contains the customer name, the salesman's name, the year, month, and day of the week of the sale, and finally the amount of the sale.

	A	B	C	D	E	F	G
1	Sale_ID	Customer	Salesman	Year	Month	Day	Amount
2	1	Acme Metal Works	Jackson	2002	Jan	Tues	$ 12,312.00
3	2	S&Q Manufacturing	Anderson	2003	Mar	Wed	$ 34,543.00
4	3	East End Inc.	Gomez	2004	Feb	Mon	$ 12,134.00
5	4	Acme Metal Works	Anderson	2002	Feb	Fri	$ 45,324.00
6	5	S&Q Manufacturing	Jackson	2004	Jan	Thu	$ 12,435.00
7	6	TechWiz Corp.	Gomez	2002	Mar	Fri	$ 12,546.00
8	7	S&Q Manufacturing	Chang	2003	Feb	Wed	$ 76,567.00
9	8	East End Inc.	Jackson	2004	Mar	Mon	$ 34,567.00
10	9	TechWiz Corp.	Chang	2002	Jan	Fri	$ 12,435.00
11	10	Acme Metal Works	Gomez	2004	Feb	Thu	$ 87,980.00
12	11	TechWiz Corp.	Anderson	2002	Mar	Fri	$ 25,432.00
13	12	Acme Metal Works	Chang	2003	Feb	Tues	$ 12,435.00
14	13	East End Inc.	Anderson	2004	Jan	Fri	$ 23,546.00
15	14	TechWiz Corp.	Chang	2004	Mar	Mon	$ 65,780.00
16	15	S&Q Manufacturing	Gomez	2002	Feb	Wed	$ 32,456.00

Figure 7-3: The sales data arranged as a flat database.

NOTE

I should point out that these data are greatly simplified from what you would find in the real world. For example, any actual sales database would include the address and phone number of each customer as well as more details about each salesman. I am trying to minimize details in order to more clearly illustrate the principles of multidimensional data.

One way to make this database more usable is to convert it to a relational structure with separate tables for customers, salesmen, days, months, and years. These are called *primary tables* because they do not depend on any other tables; for example, the Customers table contains all the information about each customer. A master table, called Sales, links to all these other tables as and contains the Amount data. The Sales table is a *dependent table* because it gets some of its information by means of relational links to the primary tables.

Figures 7-4 and 7-5 show the tables in this new relational database with the five primary tables shown in Figure 7-4 and the dependent Sales table in Figure 7-5. You can see that the "data" in most of the fields of the Sales table actually consist of links to data in the other tables. Note that any database program displays the actual data and not the link number — for example "Jackson" instead of the not-very-useful 1. I have shown the numbers here for purposes of illustration.

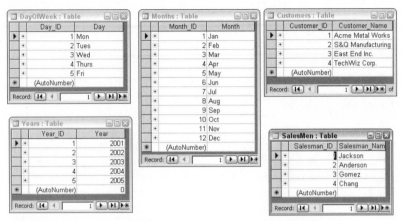

Figure 7-4: The primary tables in the relational Sales database.

Sale_ID	Customer_ID	Salesman_ID	Year_ID	Month_ID	Day_ID	Amount
1	1	1	2	1	2	$12,312.00
2	2	2	3	3	3	$34,543.00
3	3	3	4	2	1	$12,134.00
4	1	2	2	2	5	$45,324.00
5	2	2	4	1	4	$12,435.00
6	4	3	2	3	5	$12,546.00
7	2	4	3	2	3	$76,567.00
8	3	1	4	3	1	$34,567.00
9	4	4	2	1	5	$12,435.00
10	1	3	4	2	4	$87,980.00
11	4	2	4	2	4	$25,432.00
12	1	4	2	3	5	$25,432.00
13	3	2	4	1	5	$23,546.00
14	4	4	4	3	1	$65,780.00
15	2	3	2	2	3	$32,456.00
(AutoNumber)	0	0	0	0	0	$0.00

Figure 7-5: The dependent table in the relational Sales database.

As you may have guessed, a relational database does not consist of only primary and dependent tables; it also requires that you define the links, or relationships, between the tables. For example, you must specify that the Customer_ID field in the Sales table is linked to the Customer_ID field in the Customers table. This enables the database to know that the value 1 means Acme Metal Works, that 2 means S&Q Manufacturing, and so on. A database program always provides a method for defining these relationships and usually also provides a way to display them. Figure 7-6 shows the relationships in the Sales database as displayed in Microsoft Access. (Excel does not have the ability to work directly with relational databases.)

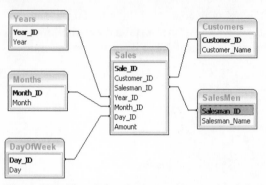

Figure 7-6: The defined relationships in the Sales database.

At this point the relational Sales database is complete and ready to use. You will find many databases essentially just like this one in use in the real world, and for many purposes they are just fine. However, for certain types of analysis with a really large database, this sort of structure is not ideal. Here's where the idea of multidimensional data comes into play. Let's take a look as this relates to the sample data.

As designed, the database includes a table for salesmen and another for customers. But perhaps you want to analyze the relationship between salesmen and customers. You may think that certain salespeople do better with certain customers. Perhaps Gomez does really well selling to Acme Metal Works but not so well with East End Inc. This kind of analysis is possible with the relational database just described, but it can be slow and cumbersome with large data sets. By adding another dimension to the data you can enable faster and more robust data analysis.

But what will this dimension be? Look at the existing data — each sales record has a Customer value and a Salesman value, currently separate. What if you combine them? In other words, instead of having a Salesman value of "Gomez" and a Customer value of "Acme Metal Works," the record had a Salesman_Customer value of "Gomez-Acme Metal Works." This will be the new dimension.

The database will still be relational. All you are doing is inserting an extra level, or dimension, of data between the dependent Sales table and the primary Customer and Salesmen tables. This new table, called Salesman_Customers, is also a dependent table because it links to the Customers and Salesmen tables. The Sales table links to the new Salesmen_Customers table rather than to the Customers and Salesmen tables individually.

To make these changes you must first remove the Customer_ID and Salesman_ID fields from the Sales table and add the Salesman_Customer_ID field. The resulting table is shown in Figure 7-7, although the Salesman_Customer_ID data have not been entered yet.

Sale_ID	Salesman_Customer_ID	Year_ID	Month_ID	Day_ID	Amount
1		2	1	2	$12,312.00
2		3	3	3	$34,543.00
3		4	2	1	$12,134.00
4		2	2	5	$45,324.00
5		4	1	4	$12,435.00
6		2	3	5	$12,546.00
7		3	2	3	$76,567.00
8		4	3	1	$34,567.00
9		2	1	5	$12,435.00
10		4	2	4	$87,980.00
11		4	2	4	$25,432.00
12		2	3	5	$25,432.00
13		4	1	5	$23,546.00
14		4	3	1	$65,780.00
15		2	2	3	$32,456.00
(AutoNumber)	0	0	0	0	$0.00

Figure 7-7: The Sales table after the field layout is changed.

Next you need the Salesman_Customer table. This table will have three fields:

- **Salesman_Customer_ID** — The table's primary key, which will be used by the Sales table to link to salesman/customer combinations.
- **Salesman_ID** — This table will link to the primary Salesmen table.
- **Customer_ID** — This table will link to the primary Customers table.

Finally, the database needs some new relationships, as follows:

- A link between the Salesman_Customer_ID field in the Sales table to the Salesman_Customer_ID field in the Salesman_Customer table.
- A link between the Customer_ID field in the Salesman_Customer table to the Customer_ID field in the Customers table.
- A link between the Salesman_ID field in the Salesman_Customer table to the Salesman_ID field in the Salesmen table.

Figure 7-8 shows the new Salesman_Customer table after it has been populated with data. It contains one record for every possible combination of the four salesmen with the four customers, for a total of 16 records.

Salesman_Customer : Table		
Salesman_Cust	Salesman_ID	Customer_ID
1	1	1
2	1	2
3	1	3
4	1	4
5	2	1
6	2	2
7	2	3
8	2	4
9	3	1
10	3	2
11	3	3
12	3	4
13	4	1
14	4	2
15	4	3
16	4	4
(AutoNumber)	0	0

Figure 7-8: The Salesman_Customer table contains one record for every possible combination of salesman and customer.

Figure 7-9 shows the new relationships for the database. The added dimension, namely the Salesman_Customer table, sits between the dependent Sales table and the primary Customers and Salesmen tables.

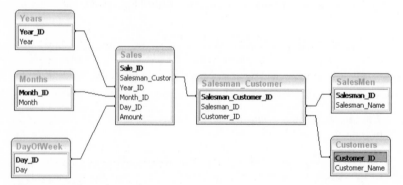

Figure 7-9: The relationships in the database now have an extra level, or dimension, represented by the Salesman_Customer table.

Finally, Figure 7-10 shows the Sales table after the Sales_Customer_ID field has been populated with data. To reiterate, here's how this works, taking the third record in Sales for an example. The Salesman_Customer_ID value for this record is 11. Because this field is linked to the Salesman_Customer table, you look at the record in that table in which the

Salesman_Customer_ID is also 11. This record has a Customer_ID field with a value of 3 and a Salesman_ID also with a value of 3. Following the links from these two fields to the Customers and Salesmen tables, you find the actual data values East End Inc. and Gomez. Therefore you know that for the sale whose data is in the specified record of the Sales table, the customer was East End Inc. and the salesman was Gomez.

Sale_ID	Salesman_Customer_ID	Year_ID	Month_ID	Day_ID	Amount
1	1	2	1	2	$12,312.00
2	6	3	3	3	$34,543.00
3	11	4	2	1	$12,134.00
4	5	2	2	5	$45,324.00
5	2	4	1	4	$12,435.00
6	12	2	3	5	$12,546.00
7	14	3	2	3	$76,567.00
8	3	4	3	1	$34,567.00
9	16	2	1	5	$12,435.00
10	9	4	2	4	$87,980.00
11	8	4	2	4	$25,432.00
12	13	2	3	5	$25,432.00
13	7	4	1	5	$23,546.00
14	16	4	3	1	$65,780.00
15	10	2	2	3	$32,456.00
(AutoNumber)	0	0	0	0	$0.00

Record: 15 of 15

Figure 7-10: The Sales table after the Salesman_Customer_ID information has been filled in.

At this point you have created a new dimension that condenses the salesman and customer data into a single table. There's more you can do, however. Take a look at the date data. They contain three pieces of information: the month of the sale, the year, and the day of the week. Can these data be condensed into a new dimension? You bet they can. By doing so you simplify and speed analyses that look at questions such as "Are more sales made on certain days of the week in January as opposed to June?"

The procedures are essentially the same as for the customer and salesman data, so I will not go into details. Briefly, the result is a new table called DayMonthYear that contains one record for each possible combination of day of the week, month, and year. The Sales table links to this new table through a field named DayMonthYear_ID, and the new table in turn links to the three primary tables DayofWeek, Months, and Years. The new DayMonthYear table — or part of it, because it contains 300 records — is shown in Figure 7-11, and the final relationship structure of the database is shown in Figure 7-12.

DayMonthYear_	Day_ID	Month_ID	Year_ID
1	1	1	1
2	2	1	1
3	3	1	1
4	4	1	1
5	5	1	1
6	1	2	1
7	2	2	1
8	3	2	1
9	4	2	1
10	5	2	1
11	1	3	1
12	2	3	1
13	3	3	1
14	4	3	1
15	5	3	1
16	1	4	1
17	2	4	1
18	3	4	1
19	4	4	1
20	5	4	1
21	1	5	1
22	2	5	1
23	3	5	1
24	4	5	1
25	5	5	1
26	1	6	1
27	2	6	1
28	3	6	1

Record: 1 of 300

Figure 7-11: The DayMonthYear table adds another dimension to the database's date data.

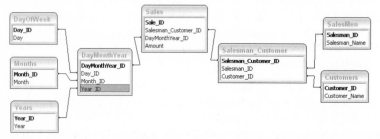

Figure 7-12: The final relationship structure in the multidimensional database.

Where Are Multidimensional Data Stored?

The term *multidimensional* describes the way the data are organized and says nothing specifically about where and how they are stored. As you have seen in the previous example, multidimensional data can be kept in an Access database. But a multidimensional data structure is often used to enable efficient queries and analysis in huge databases that are beyond the capabilities of Access, databases with tens of millions of records. Such huge databases are usually managed with specialized data-warehouse applications such as Microsoft SQL Server Analysis Server or Oracle OLAP Server. These applications are maintained by IT specialists and if you need to work with their data, these specialists will give you information about accessing them.

Multidimensional Data Terminology

When working with multidimensional data and PivotTables you will find that several terms are used in a specialized manner. You need to understand this terminology to work effectively with these tools.

A *dimension* is the highest level grouping. Dimensions are used to group data into hierarchical (parent/child) relationships. Dimensions commonly used in data analysis include people, location, time, products, and similar categories.

Within each dimension are two or more *levels*. A level represents a data element that is part of the specified dimension. For example, in the sample multidimensional database created earlier in this part you could define a dimension called People with two levels, Customers and Salesmen. This is illustrated in Figure 7-13.

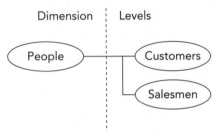

Figure 7-13: A dimension such as People contains two or more levels.

Each level contains one or more items called *members*. The Customers level contains the members Acme Metal Works, S&Q Manufacturing, and so on. Likewise, the Salesmen level contains the members Jackson, Anderson, and so on. This is shown schematically in Figure 7-14.

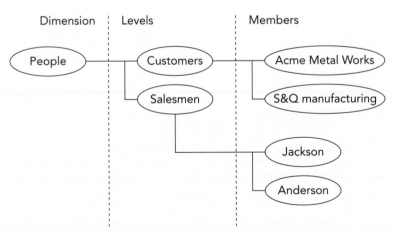

Figure 7-14: Each level within a dimension contains its own members (some members are omitted in the figure).

The example database you have been working with has another potential dimension: time. This dimension would have three levels, DayOfWeek, Month, and Year. Each of these levels would have its own members, for example Mon, Tues, Wed, Thu, and Fri for DayOfWeek.

A *measure* is a summary of a data value. You have actually worked with measures previously, although they were not called that. A sum, average, or count in a PivotTable cell, for example, is a measure. In the current example, the measure would probably be the sum of the Amount values. A cube file can have one or more measures.

The term *cube* is applied to the files used to store dimensions, levels, members, and measures. The term comes from the fact that the structure of multidimensional data is sometimes pictured as a three-dimensional cube, with each physical dimension of the cube representing a conceptual dimension in the data. This works only for data with three dimensions, of course, but the image and the name have stuck.

The important thing about cube files is that they contain already-summarized data rather than raw data. This relates to something mentioned earlier in this part: the ability to analyze huge datasets without overloading your system or experiencing long waits. There's nothing magic about this; the fact is that much of the analysis had already been made when the cube file was created. Your program, in this case Excel, needs only to retrieve the summarized data from the cube file to populate the PivotTable.

Another important thing to be aware of is that you can define multiple cube files for a given data source. When you or someone else creates a cube file, you specify what it will contain — what the dimensions will be as well as the levels and members. A large and complex database is likely to need several cube files, and you must use the one that contains the summary you need.

Creating a Cube File

You may never need to create a cube file. Often your IT department takes care of all database-related tasks at this level and the cube files are ready for you to use. In this case you can skip ahead to the tip "Creating a PivotTable from a Cube File." This tip contains a section that shows you how you can create a cube file from data in an Access database. Even if you never need to do this yourself, an understanding of the process can help you work with OLAP data efficiently and productively.

In Part II you saw how Excel enables you to import data from an Access database. One of the options available to you when you are importing Access data is to create an OLAP cube file from the data. For this tip I will use the multidimensional database that you looked at earlier in this part; if you want to work along, this database is available as `SalesData_Multidimensional Data.mdb`. This file has the same multidimensional structure described earlier but with a lot more records in the Sales table. The first part of the process is the same as for any import from an Access database:

1. Start Excel.

2. Select Import External Data from the Data menu, then select New Database Query to display the Choose Data Source dialog box (Figure 7-15).

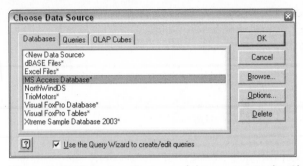

Figure 7-15: Selecting the type of data source in the Choose Data Source dialog box.

3. On the Databases tab, select the MS Access Database entry. Make sure the Use the Query Wizard to create/edit queries option is checked.

4. Click OK to display the Select Database dialog box. Navigate to the file `SalesData_Multidimensional Data.mdb`, select it, and click OK.

5. The next Query Wizard dialog box lets you choose the tables and columns you want in your query. (See Figure 7-16.) Use the right-arrow button to move all the tables to the Columns in your query list.

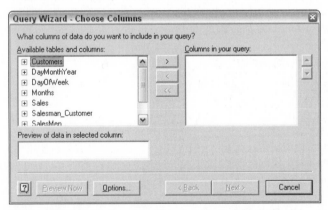

Figure 7-16: Selecting the tables and columns that will be in your query.

6. Click Next three times. (These wizard dialog boxes let you filter and sort the data, which you do not need to do).

7. In the final wizard dialog box, shown in Figure 7-17, select the Create an OLAP Cube from this query option.

8. Click Finish to close the Query Wizard and start the OLAP Cube Wizard.

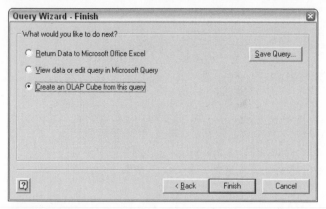

Figure 7-17: Specifying that the query be generated as an OLAP cube.

At this point you have defined the query, which determines the data that will be retrieved from the database. Because you specified the creation of an OLAP cube, the OLAP Cube Wizard will start. The next steps define the cube structure — its dimensions, levels, and so on.

If the OLAP Wizard Welcome page is displayed after you complete the Query Wizard, click Next to display Step 1 of the OLAP Cube Wizard, shown in Figure 7-18. All fields (columns) from the database are listed here. In this step of the OLAP Cube Wizard you select one or more fields to be measures — in other words, data summaries, as described earlier in this part. You also select the kind of summary — sum, average, count, and so on — to be used.

OLAP Cube Wizard Step 1 of 3

Select the source fields you want to make available as summarized data fields, and then click a function in the Summarize by column for each field.

Source field	Summarize by	Data field name
✔ Customer_ID	Count	Count Of Customer_ID
✔ DayMonthYear_ID	Count	Count Of DayMonthYear_I
✔ Day_ID	Count	Count Of Day_ID
✔ Month_ID	Count	Count Of Month_ID
✔ Year_ID	Count	Count Of Year_ID
✔ Day_ID1	Count	Count Of Day_ID1
✔ Month_ID1	Count	Count Of Month_ID1
✔ Sale_ID	Count	Count Of Sale_ID
✔ Salesman_Customer_ID	Count	Count Of Salesman_Custo
✔ DayMonthYear_ID1	Count	Count Of DayMonthYear_1
✔ Amount	Sum	Sum Of Amount
✔ Salesman_Customer_ID1	Count	Count Of Salesman_Cust1
✔ Salesman_ID	Count	Count Of Salesman_ID
✔ Customer_ID1	Count	Count Of Customer_ID1
✔ Salesman_ID1	Count	Count Of Salesman_ID1
✔ Year_ID1	Count	Count Of Year_ID1
✔ Year	Sum	Sum Of Year

Figure 7-18: In the first step of the OLAP Cube Wizard you specify the fields and summary functions to be used for the cube's measures.

Duplicate Field Names

You may be puzzling over some of the field names shown in Figure 7-18. The name Day_ID makes sense because there is such a field in the database. But what about Day_ID1? Here's what happened. The database actually contains two fields named Day_ID, one in the DayMonthYear table and another in the DayOfWeek table. Because duplicate field names can cause confusion, the wizard automatically added a 1 to one of the fields to distinguish it from the other.

For your purposes there will be one measure: the sum of the Amount field. To specify this, uncheck all the fields in the wizard except Amount, and leave Sum selected as the Summarize by value in that row. Then click Next to advance to the next step of the wizard, which is shown in Figure 7-19.

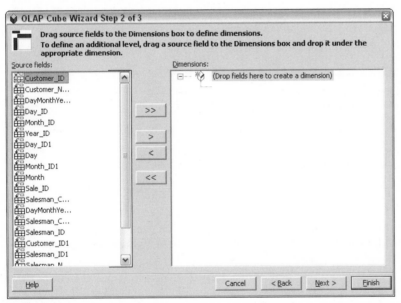

Figure 7-19: In the second step of the OLAP Cube Wizard you define the dimensions and levels for the OLAP cube.

Selecting dimensions and levels is perhaps the most important part of creating a cube file. The dimensions and levels you define determine the data available in the cube file and the ways in which users can view those data. It is somewhat simplified but accurate to say that a dimension will be available as a field in the PivotTable and that a level within that dimension will be available as detail for that field. Without experience, it can be difficult to envision the final result while you are designing the cube file. The key is to experiment by creating several cube files with different dimensions and levels and seeing what you can and cannot do with them in a PivotTable.

Each Field Only Once

Each source field can be used only once in the cube file, either as a dimension or as a level. You cannot, for example, use the same field both as a dimension and as a level under another dimension. You can, however, achieve the same effect by modifying the query or data source to include two instances of the field — in other words, two fields with different names that contain the same data.

The basic procedure in Step 2 of the OLAP Cube Wizard is to drag fields that you want as dimensions to the Drop fields here to create a dimension area, and then to drag fields that you want as levels to the parent dimension. Continuing from Figure 7-19, here's what to do:

1. Drag the field Salesman_Name from the Source fields list and drop it in the Dimensions list. The OLAP Cube Wizard will add this field as a dimension and as a level, as shown in Figure 7-20. This is automatic — a field that is a dimension is always also a level under that dimension.

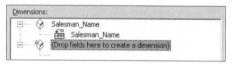

Figure 7-20: After the field Salesman_Name has been added as a dimension to the OLAP cube.

2. Right-click the Salesman_Name dimension (not the level) and select Rename from the pop-up menu.

3. Type **Person** and press Enter. The wizard now looks like the one shown in Figure 7-21. You have renamed the dimension while leaving the level with its original name.

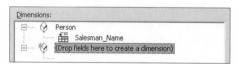

Figure 7-21: After the Salesman_Name dimension has been renamed Person.

4. Drag the Customer_Name field and drop it on the Person dimension. It becomes a level under that dimension, as shown in Figure 7-22.

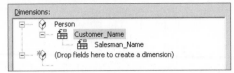

Figure 7-22: After Customer_Name has been added as a level under the Person dimension.

5. Drag the Year field and drop it where it says "Drop fields here to create a dimension."

6. Right-click the Year dimension and rename it Date.

7. Drag the Month field and drop it on the Year level. It becomes a level that is part of the Date dimension and subsidiary to the Year level.

8. Drag the Day field and drop it on the Month level. It becomes a level that is part of the Date dimension and subsidiary to the Month level. The wizard should now look like Figure 7-23.

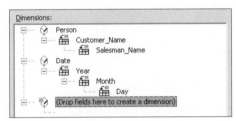

Figure 7-23: After the Year, Month, and Day fields have been added to the Date dimension.

9. Click Next to go to the final stage of the wizard (which I will discuss in a moment).

There's a subtle but important distinction to be made when dragging fields to become levels in the OLAP cube.

- If you drop the field directly on a dimension, the field becomes the top level for that dimension, displacing other existing levels downward in the hierarchy. You saw this in Step 4.

- If you drop the field on an existing level, it is placed one level lower in the hierarchy. You saw this in Steps 7 and 8.

The hierarchy of levels is important when you create the PivotTable report because it controls how the fields are arranged. The highest level becomes the outer row or column field while lower levels become the inner rows.

The final step of the OLAP Cube Wizard, shown in Figure 7-24, enables you to specify when the cube is updated and the name and location for the cube file. The three options are:

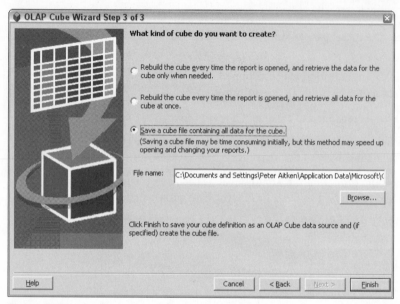

Figure 7-24: The final step of the OLAP Cube Wizard lets you specify cube update options.

- **Retrieving data on demand** — Saves the instructions for creating the cube file. The data are retrieved, and the cube file created, only when the report is created. If the report is changed, new data are retrieved only when needed. Use this option when the PivotTable report will be viewed but seldom changed.

- **Retrieving data all at once** — Similar to the first option except that when the report is created, all the data, not just the needed data, are retrieved. This setting enables users to make changes to the report quickly without having to wait for data retrieval. Use for PivotTable reports that will be changed frequently.

- **Saving a cube file** — Creates a cube file that contains all the data as well as the instructions. It takes more time to create initially, but enables use of the cube file when the connection to the data source is not available.

The first two options result in the creation of a file with the .oqy extension, using the name and location you specify in the dialog box. The third option saves both an OQY file containing the instructions for the cube and a CUB file containing the actual data.

After selecting the desired option click the Finish button. The OLAP Cube Wizard completes its work and returns you to Excel. Excel assumes that you are creating a PivotTable report and displays a dialog box asking where the report should be placed. (This is actually Step 3 of the PivotTable Wizard.) After entering the required information, click Finish to create the blank PivotTable report. Working with the report is the topic of the next tip.

Creating a PivotTable from a Cube File

To be honest, creating a PivotTable from a cube file is not all that different from creating a PivotTable from other kinds of data, as covered in previous parts. There are, however, a few differences of which you need to be aware.

This walkthough continues from the previous tip, which ended with the blank PivotTable created and ready for fields to be dragged and dropped. However, you can also create a PivotTable report from an existing cube file, as follows:

1. Select PivotTable and PivotChart Report from the Data menu to start the PivotTable Wizard.

2. In the first step of the Wizard select the External Data Source option.

3. Click Next to proceed to Step 2 of the wizard.

4. Click the Get Data button to display the Choose Data Source dialog box, then click the OLAP Cubes tab, shown in Figure 7-25.

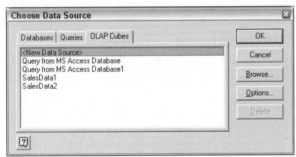

Figure 7-25: Selecting an existing OLAP cube as the data source in the PivotTable Wizard.

5. Select the desired cube file and click OK. If the cube file is not stored in the standard location, use the Browse button to find it.

6. Complete the PivotTable Wizard steps as usual.

After a PivotTable report is created based on an OLAP cube file, the blank PivotTable is displayed in Excel as usual. Figure 7-26 demonstrates this for the cube file created in the previous tip.

Part VII

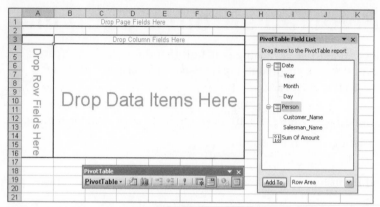

Figure 7-26: The blank PivotTable report created from the OLAP cube file.

For the most part, this looks like a regular PivotTable. The two dimensions, Date and Person, are listed in the PivotTable Field List. In fact, they are fields, and can be dragged to the PivotTable to define its structure. Note also that the levels are listed under each dimension — Year, Month, and Day for the Date dimension, for example. These are not fields, and you can't drag them to the PivotTable. They are listed to show you what each dimension contains. When you add a dimension to the PivotTable, its levels go along automatically. You'll see how this works in a minute.

The Sum Of Amount field is present too. This is what you specified as the summary data item in the cube. If you had specified other summary data items, they would be listed as well.

To complete the PivotTable follow these steps:

1. Drag the Date field (dimension) and drop it in the Column area of the PivotTable. In the table the field is given the name of its top level, Year, rather than the name of the dimension.

2. Drag the Person field and drop it in the Row area.

3. Drag the Sum Of Amount field and drop it in the Data area.

OLAP Icons

In the PivotTable Field List, items from an OLAP cube are displayed with one of two icons.

This icon marks a dimension; a dimension can be dropped only on a Row, Column, or Page area of a PivotTable.

This icon marks a measure, or data summary, which can be dropped only on the Data area of the PivotTable.

4. Right-click the Sum Of Amount field button and select Format Cells from the pop-up menu.

5. Specify Currency format with no decimal places, then click OK.

At this point the PivotTable looks like Figure 7-27. So far it looks like any other PivotTable report; what happened to all the levels? Only the top level in each dimension is represented, and the Month, Day, and Salesman levels are nowhere to be seen. What's going on?

	A	B	C	D	E	F	G
1				Drop Page Fields Here			
2							
3	Sum Of Amount	Year	▼				
4	Customer_Name ▼	2001	2002	2003	2004	2005	Grand Total
5	Acme Metal Works	$2,578,780	$3,217,125	$3,067,206	$2,651,146	$2,303,556	$13,817,813
6	East End Inc.	$3,491,924	$3,048,653	$2,715,097	$2,820,127	$2,628,418	$14,704,219
7	S&Q Manufacturing	$3,135,986	$2,616,058	$2,614,124	$3,057,470	$2,982,308	$14,405,946
8	TechWiz Corp.	$3,401,171	$3,233,254	$3,069,649	$3,478,283	$2,865,070	$16,047,427
9	Grand Total	$12,607,861	$12,115,090	$11,466,076	$12,007,026	$10,779,352	$58,975,405

Figure 7-27: The initial PivotTable report after dimensions are added.

In fact those levels are present in the table but currently hidden. To see what I mean, right-click the Customer_Name field, select Group and Show Detail from the pop-up menu, and then select Show Detail from the next menu. The next level in the hierarchy, Salesman_Name, is now displayed, as shown in Figure 7-28.

	A	B	C	D	E	F	G	H
1				Drop Page Fields Here				
2								
3	Sum Of Amount		Year	▼				
4	Customer_Name ▼	Salesman_Name	2001	2002	2003	2004	2005	Grand Total
5	Acme Metal Works	Anderson	$524,386	$1,026,747	$744,745	$783,215	$600,159	$3,679,252
6		Chang	$471,305	$794,316	$783,444	$856,150	$517,407	$3,422,622
7		Gomez	$829,067	$742,508	$863,707	$532,747	$592,409	$3,560,438
8		Jackson	$754,022	$653,554	$675,310	$479,034	$593,581	$3,155,501
9	Acme Metal Works Total		$2,578,780	$3,217,125	$3,067,206	$2,651,146	$2,303,556	$13,817,813
10	East End Inc.	Anderson	$930,450	$1,038,150	$642,544	$577,364	$630,268	$3,818,776
11		Chang	$811,462	$556,729	$729,496	$685,463	$618,098	$3,401,248
12		Gomez	$765,165	$665,607	$642,664	$615,168	$694,504	$3,383,108
13		Jackson	$984,847	$788,167	$700,393	$942,132	$685,548	$4,101,087
14	East End Inc. Total		$3,491,924	$3,048,653	$2,715,097	$2,820,127	$2,628,418	$14,704,219
15	S&Q Manufacturing	Anderson	$796,932	$585,133	$453,235	$718,402	$918,925	$3,472,627
16		Chang	$814,178	$501,243	$839,527	$658,922	$725,667	$3,539,537
17		Gomez	$820,306	$918,251	$679,725	$742,660	$563,012	$3,723,954
18		Jackson	$704,570	$611,431	$641,637	$937,486	$774,704	$3,669,828
19	S&Q Manufacturing Total		$3,135,986	$2,616,058	$2,614,124	$3,057,470	$2,982,308	$14,405,946
20	TechWiz Corp.	Anderson	$944,132	$534,960	$742,579	$978,110	$691,771	$3,891,552
21		Chang	$542,071	$720,038	$870,797	$874,893	$617,314	$3,625,113
22		Gomez	$1,076,951	$904,470	$609,609	$1,036,611	$899,058	$4,526,699
23		Jackson	$838,017	$1,073,786	$846,664	$588,669	$656,927	$4,004,063
24	TechWiz Corp. Total		$3,401,171	$3,233,254	$3,069,649	$3,478,283	$2,865,070	$16,047,427
25	Grand Total		$12,607,861	$12,115,090	$11,466,076	$12,007,026	$10,779,352	$58,975,405

Figure 7-28: Showing detail for the Customer_Name field makes the Salesman_Name level visible in the PivotTable report.

It works the same way for the Year field. Show its detail and the next level in the hierarchy, Month, becomes visible. Show detail for the Month field and the final level, Day, becomes visible. The PivotTable with all the detail visible is shown in Figure 7-29. This figure actually shows only a small part of the table because it is quite large.

	Sum Of Amount		Year ▼	Month	Day									
			2001											
			Apr					Apr Total	Aug					Aug Total
	Customer_Name ▼	Salesman_Name	Fri	Mon	Thurs	Tues	Wed		Fri	Mon	Thurs	Tues	Wed	
7	Acme Metal Works	Anderson		$14,701	$115,189		$9,590	$139,480					$36,498	$36,49
8		Chang								$35,192			$23,128	$58,32
9		Gomez			$35,552			$35,552						
10		Jackson	$9,649	$9,793				$19,442	$36,213	$36,150		$76,862		$149,22
11	Acme Metal Works Total		$9,649	$24,494	$150,741		$9,590	$194,474	$36,213	$71,342		$76,862	$59,626	$244,04
12	East End Inc.	Anderson				$40,426		$40,426	$44,461		$27,125		$38,730	$110,31
13		Chang	$48,160					$48,160	$12,144	$12,738			$76,441	$101,32
14		Gomez	$19,118		$33,857		$25,853	$78,828		$35,974		$37,764		$73,73
15		Jackson		$31,842		$38,797		$70,639		$28,270	$33,541			$61,81
16	East End Inc. Total		$67,278	$31,842	$33,857	$79,223	$25,853	$238,053	$56,605	$76,982	$60,666	$37,764	$115,171	$347,18
17	S&Q Manufacturing	Anderson												
18		Chang		$17,841	$41,835	$20,811	$50,764	$131,251		$65,084				$65,08
19		Gomez					$49,418	$49,418	$37,775			$44,397		$82,17
20		Jackson				$37,045	$94,232	$131,277						
21	S&Q Manufacturing Total			$17,841	$41,835	$57,856	$194,414	$311,946	$37,775	$65,084		$44,397		$147,25
22	TechWiz Corp.	Anderson		$30,624			$46,408	$77,032			$30,838		$40,513	$71,35
23		Chang			$17,311			$17,311			$30,682	$57,509		$88,19
24		Gomez	$66,762	$20,224	$61,895	$38,322		$187,203				$48,215	$67,561	$115,77
25		Jackson	$94,578	$26,596				$121,174	$44,848	$39,279				$84,12
26	TechWiz Corp. Total		$161,340	$77,444	$79,206	$38,322	$46,408	$402,720	$44,848	$39,279	$61,520	$105,724	$108,074	$359,44
27	Grand Total		$238,267	$151,621	$305,639	$175,401	$276,265	$1,147,193	$175,441	$252,687	$122,186	$264,747	$282,871	$1,097,93

Figure 7-29: With all detail shown, all the hierarchical levels in the OLAP cube are displayed in the PivotTable.

Working with OLAP PivotTables

In most respects, a PivotTable created from OLAP data is the same as any other PivotTable. There are some differences, however, and you need to be aware of them.

You cannot drill down in the data of an OLAP-based PivotTable by double-clicking a data cell. This makes sense, of course: the data have already been summarized in the OLAP cube, and the raw data are located in the data source, to which Excel is not connected. Also, you can't change the measure used, such as by changing a Sum to an Average. Again, the summary calculation is done when the cube is created — remember, you specified the summary measure when defining the cube — and you can't change it from within Excel.

On the PivotTable menu, the Formulas commands are not available because a PivotTable based on multidimensional data does not permit the use of formulas. Likewise, the Show Pages command is not available.

Part VIII

Getting Hard Data from a PivotTable

After you have created your PivotTable report, then what? Of course, many reports are simply viewed and/or printed, but in other situations you will want to make use of the report data in the worksheet. For example, you may want to use Excel's various tools, such as formulas and functions, to perform additional analyses of the PivotTable data including the creation of charts (standard Excel charts as opposed to PivotCharts). How do you make those data available in other parts of the workbook? That's the topic of this chapter.

Tips and Where to Find Them

Understanding the GETPIVOTDATA Function

Suppose you want to write a formula that references a number in a PivotTable, and that number happens to be in cell G15. Well, you can simply use the cell reference G15 (or perhaps G15), right? Unfortunately, things aren't that simple. Just think of some of the things you can do with a PivotTable: pivoting it, of course, as well as showing or hiding detail and changing the sort order. These and other manipulations can cause a particular number to change its position. The summary data that were in cell G15 may now be in cell H22! Obviously you can't reliably retrieve data from a PivotTable using the standard Excel cell references. What to do? Enter the GETPIVOTDATA function.

GETPIVOTDATA Function Basics

The GETPIVOTDATA function is designed specifically to retrieve data from a PivotTable based not on the data's cell address but rather on its logical position in the table. Let's look at the syntax for this function:

```
GETPIVOTDATA(data_field,pivot_table,field1,item1,field2,item2,...)
```

- data_field is the name of the data field that you want to retrieve — in other words, the name of the field that you dropped on the Data area of the PivotTable.

- pivot_table is a reference to any cell or range of cells in the PivotTable.

- field1 and item1 are respectively the name of the first field and the first data value associated with the data you want to retrieve.

- field2 and item2 are respectively the name of the second field and the second data value associated with the data you want to retrieve.

You can have as many as 14 field and item pairs. All arguments to GETPIVOTDATA except for the cell reference must be enclosed in quotes. An example will help to clarify how these arguments are used. I will use the PivotTable report shown in Figure 8-1.

	A	B	C	D	E	F	G
1							
2							
3	Sum of Sales	Category ▼					
4	Month ▼	Accessories	Outerwear	Pants	Shirts	Shoes	Grand Total
5	Jan	$1,845	$2,820	$2,150	$2,397	$1,769	$10,981
6	Feb	$2,718	$2,606	$2,814	$2,846	$2,192	$13,176
7	Mar	$2,078	$1,606	$1,187	$2,319	$1,055	$8,245
8	Apr	$2,195	$2,255	$1,873	$2,648	$2,919	$11,890
9	May	$1,590	$1,714	$1,880	$2,798	$2,742	$10,724
10	June (projected)	$2,271	$2,381	$2,252	$3,268	$3,397	$13,568
11	Grand Total	$12,697	$13,382	$12,156	$16,276	$14,074	$68,584

Figure 8-1: The sample PivotTable report.

Suppose you want to retrieve the sum of sales in the Accessories category for the month of Jan. The proper function would be

```
=GETPIVOTDATA("Sales",$A$3,"Month","Jan","Category","Accessories")
```

Let's dissect these arguments.

- The `"Sales"` argument is used because the name of the data field in this PivotTable is Sales. That is, when the PivotTable was created, the Sales field was dragged from the Field List to the Data area of the PivotTable.

- The `$A$3` argument identifies a cell in the PivotTable.

- The `"Month"` and `"Jan"` arguments go together. They specify that you want to retrieve a value where the Month field contains the value Jan.

- The `"Category"` and `"Accessories"` arguments also go together. They specify that you want to retrieve a value where the Category field contains the value Accessories.

Looking at the PivotTable in Figure 8-1 you can see that the desired value, where Category=Accessories and Month=Jan, is in cell B5, so the function will return the value 1845.

If you include only a single field/item pair in the argument list, the function returns the corresponding total. For example, the function

```
=GETPIVOTDATA("Sales",$A$3,"Month","Jan")
```

returns the total for all data where Month=Jan, in this case the value 10981. Likewise the function

```
=GETPIVOTDATA("Sales",$A$3,"Category","Pants")
```

returns the sum for all data where Category=Pants, 12156. If you omit any mention of field and item, the GETPIVOTDATA function returns the overall total for the specified data item.

`=GETPIVOTDATA("Sales",$A$3)` returns the value 68548, the overall total of Sales items.

The Dreaded #REF

A restriction on using the GETPIVOTDATA function is that the PivotTable cell it references must be visible. If you change the PivotTable, for example by hiding detail or filtering detail, and the cell is no longer visible, the GETPIVOTDATA function will return #REF.

Copying Formulas that Contain GETPIVOTDATA

You can copy a formula that contains the GETPIVOTDATA function, just as you can any other Excel formula. However, the concept of relative cell addresses does not apply. In other words, the PivotTable cell that the GETPIVOTDATA function refers to will not be adjusted according to where you copy the formula. This make sense, of course, because the concept of a relative address is meaningless in terms of PivotTable data.

When using the GETPIVOTDATA function, you need to keep the following factors in mind:

- If the pivot_table argument refers to a range that contains two or more PivotTable reports, data are returned from whichever PivotTable was most recently created.

- Calculated fields, calculated items, and custom calculations can all be returned by GETPIVOTDATA.

- If the pivot_table argument refers to a cell or range where no PivotTable is located, the function returns #REF.

- If the field and item arguments refer to data that do not exist in the PivotTable, the function returns #REF.

A GETPIVOTDATA Shortcut

Excel makes entering the GETPIVOTDATA function really easy for most situations. All you need to do is to enter the equals sign in a cell, either at the beginning or as part of a formula, and then click the cell in the PivotTable whose data you want. This cell can be an individual data cell or a total cell. Excel will then automatically enter the correct GETPIVOTDATA function in the formula.

Referencing PivotTable Cells by Address

There may be times when you want to reference a cell in a PivotTable report by its cell address rather than by generating a GETPIVOTDATA function. For example, if you are writing some formulas outside of the PivotTable to perform calculations on its data, you may want relative cell addresses to adjust automatically when you copy the formula to other cells. You can set this up simply by typing the address into your formula rather than by clicking the cell. You can also turn off the PivotTable feature that automatically generates

GETPIVOTDATA functions when a cell is clicked. To do so, you must add a button to one of your toolbars as follows:

1. Select Customize from the Tools menu to display the Customize dialog box. (See Figure 8-2.)

2. Select Data in the categories list.

3. Select Generate GetPivotData from the Commands list.

4. Drag the button from the Commands list to one of your toolbars and drop it at the desired location.

5. Click Close to close the Customize dialog box.

The Generate GetPivotData button looks like this:

 Click it to toggle the feature on and off. When it is off, if you click a PivotTable cell while entering a formula, a cell reference is generated instead of a GETPIVOTDATA function.

Figure 8-2: Adding the Generate GetPivotData button to a toolbar.

Page Fields and the GETPIVOTDATA Function

The GETPIVOTDATA function does not use any reference to the page fields in a PivotTable report. For example, look at the PivotTable in Figure 8-3, which has three page fields.

	A	B	C	D	E
1	Color	(All) ▼			
2	Item	2 ▼			
3	Size	Large ▼			
4					
5	Sum of Amount	Month ▼			
6	Store ▼	Jan	Feb	Mar	Grand Total
7	Downtown		$33.96		$33.96
8	East End	$20.94			$20.94
9	Northside		$16.86	$32.04	$48.90
10	South Plaza			$25.52	$25.52
11	Grand Total	$20.94	$50.82	$57.56	$129.32

Figure 8-3: A PivotTable report with three page fields.

Suppose you create a GETPIVOTDATA function to retrieve the data in cell D11, the total for March. The function will look like this:

```
=GETPIVOTDATA("Amount",$A$5,"Month","Mar")
```

The function contains no reference to the settings for the three page fields: For example, there is no information relating to the fact that the Size field is filtered on the value Large. This is correct. The page fields control which data are summarized in the PivotTable, while the GETPIVOTDATA function returns a specific piece of those data. Changing the page field filtering may change the value returned by the GETPIVOTDATA function, of course.

GETPIVOTDATA and OLAP Data

You can use the GETPIVOTDATA function on PivotTable reports based on OLAP data. One difference is that in the function arguments, the item can specify the source name of the dimension as well as the item name itself. Also, arguments are enclosed in brackets. For example, look at the PivotTable that you created from OLAP data in the walkthrough in Part VII, as shown in Figure 8-4.

3	Sum Of Amount		Year ▼					
4	Customer Name ▼	Salesman Name	2001	2002	2003	2004	2005	Grand Total
5	Acme Metal Works	Anderson	$524,386	$1,026,747	$744,745	$783,215	$600,159	$3,679,252
6		Chang	$471,305	$794,316	$783,444	$856,150	$517,407	$3,422,622
7		Gomez	$829,067	$742,508	$863,707	$532,747	$592,409	$3,560,438
8		Jackson	$754,022	$653,554	$675,310	$479,034	$593,581	$3,155,501
9	Acme Metal Works Total		$2,578,780	$3,217,125	$3,067,206	$2,651,146	$2,303,556	$13,817,813
10	East End Inc.	Anderson	$930,450	$1,038,150	$642,544	$577,364	$630,268	$3,818,776
11		Chang	$811,462	$556,729	$729,496	$685,463	$618,098	$3,401,248
12		Gomez	$765,165	$665,607	$642,664	$615,168	$694,504	$3,383,108
13		Jackson	$984,847	$788,167	$700,393	$942,132	$685,548	$4,101,087
14	East End Inc. Total		$3,491,924	$3,048,653	$2,715,097	$2,820,127	$2,628,418	$14,704,219
15	S&Q Manufacturing	Anderson	$796,932	$585,133	$453,235	$718,402	$918,925	$3,472,627
16		Chang	$814,178	$501,243	$839,527	$658,922	$725,667	$3,539,537
17		Gomez	$820,306	$918,251	$679,725	$742,660	$563,012	$3,723,954
18		Jackson	$704,570	$611,431	$641,637	$937,486	$774,704	$3,669,828
19	S&Q Manufacturing Total		$3,135,986	$2,616,058	$2,614,124	$3,057,470	$2,982,308	$14,405,946
20	TechWiz Corp.	Anderson	$944,132	$534,960	$742,579	$978,110	$691,771	$3,891,552
21		Chang	$542,071	$720,038	$870,797	$874,893	$617,314	$3,625,113
22		Gomez	$1,076,951	$904,470	$609,609	$1,036,611	$899,058	$4,526,699
23		Jackson	$838,017	$1,073,786	$846,664	$588,669	$656,927	$4,004,063
24	TechWiz Corp. Total		$3,401,171	$3,233,254	$3,069,649	$3,478,283	$2,865,070	$16,047,427
25	Grand Total		$12,607,861	$12,115,090	$11,466,076	$12,007,026	$10,779,352	$58,975,405

Figure 8-4: A PivotTable report created from OLAP data.

Suppose you want to use the GETPIVOTDATA function to retrieve the total sales made by Anderson to Acme Metal Works in the year 2003. The function will look like this:

```
=GETPIVOTDATA("[Measures].[Sum Of Amount]",
$A$3,"[Date]","[Date].[All].[2003]","[Person]",
"[Person].[All].[Acme Metal Works].[Anderson]")
```

If you refer to Part VII, you will recall that the year is actually represented in a level named Year, and also that when you designed the cube file, you placed that level in a dimension named Date. The same is true for the Customer_Name and Salesman_name fields (levels), which were placed in a dimension named Person. And you can see that the dimension names Date and Person are used in the GETPIVOTDATA function rather than the level names.

Because the syntax of GETPIVOTDATA can be rather complex when working with OLAP data, I recommend that you always use the shortcut and let Excel generate the function arguments for you.

GETPIVOTDATA and Show/Hide Detail

One of the nice aspects of the GETPIVOTDATA function is that the result it returns does not change when you show additional levels of detail. For example, look at the PivotTable report in Figure 8-4. This is the PivotTable that you created from OLAP data in Part VII. You can see that no detail is shown under the Year dimension; the Month and DayOfWeek levels are hidden. This means that each result cell is the sum across all days and months. For example, cell 5 shows the sum of all sales that Anderson made to Acme Metal Works in 2001. If you used the GETPIVOTDATA function to reference this cell, it would return the value in the cell — $524,386.

Suppose that now you use the Show Detail command to display additional detail for the Year field. The result, shown in Figure 8-5, is that the Month detail is displayed in the PivotTable report. There is no cell in the report that sums all sales that Anderson made to Acme Metal Works in 2001 because this total is now broken down by months. Yet the GETPIVOTDATA function that you created still shows the same total. This is a very useful feature of this function.

Of course the opposite is not true. If you create a GETPIVOTDATA function that refers to a cell in a PivotTable report and hide that cell with the Hide Detail command, the function will return #REF.

#	Sum Of Amount	Year	Month									
3	Sum Of Amount	Year	Month									
4		2001										
5	Customer_Name	Salesman_Name	Apr	Aug	Dec	Feb	Jan	Jul	Jun	Mar	May	Nov	O
6	Acme Metal Works	Anderson	$139,480	$36,498		$74,967		$10,419	$25,148	$25,828	$93,897	$24,497	
7		Chang		$58,320	$78,079	$51,886	$71,355	$21,930	$30,812	$9,584		$61,374	
8		Gomez	$35,552		$94,070	$76,947	$103,806	$50,128	$50,898	$46,228	$141,286	$146,030	
9		Jackson	$19,442	$149,225	$149,305	$145,683	$25,806		$50,408		$102,146	$102,916	
10	Acme Metal Works Total		$194,474	$244,043	$321,454	$349,483	$200,967	$82,477	$157,266	$81,640	$337,329	$334,817	
11	East End Inc.	Anderson	$40,426	$110,316	$11,712	$71,333	$37,607	$43,461	$16,483	$110,008	$51,714	$214,703	
12		Chang	$48,160	$101,323	$114,245	$97,421	$93,418	$56,735	$14,090	$58,768	$21,935	$57,218	
13		Gomez	$78,828	$73,738	$77,684	$113,138	$33,180	$108,584	$30,675	$122,300	$26,628	$88,984	
14		Jackson	$70,639	$61,811	$103,148	$125,286	$76,688	$102,859	$47,002	$162,594	$45,856	$39,235	
15	East End Inc. Total		$238,053	$347,188	$306,789	$407,178	$240,893	$311,639	$108,250	$453,670	$146,133	$400,140	
16	S&Q Manufacturing	Anderson				$19,519	$60,213	$108,452	$146,999	$121,793	$99,761	$87,893	$119,564
17		Chang	$131,251	$65,084	$74,239	$61,118	$30,734	$148,947		$60,863	$72,155	$102,085	
18		Gomez	$49,418	$82,172	$119,550	$63,727		$39,642	$102,890	$87,297	$179,506	$71,794	
19		Jackson	$131,277		$109,507	$33,849	$114,245	$143,239	$8,507		$52,289	$39,558	
20	S&Q Manufacturing Total		$311,946	$147,256	$322,815	$218,907	$253,431	$478,827	$233,190	$247,921	$391,843	$333,001	
21	TechWiz Corp.	Anderson	$77,032	$71,351	$86,722	$88,692	$115,834	$104,572	$51,540	$66,511	$61,496	$80,418	
22		Chang	$17,311	$88,191	$63,974	$27,183		$16,848	$89,546		$60,374	$88,270	
23		Gomez	$187,203	$115,776		$115,978		$154,324	$169,258	$144,979	$36,299	$19,236	
24		Jackson	$121,174	$84,127	$30,361	$77,105	$42,559	$42,122	$99,841	$20,506	$69,689	$92,277	
25	TechWiz Corp. Total		$402,720	$359,445	$181,057	$308,958	$158,393	$317,866	$410,185	$231,996	$227,858	$280,201	
26	Grand Total		$1,147,193	$1,097,932	$1,132,115	$1,284,526	$853,684	$1,190,809	$908,891	$1,015,227	$1,103,163	$1,348,159	

Figure 8-5: Increasing the level of detail shown in a PivotTable does not change the result of the GETPIVOTDATA function.

Using GETPIVOTDATA to Analyze PivotTable Data

For this walkthrough, you continue with the PivotTable you created from OLAP data. It is shown again in Figure 8-6 with all the detail under the Year dimension hidden. Your goal is to create a chart — a standard Excel chart, not a PivotChart — that compares the sales each salesman made to each customer in the year 2005.

The strategy you will follow has two parts. The first is to use the GETPIVOTDATA function to pull the required numbers out of the PivotTable and place them in a regular Excel table. The second and easier part is to create a chart from this new table.

1. Open the workbook containing the PivotTable that you created from OLAP data in Part VII.

2. Decide on a location for the new table. It can be in a new worksheet or the one that contains the PivotTable.

3. Enter a title for the table, Sales for 2005, in a cell.

4. In the row below the title, enter the four customer names in four columns. Adjust the column widths, if needed, to show the full names.

5. In the column to the left, enter the four salesman names in four rows.

6. Format all the text you entered as bold. At this point the table will look like Figure 8-7.

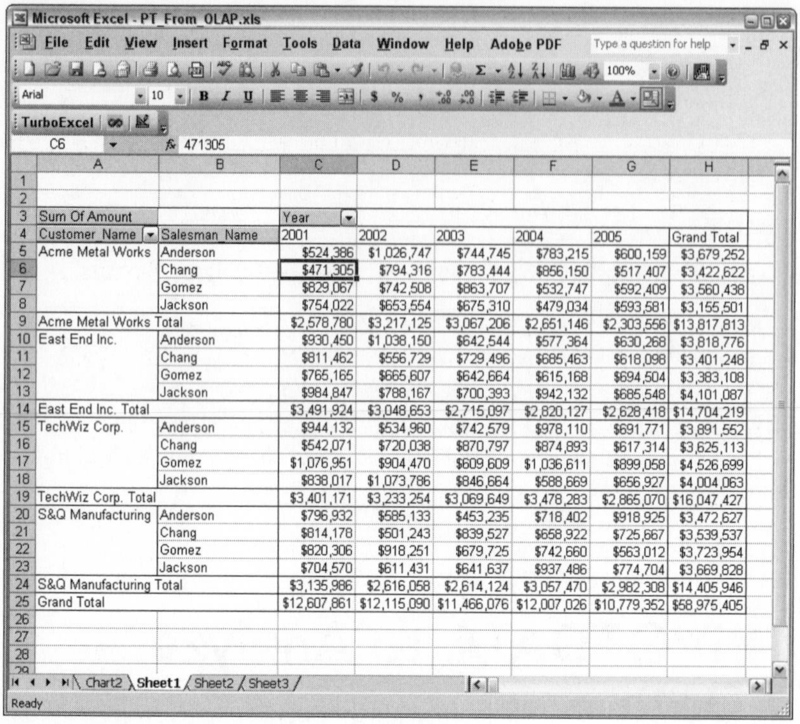

Sum Of Amount		Year					
Customer_Name	Salesman_Name	2001	2002	2003	2004	2005	Grand Total
Acme Metal Works	Anderson	$524,386	$1,026,747	$744,745	$783,215	$600,159	$3,679,252
	Chang	$471,305	$794,316	$783,444	$856,150	$517,407	$3,422,622
	Gomez	$829,067	$742,508	$863,707	$532,747	$592,409	$3,560,438
	Jackson	$754,022	$653,554	$675,310	$479,034	$593,581	$3,155,501
Acme Metal Works Total		$2,578,780	$3,217,125	$3,067,206	$2,651,146	$2,303,556	$13,817,813
East End Inc.	Anderson	$930,450	$1,038,150	$642,544	$577,364	$630,268	$3,818,776
	Chang	$811,462	$556,729	$729,496	$685,463	$618,098	$3,401,248
	Gomez	$765,165	$665,607	$642,664	$615,168	$694,504	$3,383,108
	Jackson	$984,847	$788,167	$700,393	$942,132	$685,548	$4,101,087
East End Inc. Total		$3,491,924	$3,048,653	$2,715,097	$2,820,127	$2,628,418	$14,704,219
TechWiz Corp.	Anderson	$944,132	$534,960	$742,579	$978,110	$691,771	$3,891,552
	Chang	$542,071	$720,038	$870,797	$874,893	$617,314	$3,625,113
	Gomez	$1,076,951	$904,470	$609,609	$1,036,611	$899,058	$4,526,699
	Jackson	$838,017	$1,073,786	$846,664	$588,669	$656,927	$4,004,063
TechWiz Corp. Total		$3,401,171	$3,233,254	$3,069,649	$3,478,283	$2,865,070	$16,047,427
S&Q Manufacturing	Anderson	$796,932	$585,133	$453,235	$718,402	$918,925	$3,472,627
	Chang	$814,178	$501,243	$839,527	$658,922	$725,667	$3,539,537
	Gomez	$820,306	$918,251	$679,725	$742,660	$563,012	$3,723,954
	Jackson	$704,570	$611,431	$641,637	$937,486	$774,704	$3,669,828
S&Q Manufacturing Total		$3,135,986	$2,616,058	$2,614,124	$3,057,470	$2,982,308	$14,405,946
Grand Total		$12,607,861	$12,115,090	$11,466,076	$12,007,026	$10,779,352	$58,975,405

Figure 8-6: The PivotTable for this walkthrough.

	Sales for 2005			
	Acme Metal Works	East End Inc.	TechWiz Corp.	S&Q Manufacturing
Anderson				
Chang				
Gomez				
Jackson				

Figure 8-7: The new data table after the row and column headings are entered.

The next step is to enter a GETPIVOTDATA function in the table cells to refer to the proper cells in the PivotTable report. For example, consider the cell in the new table at the intersection of the Anderson row and the Acme Metal Works column. Obviously this cell should display the total sales in 2005 for Anderson to Acme Metal Works. In the PivotTable this is cell G5, although it might be different in your PivotTable, depending on where you put it. Thus, the next steps are:

1. Place the cell pointer in the new table at the intersection of the Anderson column and the Acme Metal Works row.
2. Type = (an equals sign).

3. Click the Anderson/Acme Metal Works/2005 cell in the PivotTable. (In Figure 8-6 this is cell G5.)

4. Press Enter to complete entry of the GETPIVOTDATA function.

5. Move the cell pointer to the cell in the new table at the intersection of the Chang column and the Acme Metal Works row.

6. Type = (an equals sign).

7. Click the Chang/Acme Metal Works/2005 cell in the PivotTable. In Figure 8-6 this is cell G6.

8. Continue in this manner until all 16 data cells in the new table have the appropriate GETPIVOTDATA function in them.

9. Format all the number cells in the new table as Currency with no decimal places.

At this point the data table is complete and should look like Figure 8-8.

	Sales for 2005			
	Acme Metal Works	East End Inc.	TechWiz Corp	S&Q Manufacturing
Anderson	$600,159	$630,268	$691,771	$918,925
Chang	$517,407	$618,098	$617,314	$725,667
Gomez	$592,409	$694,504	$899,058	$563,012
Jackson	$593,581	$685,548	$656,927	$774,704

Figure 8-8: The new data table after GETPIVOTDATA functions are entered in each cell.

The final steps of this tip are quite simple, and require only that you use the PivotChart Wizard to make a chart from the new data table you just created.

1. Select the entire data table, excluding the cell with the title in it.

2. Click the Chart Wizard button on the toolbar.

3. In the first Chart Wizard dialog box, leave the default Column type selected, then click Next.

4. Accept the default chart settings in the next two wizard dialog boxes, clicking Next until you reach Step 4.

5. Specify that the chart be created as a new sheet.

6. Click Finish.

The final chart is shown in Figure 8-9. As with any Excel chart, you can customize it as desired, adding titles and other elements.

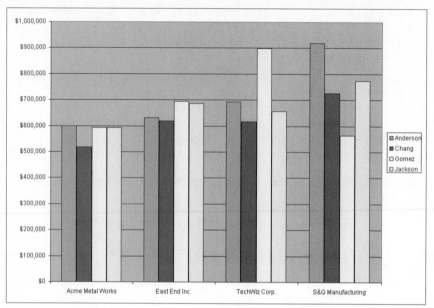

Figure 8-9: The final chart based on the data extracted with the GETPIVOTDATA function.

Copying and Pasting PivotTables

You can copy a PivotTable and paste it in a new location, even in a new workbook, and the copy will continue to function just like the original. You'll be able to refresh data, pivot the table, and so on. If you copy the PivotTable to a new workbook, and the original data are in another Excel workbook, the data reference in the copied PivotTable will still reference the original data location. You can use this ability to copy a PivotTable and retain full functionality to create a master PivotTable workbook that contains multiple PivotTable reports copied from multiple workbooks. PivotTables based on external data, including OLAP cubes, can be copied in the same way. Another reason to create a copy of a PivotTable is that it enables you to pivot or filter the copy differently from the original and display both versions at the same time. To copy a PivotTable, do the following:

1. Click any cell in the PivotTable.

2. From the PivotTable menu choose Select, then choose Entire Table.

3. Press Ctrl+C or select Copy from the Edit menu.

4. Click the cell in which you want to place the top left of the PivotTable. The cell can be in the same worksheet, in another worksheet in the same workbook, or in another workbook.

5. Press Ctrl+V or select Paste from the Edit menu.

If the PivotTable is in its final form, you can use Paste Special to copy the displayed data only. The result is plain data, not a PivotTable, just as if you had typed the data in. You cannot refresh or pivot the table. To copy a PivotTable as data, follow these steps:

1. Click any cell in the PivotTable.

2. From the PivotTable menu choose Select, then choose Entire Table.

3. Press Ctrl+C or select Copy from the Edit menu.

4. Click the cell in which you want to place the top left of the data.

5. Select Paste Special from the Edit menu to display the Paste Special dialog box.

6. Select the Values option.

7. Click OK.

Of course you can use Paste Special to copy any part of a PivotTable, such as a single cell or an entire column or row.

Part IX

PivotTable Alternatives

Excel offers a wide range of data-analysis tools in addition to PivotTables. It's a good idea to know about these techniques so that when you are faced with a data-analysis task, you can choose the best technique. As powerful as PivotTables are, they are not always the best choice — in fact, sometimes they are too powerful and something simpler will serve you better. This chapter provides an overview of some of the other data-analysis techniques that perform analysis tasks similar to PivotTables.

Tips and Where to Find Them

Working with Subtotals

Excel's subtotal tool makes it easy to generate subtotals based on values in the data. For example, look at the Excel database in Figure 9-1. This database contains data for a video rental chain, specifically the number of titles in stock for each genre at each store. This is typical of the kind of data you might analyze with a PivotTable.

	A	B	C
1	**Store**	**Genre**	**Titles in Stock**
2	Downtown	Adventure	121
3	North Hills	Adventure	199
4	Southpoint	Adventure	301
5	Downtown	Classics	412
6	North Hills	Classics	189
7	Southpoint	Classics	312
8	Downtown	Comedy	340
9	North Hills	Comedy	324
10	Southpoint	Comedy	299
11	Downtown	Drama	132
12	North Hills	Drama	209
13	Southpoint	Drama	178
14	Downtown	Sci-Fi	212
15	North Hills	Sci-Fi	287
16	Southpoint	Sci-Fi	312

Figure 9-1: Video store stock data.

Suppose you want titles in stock for each genre totaled across all stores. Sure, you can create a PivotTable report for this purpose, as shown in Figure 9-2. But you can also use subtotals.

Sum of Titles in Stock	
Genre	Total
Adventure	621
Classics	913
Comedy	963
Drama	519
Sci-Fi	811
Grand Total	3827

Figure 9-2: Using a PivotTable to total the number of titles in each genre across all stores.

If you want to use subtotals, the data must be sorted on the field on which you want to subtotal — in this case, Genre. Then, do the following:

1. Place the cell pointer on any cell in the data table.

2. Select Subtotals from the Data menu to display the Subtotal dialog box, shown in Figure 9-3.

Part IX

Figure 9-3: You use the Subtotal dialog box to define subtotals.

3. In the At each change in list, select the field on which the subtotals will be based; in this example, this field is Genre.

4. In the Use function list, select the subtotal function. You can choose between Sum (appropriate for this example) and several other measures (explained in the list following Step 6).

5. In the Add subtotal to list, place a checkmark next to the field or fields you want subtotaled. For this example you will place a check next to Titles in Stock.

6. Select the following as desired:

   • **Replace Current Subtotals** — If this option is selected, any subtotals already in the data table will be replaced with the new ones. If it is not selected, the new subtotals will be included in the data table along with any existing ones.

   • **Page Break Between Groups** — Excel inserts a page break after each group. (This is relevant for printing.)

   • **Summary Below Data** — If this option is selected, each subtotal will be displayed below the group of records it is subtotaling, and the grand total will be displayed in the last row. If this option is not selected, each subtotal will be displayed above the group of records it is subtotaling, and the grand total will be displayed in the first row.

7. Click OK.

Figure 9-4 shows the data subtotaled by Genre. You can see that the same subtotals are calculated as in the PivotTable report shown in Figure 9-2. The arrangement is different, of course, with the analysis results interspersed in the data table rather than in their own separate table.

	A	B	C
1	**Store**	**Genre**	**Titles in Stock**
2	Downtown	Adventure	121
3	North Hills	Adventure	199
4	Southpoint	Adventure	301
5		**Adventure Total**	621
6	Downtown	Classics	412
7	North Hills	Classics	189
8	Southpoint	Classics	312
9		**Classics Total**	913
10	Downtown	Comedy	340
11	North Hills	Comedy	324
12	Southpoint	Comedy	299
13		**Comedy Total**	963
14	Downtown	Drama	132
15	North Hills	Drama	209
16	Southpoint	Drama	178
17		**Drama Total**	519
18	Downtown	Sci-Fi	212
19	North Hills	Sci-Fi	287
20	Southpoint	Sci-Fi	312
21		**Sci-Fi Total**	811
22		**Grand Total**	3827

Figure 9-4: Totals by Genre calculated with Excel's subtotal tool.

When defining subtotals, you can choose from a number of summary calculations. You have the following at your disposal:

- **Average** — The average of the values (sum divided by number of values).
- **Count** — The number of values, including blank cells.
- **CountA** — The number of values, excluding blank cells.
- **Max** — The largest value.
- **Min** — The smallest value.
- **Product** — The product of the values.
- **StDev** — The standard deviation of the values, estimated for the sample.
- **StDevP** — The standard deviation of the values, estimated for the population.
- **Sum** — The sum of the values.
- **Var** — The variance of the values, estimated for the sample.
- **VarP** — The variance of the values, estimated for the population.

Removing Subtotals

To remove all subtotals from a data range, click the Remove All button in the Subtotal dialog box.

Nesting Subtotals

You are not limited to creating one level of subtotals for your data. You can nest them, subtotaling by one field and then, within those groupings, by another. Look, for example, at Figure 9-5. This is an expansion of the video store data from Figure 9-1, with an additional field that breaks down the titles by rating — G, PG, or R. These data are in the file `VideoDataWithRatings.xls`.

	A	B	C	D
1	Store	Genre	Rating	Titles in Stock
2	Downtown	Adventure	G	99
3	Downtown	Classics	G	123
4	Downtown	Comedy	G	114
5	Downtown	Drama	G	56
6	Downtown	Sci-Fi	G	98
7	Downtown	Adventure	PG	78
8	Downtown	Classics	PG	98
9	Downtown	Comedy	PG	90
10	Downtown	Drama	PG	45
11	Downtown	Sci-Fi	PG	95
12	Downtown	Adventure	R	89
13	Downtown	Classics	R	56
14	Downtown	Comedy	R	101
15	Downtown	Drama	R	78
16	Downtown	Sci-Fi	R	76
17	North Hills	Adventure	G	109
18	North Hills	Classics	G	87
19	North Hills	Comedy	G	123

Figure 9-5: The video-store data with an additional field for rating.

Here are the steps required to create nested subtotals for these data. First, you sort the data, and then you create the subtotals:

1. Open the file `VideoDataWithRatings.xls` in Excel.

2. Place the cell pointer anywhere in the data table.

3. Select Sort from the Data menu to display the Sort dialog box. (See Figure 9-6.)

4. Under Sort by, select Genre and Ascending.

5. Under Then by, select Rating and Ascending.

6. Make sure that the Header row option is selected.

7. Click OK to perform the sort.

8. Select Subtotal from the Data menu to display the Subtotal dialog box (shown earlier in Figure 9-3).

9. Select Genre in the At each change in list.

10. Select Sum in the Use function list.

11. In the Add subtotal to list, place a check next to Titles in Stock and remove any other checks.

12. Make sure the Page break between groups option is off and the Summary below data option is on.

13. Click OK.

Figure 9-6: Sorting the data before applying subtotals.

At this point the data look like Figure 9-7. You can see that it includes subtotals for Genre. The next step is to add the nested subtotals for Rating.

	A	B	C	D
1	Store	Genre	Rating	Titles in Stock
2	Downtown	Adventure	G	99
3	North Hills	Adventure	G	109
4	Southpoint	Adventure	G	102
5	Downtown	Adventure	PG	78
6	North Hills	Adventure	PG	45
7	Southpoint	Adventure	PG	98
8	Downtown	Adventure	R	89
9	North Hills	Adventure	R	78
10	Southpoint	Adventure	R	90
11		**Adventure Total**		788
12	Downtown	Classics	G	123
13	North Hills	Classics	G	87
14	Southpoint	Classics	G	99
15	Downtown	Classics	PG	98
16	North Hills	Classics	PG	78
17	Southpoint	Classics	PG	78
18	Downtown	Classics	R	56
19	North Hills	Classics	R	65
20	Southpoint	Classics	R	89
21		**Classics Total**		773
22	Downtown	Comedy	G	114
23	North Hills	Comedy	G	123
24	Southpoint	Comedy	G	79
25	Downtown	Comedy	PG	90
26	North Hills	Comedy	PG	45
27	Southpoint	Comedy	PG	87
28	Downtown	Comedy	R	101
29	North Hills	Comedy	R	78
30	Southpoint	Comedy	R	91
31		**Comedy Total**		808

Figure 9-7: Subtotaling the data by Genre.

1. Select Subtotal from the Data menu to display the Subtotal dialog box.

2. Select Rating in the At each change in list.

3. Select Sum in the Use function list.

4. In the Add subtotal to list, place a check next to Titles in Stock and remove any other checks.

5. Make sure the Page break between groups options is off and the Summary below data option is on. Most important, make sure the Replace current subtotals option is off.

6. Click OK.

The new subtotal is added, as shown in Figure 9-8. Now you can see that within each Genre group, the data for each rating are broken out and subtotaled separately.

	A	B	C	D
1	**Store**	**Genre**	**Rating**	**Titles in Stock**
2	Downtown	Adventure	G	99
3	North Hills	Adventure	G	109
4	Southpoint	Adventure	G	102
5			**G Total**	310
6	Downtown	Adventure	PG	78
7	North Hills	Adventure	PG	45
8	Southpoint	Adventure	PG	98
9			**PG Total**	221
10	Downtown	Adventure	R	89
11	North Hills	Adventure	R	78
12	Southpoint	Adventure	R	90
13			**R Total**	257
14		**Adventure Total**		788
15	Downtown	Classics	G	123
16	North Hills	Classics	G	87
17	Southpoint	Classics	G	99
18			**G Total**	309
19	Downtown	Classics	PG	98
20	North Hills	Classics	PG	78
21	Southpoint	Classics	PG	78
22			**PG Total**	254
23	Downtown	Classics	R	56
24	North Hills	Classics	R	65
25	Southpoint	Classics	R	89
26			**R Total**	210
27		**Classics Total**		773
28	Downtown	Comedy	G	114
29	North Hills	Comedy	G	123
30	Southpoint	Comedy	G	79
31			**G Total**	316

Figure 9-8: The data are subtotaled at two levels, Genre and Rating.

Hiding and Showing Subtotal Detail

When you add subtotals to a data list in Excel, you see a vertical area immediately to the left of the row numbers at the left edge of the worksheet. This is called the *outline section*, and the controls in this area enable you to hide and display different levels of detail. Look at Figure 9-9, which is again the data from the previous tip.

Outline area

1 2 3 4		A	B	C	D
	1	Store	Genre	Rating	Titles in Stock
+	5			G Total	310
+	9			PG Total	221
+	13			R Total	257
−	14		Adventure Total		788
·	15	Downtown	Classics	G	123
·	16	North Hills	Classics	G	87
·	17	Southpoint	Classics	G	99
−	18			G Total	309

Figure 9-9: You can use the outline area to control the level of detail displayed.

Three controls are available in the outline area:

- The Hide Detail button is displayed when the rows in a group are visible. Clicking the Hide Detail button hides the rows.

- The Show Detail button is displayed when the rows in a group are hidden. Clicking the Show Detail button displays the rows.

- The Level buttons each represent a level of organization in the list. Click a Level button to show all the detail for the level of the button and hide all detail below.

Subtotals Versus PivotTables

Subtotals are easy to use and the fact that the subtotals are displayed along with the data may be an advantage in some situations. However, the use of subtotals is dependent on the data being organized in a certain way, and restricts the ways in which they can be sorted. Also, there is no reliable way to get data out of a data table that includes subtotals — in other words, there is no equivalent of the GETPIVOTDATA function. Subtotals certainly have their uses but are not capable of performing most of the robust types of analysis for which PivotTables are designed.

Working With Database Functions

Excel has a special category of functions intended specifically for working with databases. In this context, a database is any table of data with column headings identifying the fields, just the kind of data that is commonly analyzed with PivotTables. The database functions perform the same calculations as other Excel functions, such as sum, average, and standard deviation. What sets them apart is that they include only values that meet one or more criteria.

To illustrate, look at the video store data presented in Figure 9-5. You have already seen how you can use a PivotTable or subtotals to extract summary data that will answer questions such as "What's the total number of videos in the Drama genre?" Database functions can perform much the same task.

The database function names all start with *D*. The remainder of the name describes the function and is the same as the name of the equivalent non-database function. The following list describes the database functions:

- DAVERAGE returns the average of selected database entries.

- DCOUNT counts the cells that contain numbers in a database.

- DCOUNTA counts nonblank cells in a database.

- DMAX returns the maximum value from selected database entries.

- DMIN returns the minimum value from selected database entries.

- DPRODUCT multiplies the values in a particular field of records that match the criteria in a database.

- DSTDEV estimates the standard deviation based on a sample of selected database entries.

- DSTDEVP calculates the standard deviation based on the entire population of selected database entries.

- DSUM adds the numbers in the field column of records in the database that match the criteria.

- DVAR estimates variance based on a sample from selected database entries.

- DVARP calculates variance based on the entire population of selected database entries.

The functions all take the same arguments, as follows:

DXXXXX(*Database, Field, Criteria*)

- *Database* is the worksheet range containing the data, including the first row of column or field names. It can be a range address such as A1:J150 or an assigned range name.

- *Field* is the name of the field or column whose values will be summarized by the function.

- *Criteria* is the worksheet range where the criteria for the database function is located.

Defining Criteria

The criteria is the only tricky part of using database functions. They tell the function which rows, or records, to include in its calculation. For example, to calculate the total number of titles for the Drama genre, the criteria would in effect tell the DSUM function to include only those records where the Genre field contains the value Drama.

At a minimum, the criteria range contains two cells in one column. The top cell contains the name of the field the criterion applies to, and the lower cell contains the criterion itself. For example, the criterion in Figure 9-10 specifies that only those records which contain Adventure in the Genre column will be included in the calculation.

Figure 9-10: A simple criterion for a database function.

To see a real example, return to the video store data and calculate the sum of titles in stock for the Adventure genre. Assuming that you placed the criterion in cells G2:G3, the database function will be

```
=DSUM(A1:D46, "Titles in Stock", G2:G3)
```

The three arguments are as follows:

- A1:D46 is the range of cells containing the data, including the row of field names at the top.

- "Titles in Stock" is the name of the column whose values we want to sum.

- G2:G3 is the range containing the criterion.

For text criteria, such as in the previous example, simply type in the text you want to match. For numbers, if you want an exact match simply enter the number. For example, the criterion range in Figure 9-11 matches records in which the Age field is equal to 23.

Where to Put Your Criteria

You can put your criteria essentially anywhere in the workbook. The only place you should avoid is below the data table. It's a good idea to leave this area blank in case you need to add data to the table

Figure 9-11: A numeric criterion for a database function.

Numeric criteria that are not exact matches are specified with the symbols in the following table:

Symbol	Meaning	Example	Matches
>	Greater than	>15	Values greater than 15
<	Less than	<0	Values less than 0
>=	Greater than or equal to	>=15	Values of 15 or greater
<=	Less than or equal to	<=0	Values of 0 or less

You can also define a criteria range for more complex criteria. To match more than one value in a field, place the values in two or more cells below the field name. For example, the criterion range shown in Figure 9-12 will match records in which the Genre field contains either Adventure or Drama. Of course, the range passed as the criterion argument to the database function must specify all the cells in the criterion range.

Figure 9-12: A criterion that matches two values in the Genre field.

To define criteria that include two or more fields, create a criterion range with two or more columns. Place a field name at the top of each column and the criteria in the cells below. The example shown in Figure 9-13 will match only those records in which the Genre field contains Adventure and the Rating field contains PG. As before, the criterion range passed to the database function must include all the rows and columns of the range.

Genre	Rating
Adventure	PG

Figure 9-13: A criterion that specifies matches for two database fields.

Database Functions Versus PivotTables

Database functions are very powerful, although they can be a little tricky to use. They are at their best when you need to pull specific summary information out of a database without necessarily summarizing all the information. They are also more appropriate when you know in advance the type of analysis you will be performing and know that it will not change down the road. A PivotTable report is a better choice for summarizing an entire database or significant parts of it, or if you want to be able to vary the type of analysis you perform.

Working with Crosstabs

You may have heard of *crosstabs,* short for *cross tabulations,* as an Excel data-analysis tool. A crosstab is a table of sums, averages, or other summary calculations arranged in row-and-column format. Sounds sort of like a PivotTable, doesn't it? In fact, PivotTables were developed as a much more powerful replacement for crosstabs, and crosstabs are not even supported in recent versions of Excel. (Although you can create your own, it's a tedious process.) If you happen across an old workbook that contains a crosstab, you can convert it to a PivotTable report as follows:

1. Open the workbook that contains the crosstab table.

2. Click any cell in the crosstab table.

3. Select PivotTable and PivotChart Report from the Data menu.

4. Click Finish and then click OK in response to any prompts.

5. Save the workbook in the current Excel version.

Working with Filters

Filters are very useful Excel database tools that enable you to filter your data, showing only those records that meet certain criteria. Other non-matching records are still present in the database, but they are hidden while the filter is applied.

To create a filter, first place the cell pointer anywhere in the database table, select Filter from the Data menu, and then select AutoFilter from the next menu. Excel will place a drop-down list at the top of each column in the table, as shown for the video store data in Figure 9-14.

Part IX

	A	B	C	D
1	Store ▾	Genre ▾	Rating ▾	Titles in Stock ▾
2	Downtown	Adventure	G	99
3	Downtown	Adventure	PG	78
4	Downtown	Adventure	R	89
5	Downtown	Classics	G	123
6	Downtown	Classics	PG	98

Figure 9-14: When you add filters to a database, each column heading becomes a drop-down list.

Next, use these drop-down lists to define your filter. You can also sort the database on the field. The drop-down list for the Genre field is shown in Figure 9-15. The choices on the list are:

Figure 9-15: A drop-down filter list enables you to define your filter and/or sort the database.

- **Sort Ascending** — Sorts the database on this field in ascending order (A–Z, 1–10).

- **Sort Descending** — Sorts the database on this field in descending order (Z–A, 10–1).

- **(All)** — Removnves any filter for this field.

- **(Top 10)** — Displays only the top 10 records. (That is, the 10 records with the highest values in the field. Appropriate for number fields only.)

- **(Custom)** — Lets you define a custom filter (which is beyond the scope of this chapter).

- **[Individual data values]** — Displays only those records with the selected value.

You can filter a database table on one or more fields as needed. To remove all filters from the database, select Filter from the Data menu and then select Show All from the next menu. To remove the filter drop-down lists, select Filter from the Data menu and then select AutoFilter from the next menu.

Filters Versus PivotTables

Filters are not really an alternative to PivotTables. They can be very useful tools for some data-presentation and -analysis tasks, but they do not provide the kind of summary analyses that PivotTables, subtotals, and database functions do.

Part **X**

Programming PivotTables with VBA

Excel includes a powerful programming language called Visual Basic for Applications, or VBA. With VBA you can automate essentially any task in Excel, including the creation and manipulation of PivotTable reports. This part provides you with the information you need to create VBA programs to work with PivotTables and contains numerous working examples. This part does not, however, teach the fundamentals of VBA programming. After all, that is a topic that can fill an entire book! For the purposes of this part I assume you have at least intermediate-level experience working with VBA and the VBA editor.

Tips and Where to Find Them

Understanding the PivotTable Object Model

In VBA, PivotTables and all their various parts and components are represented by *object models*. This means that everything is represented by a specific kind of object. For example, the PivotTable itself is represented by a PivotTable object, an individual cell in a PivotTable is represented by a PivotCell object, and so on. Programming PivotTables essentially means manipulating the underlying objects.

The PivotTable object model has two basic features:

- It is hierarchical, meaning that every object has a parent object and most objects also have child objects.
- It uses *collections,* a special kind of object designed to hold other objects. By convention, a collection object has a name that is the plural of the name of the type of objects it contains. For example, the PivotTables collection contains each PivotTable in a given workbook. There are exceptions to this naming rule, however.

To manipulate an object in code you must first get a reference to it, a variable name that you use in code to refer to the object. If the object already exists, such as a PivotTable already present in a workbook, you retrieve the reference from the appropriate collection. The most important objects and collections in the PivotTable object model are described in the following table. The relationships among these objects and collections are diagrammed in Figure 10-1.

Object/collection	Description
PivotTable PivotTables	The PivotTable object represents a single PivotTable. The PivotTables collection contains all the PivotTables on a single worksheet.
PivotField PivotFields	The PivotField object represents a field in a PivotTable. The PivotFields collection contains all the fields in a single PivotTable.
PivotItem PivotItems	The PivotItem object represents a single item (an individual data entry) in a field. The PivotItems collection contains all the items for a single field.
CalculatedFields	The CalculatedFields collection contains all the calculated fields in the PivotTable. Each calculated field is represented by a PivotField object.

continued

Object/collection	Description
CalculatedMembers CalculatedMember	The CalculatedMembers collection contains all the calculated measures in the PivotTable. Each calculated measure is represented by a CalculatedMember object.
PivotFormula PivotFormulas	Each formula used to calculate results (sum, average, and so on) in a PivotTable is represented by a PivotFormula object. The PivotFormulas collection contains all the formulas for a single PivotTable.

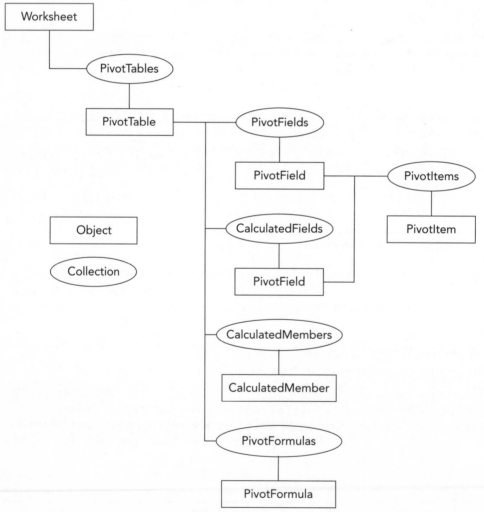

Figure 10-1: The hierarchy of the most important objects and collections in the PivotTable object model.

Referencing and Creating PivotTables

The first step in manipulating a PivotTable is to obtain a reference to it. How you do this depends on whether the PivotTable already exists. If it does, you obtain a reference to the existing PivotTable. If it doesn't, you create the PivotTable and, in the process, obtain the reference. The following sections explain both techniques.

Referencing an Existing PivotTable

A PivotTable that already exists will be present in the PivotTables collection for the worksheet in which it is located. Assuming that the variable is a reference to that worksheet, the syntax is as follows. First, declare a variable of the proper type to hold the reference:

```
Dim pt As PivotTable
```

Then retrieve the reference and store it in the variable:

```
Set pt = ws.PivotTables(index)
```

The *index* argument identifies the PivotTable. It can be either of the following:

- *A number that identifies the position of the PivotTable on the worksheet.* The first PivotTable created on a worksheet has index=1, the next one created has index-2, and so on.

- *A string specifying the name of the PivotTable.* By default PivotTables on a given worksheet are assigned the names PivotTable1, PivotTable2, and so on. You can change the name in the Table Options dialog box. To display this dialog box, right-click the PivotTable and select Table options from the pop-up menu.

If you specify a PivotTable that does not exist, a run-time error occurs. The code in Listing 10-1 illustrates this technique for obtaining a reference to an existing PivotTable. It opens a workbook and gets a reference to the first PivotTable on Sheet4.

The PivotTables Collection

You might think that all the PivotTables in a workbook would be organized together in a PivotTables collection that belongs to the workbook itself, but that's not the way Excel does things. Instead, each worksheet has its own PivotTables collection.

Listing 10-1: A VBA procedure that opens a workbook and gets a reference to a PivotTable.

```
Sub GetPivotTableReference()

Dim wb As Workbook
Dim pt As PivotTable

On Error GoTo ErrorHandler

' Open the workbook.
Set wb = Workbooks.Open("c:\PivotData\SurveyResults.xls")
' Get the PivotTable reference.
Set pt = wb.Worksheets("Sheet4").PivotTables(1)

' Code here can use the variable pt to work with the PivotTable

EndOfSub:
Exit Sub

ErrorHandler:

If Err.Number = 5 Or Err.Number = 9 then
    MsgBox "The workbook file could not be found"
ElseIf Err.Number = 1004 Then
    MsgBox "The PivotTable could not be found"
Else
    MsgBox "Error " & Err & " - " & Err.Description
End If

Resume EndOfSub

End Sub
```

Creating a New PivotTable in Code

You can create a new PivotTable using VBA code in two ways. The easiest, and the one you should use whenever possible, involves the PivotTableWizard method. Despite its name, this method doesn't display the PivotTable Wizard, but rather uses it behind the scenes to create a PivotTable based on options that you specify in code. The limitation of this method is that it cannot be used with OLE DB data sources. When you are using such a data source, you must use the second method, which does not involve the PivotTableWizard method. These two techniques are explained in the following sections.

Using the PivotTableWizard Method

To create a new PivotTable in a worksheet, call the PivotTableWizard method on the Worksheet object where you want the PivotTable located. The syntax of this method is quite complex, with numerous optional arguments that are infrequently used. For your present purposes, it will be most helpful to look at some examples. (You can also get the full details from the VBA online Help.)

At its simplest, the PivotTableWizard method requires that you specify the type of the source data and their location. For data in an Excel list, you use the constant xlDatabase to specify the type. For example, this line of code creates a PivotTable based on the data in the range A4:E250 on Sheet1. The PivotTable is placed on Sheet2, by default in the active cell.

```
Worksheets("Sheet2").PivotTableWizard SourceType:=xlDatabase, _
    SourceData:=Range("Sheet1!A4:E250")
```

You can specify a location other than the active cell for the PivotTable, and you can also assign a name to the report when it is created:

```
Worksheets("Sheet2").PivotTableWizard SourceType:=xlDatabase, _
  SourceData:=Range("Sheet1!A4:E250"), _
  TableDestination:=Range("D4"), _
  TableName:="My Pivot Table"
```

Finally, you can specify that the PivotTable include grand totals for the rows and/or the columns:

```
Worksheets("Sheet2").PivotTableWizard SourceType:=xlDatabase, _
  SourceData:=Range("Sheet1!A4:E250"), _
  TableDestination:=Range("D4"), _
  TableName:="My Pivot Table", _
  RowGrand:=True, ColumnGrand:=True
```

Figure 10-2 shows a data table in Excel on which the example PivotTable report used here will be based.

You can create a PivotTable report based on these data with the following VBA code:

```
Worksheets("Sheet2").PivotTableWizard SourceType:=xlDatabase, _
    SourceData:=Range("Sheet1!A4:C28"), _
    TableDestination:=Range("B2")
```

	A	B	C
1			
2	Popcorn Video Rentals		
3			
4	Store	Category	Titles
5	Main Street	Action	374
6	Main Street	Drama	180
7	Main Street	Childrens	63
8	Main Street	Sci-Fi	324
9	Main Street	Classics	203
10	Main Street	Comedy	145
11	Northgate	Action	45
12	Northgate	Drama	287
13	Northgate	Childrens	320
14	Northgate	Sci-Fi	36
15	Northgate	Classics	79
16	Northgate	Comedy	225
17	Clarkville	Action	22
18	Clarkville	Drama	172
19	Clarkville	Childrens	203
20	Clarkville	Sci-Fi	324
21	Clarkville	Classics	251
22	Clarkville	Comedy	345
23	West End	Action	310
24	West End	Drama	369
25	West End	Childrens	220
26	West End	Sci-Fi	236
27	West End	Classics	145
28	West End	Comedy	296

Figure 10-2: The data for the PivotTable report.

The resulting PivotTable is shown in Figure 10-3. But wait, something is missing! The report doesn't contain the areas with labels such as "Drop Row Fields Here" that you are used to seeing when you create a PivotTable manually using the PivotTable Wizard. Nothing is wrong; that's the way it works when you create a PivotTable in code. You can still drag fields from the Field List and drop them to define the report, but when creating a PivotTable in code, you usually also define the layout in code rather than letting the user do it. Adding fields and other parts of defining a PivotTable in code are covered later in the part.

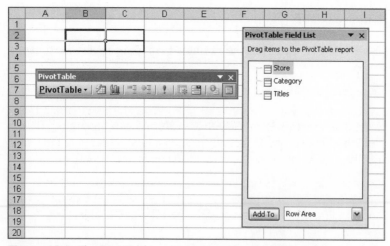

Figure 10-3: The PivotTable report created by the VBA code.

After you have created the PivotTable, you can get a reference to it using the techniques I explained earlier in this part in the section "Referencing an Existing PivotTable." You can also get the reference at the same time that the PivotTable is created because the PivotTableWizard method returns a reference to the newly created PivotTable. For example:

```
Dim pt As PivotTable
Set pt = Worksheets("Sheet3").PivotTableWizard _
  (SourceType:=xlDatabase, _
  SourceData:=Range("Sheet1!A4:C28"), _
  TableDestination:=Range("B2"))
```

Note that when you use the return value of the method, its arguments must be enclosed in parentheses. This is required by VBA syntax rules.

Creating a New PivotTable Without the PivotTableWizard Method

Creating a new PivotTable using VBA code but without the PivotTableWizard method is a bit more complicated that you might think at first glance. This is because an object called PivotCache is involved. When you create a PivotTable manually in a worksheet or in code using the PivotTableWizard, the PivotCache object is created automatically. It exists behind the scenes and the user never has to be concerned with it. When you are working in VBA, however, you must attend to these details.

The memory dedicated to a PivotTable report is represented by a PivotCache object, and each PivotTable has its own PivotCache (although in certain situations you can have two or more PivotTables based on a single PivotCache). All the PivotCache objects in a workbook are represented in the PivotCaches collection. Thus, there are two steps in creating a new PivotTable:

1. Create a new PivotCache object by calling the Add method of the PivotCaches collection. At this time you specify the data source for the PivotTable.

2. Create the new PivotTable by calling the CreatePivotTable method of the PivotCache object you created in Step 1. In this step you specify the location for the new PivotTable and, optionally, assign a name to it.

The VBA example in Listing 10-2 shows you how to create a PivotTable from data in a list in an Excel workbook. You can also create a PivotTable from external data (including OLE DB data), from another PivotTable report, and from multiple consolidation ranges. (You can find detailed descriptions of these techniques in the VBA online documentation.)

This example uses the video store data we used in Part IX, and which you saw earlier in Figure 10-2. It's important to note the location of the source data — cells A4:C28 on Sheet1 — because you need this information when creating the PivotCache object.

Part X

Listing 10-2: A VBA procedure that creates a new PivotTable based on data in an Excel list.

```
Public Sub CreatePivotTable()

Dim wb As Workbook
Dim pt As PivotTable
Dim pc As PivotCache

On Error GoTo ErrorHandler

' Open the workbook.
Set wb = Workbooks.Open("c:\PivotData\VideoStoreRawData.xls")

' Create the PivotCache.
Set pc = wb.PivotCaches.Add(SourceType:=xlDatabase, _
    SourceData:="[VideoStoreRawData.xls]Sheet1!A4:C28")

' Create the PivotTable on Sheet 2 of the same workbook.
Set pt = pc.CreatePivotTable _
    TableDestination:="[VideoStoreRawData.xls]Sheet2! ", _
    TableName:="Video Data"

' At this point the variable pt refers to the new PivotTable and
' can be used to manipulate it.

' Activate the worksheet containing the PivotTable.
wb.Worksheets("Sheet2").Activate

EndOfSub:

Exit Sub

ErrorHandler:

If Err.Number = 5 Or Err.Number = 9 Then
    MsgBox "The file could not be found"
ElseIf Err.Number = 1004 Then
    MsgBox "There is already a PivotTable at that location"
Else
    MsgBox "Error " & Err & " - " & Err.Description
End If

Resume EndOfSub

End Sub
```

When you run this VBA procedure it creates a new blank PivotTable, similar to what you see at the completion of the PivotTable Wizard when you are creating a PivotTable manually. As when you use the PivotTable Wizard, the new PivotTable doesn't have the "Drop Here" labels. Users can still drop fields on the PivotTable, but as I mentioned before, you will most often be completing the PivotTable layout in code rather than letting the user do it manually.

Working with the PivotTable Object

Manipulating the PivotTable object is, as you might expect, at the heart of working with PivotTables in code. Given the power and flexibility of PivotTables, it is not too surprising that the PivotTable object is quite complex. It has over a dozen methods and several dozen properties with which you can work. Some of these are essential and are used almost every time you need to manipulate a PivotTable in VBA code. Others are relatively obscure and are rarely used. Tables 10-1 and 10-2 list the more important properties and methods of this object with a brief description of each. Then, the following sections show you how to perform real-world tasks with PivotTables using VBA code. Properties marked Read Only can be read but not set in code. Properties marked Read/Write can be read and set.

TABLE 10-1   IMPORTANT PROPERTIES OF THE PIVOTTABLE OBJECT

Property	Read Only (R) or Read/Write (R/W)	Description
CalculatedMembers	R	Returns a CalculatedMembers collection representing all the calculated members and measures for an OLAP-based PivotTable.
ColumnFields	R	If the PivotTable has only one column field, returns a PivotField object representing the field. If the PivotTable has more than one column field, returns a PivotFields collection containing one PivotField object for each column field.
ColumnGrand	R/W	True if the PivotTable displays column grand totals, false if not.
DataFields	R	If the PivotTable has only one data field, returns a PivotField object representing the field. If the PivotTable has more than one data field, returns a PivotFields collection that contains one PivotField object for each data field.

continued

Part X

TABLE 10-1   IMPORTANT PROPERTIES OF THE PIVOTTABLE OBJECT *(continued)*

Property	Read Only (R) or Read/Write (R/W)	Description
EnableDrillDown	R/W	Returns true (the default) if drill-down is enabled, false if not.
GrandTotalName	R/W	Specifies the heading label for grand total rows and columns. The default is "Grand Total."
Name	R/W	The name of the PivotTable.
PageFields	R	If the PivotTable has only one visible page field, returns a PivotField object representing the field. If the PivotTable has more than one visible page field, returns a PivotFields collection that contains one PivotField object for each page field.
PivotFormulas	R	Returns a PivotFormulas object that represents the collection of formulas for the PivotTable.
PreserveFormatting	R/W	Returns true if the table's formatting is preserved when refreshed or recalculated, false if it is not.
RowFields	R	If the PivotTable has only one row field, returns a PivotField object representing the field. If the PivotTable has more than one row field, returns a PivotFields collection containing one PivotField object for each row field.
RowGrand	R/W	Returns true if the PivotTable displays row grand totals, false if it does not.

TABLE 10-2   IMPORTANT METHODS OF THE PIVOTTABLE OBJECT

Method	Description	Return value
AddDataField	Adds a data field to the PivotTable report.	A reference to the PivotField object for the added field.
AddFields	Adds row, column, and/or page fields to the PivotTable report. (Not available with OLAP data sources.)	N/A

Method	Description	Return value
Format	Applies one of several predefined formats to the PivotTable.	N/A
GetData	Returns data from a specified cell in the PivotTable report.	The returned data as a string.
GetPivotData	Returns a range object representing specified data in the PivotTable report.	A range object.
ListFormulas	Creates a new worksheet containing a list of all calculated PivotTable items and fields.	N/A
PivotFields	Returns visible and hidden PivotTable fields (all in the Field List).	A PivotField object representing a single PivotTable field or a PivotFields collection of multiple visible and hidden fields.
PivotSelect	Selects part of a PivotTable report.	N/A
RefreshTable	Refreshes the PivotTable report.	True if successful, false if not.
ShowPages	Creates a new PivotTable report, on a new worksheet, for each item in the page field.	N/A

Part X

Adding and Removing Row, Column, and Page Fields

A PivotTable report is largely defined by its row, column, a page fields. When you first create a PivotTable report using the methods described earlier in this part, it has no fields at all and you must add them. After a report has been defined, you may want to remove certain fields and add others, or move a field from the Row area to the Column area. You can do all these things with the AddFields method.

```
AddFields(RowFields, ColumnFields, PageFields, _ AddToTable)
```

The first three arguments specify the fields to be added to the Row, Column, and/or Page areas respectively. You must specify at least one of these arguments, and you can also specify two or three of them in a single call. The argument takes one of two forms:

- If you are adding a single field, it is the field name.

- If you are adding more then one field, it is an array containing the names.

The AddToTable argument determines whether existing fields are replaced. If this argument is True, the specified fields are added to the report without any existing fields being deleted. If this argument is False or is omitted, existing fields are deleted and replaced with the new ones.

The following code adds the field named Region to the Column area of the first PivotTable on Sheet1, adding it to any existing column fields:

```
Worksheets("Sheet1").PivotTables(1).AddFields _
    (ColumnFields:="Region", AddToTable:=True)
```

This code adds the fields named Status and DueDate to the Row area of the PivotTable referenced by the variable myPivotTable, replacing any existing row fields:

```
myPivotTable.AddFields(RowFields:=Array("Status", "DueDate"))
```

This final example adds two page fields, one row field, and one column field to a PivotTable report, replacing any existing fields:

```
myPivotTable.AddFields(RowFields:="Region", _
    ColumnFields:="Quarter", _
    PageFields:=Array("Status", "DueDate"))
```

After you learn how to add data fields to a PivotTable I will put everything together in a real-world example.

Adding and Removing Data Fields

In addition to row, column, and page fields, a PivotTable report needs one or more data fields. You add a data field to a PivotTable report with the AddDataField method. It has the following syntax:

```
AddDataField(Field, Caption, Function)
```

- The Field argument specifies the field to add. You might think you could just specify the field name, but you cannot; you must pass a reference to the field. I'll show you how later in this tip.

- The `Caption` argument specifies the caption that will be used for the field — in other words the label displayed in the PivotTable report.

- The `Function` argument specifies the function that the added field uses. The default is `Sum`.

The function returns a reference to the added field.

The first argument specifies the field to add, but it must be a reference to a PivotField object for that field and not just the field name. This seems like an unnecessary complication, but that's the way it works. You can get this reference from the PivotTable's PivotFields method as follows, where *Name* is the name of the field:

```
PivotFields(Name)
```

Here's an example of adding a data field. This code first gets a reference to the PivotTable named PivotTable1 on Sheet1. Then it adds the field named Sales with the caption Total Sales. The field will use the default `Sum` function:

```
Dim pt As PivotTable
Set pt = Worksheets("Sheet1").PivotTables("PivotTable1")
pt.AddDataField pt.PivotFields("Sales"), "Total Sales"
```

Creating a PivotTable Using VBA Code

The code presented in this tip builds on the code examples presented earlier that showed you how to create a PivotTable using the PivotTableWizard. Listing 10-3 contains a complete VBA procedure that creates a PivotTable and populates it with row, column, and data fields. The code creates a PivotTable from the data shown in Figure 10-2. The code performs the following steps:

1. Opens the worksheet c:\PivotData\VideoStoreRawData.xls. (You'll need to change this if you have placed the file in a different location.)

2. Creates the PivotTable report at cell B2 in Sheet 2.

3. Adds Store as a row field and Category as a column field.

4. Adds Titles as the data field with the caption Total Titles.

The resulting PivotTable report is shown in Figure 10-4. You can see that this is a complete PivotTable, with all required fields in place. With code such as this you can automate the procedure of creating a PivotTable, letting users create a PivotTable with the least effort. Of course, you need to know something about the data, specifically their location and the field names.

Let Excel Find the Data Range

Suppose you know where the data are located but not the precise number of rows they contain. Can you still create a PivotTable in code? You bet, using the CurrentRegion property. All you need to know is the address of any single cell in the data range: then this property returns the range of surrounding cells that contain data. Specifically, it returns the range of data bounded by empty rows, empty columns, and/or the edges of the worksheet. For example, the expression

```
Range("Sheet1!A4").CurrentRegion,
```

returns the range of data surrounding cell A4 on Sheet1 — in this case A4:C28.

Listing 10-3: A VBA procedure that creates a PivotTable and adds all required fields to it.

```
Public Sub CreateCompletePivotTable()

Dim wb As Workbook
Dim pt As PivotTable

On Error GoTo ErrorHandler

' Open the workbook.
Set wb = Workbooks.Open("c:\PivotData\VideoStoreRawData.xls")

' Create the PivotTable and get a reference to it.
Set pt = Worksheets("Sheet2").PivotTableWizard _
  (SourceType:=xlDatabase, _
  SourceData:=Range("Sheet1!A4:C28"), _
  TableDestination:=Range("Sheet2!B2"))

' Add row and column fields.
pt.AddFields RowFields:="Store", ColumnFields:="Category"

' Add data field.
pt.AddDataField pt.PivotFields("Titles"), "Total Titles"

EndOfSub:
Exit Sub

ErrorHandler:

If Err.Number = 5 Or Err.Number = 9 Then
    MsgBox "The file could not be found"
```

```
ElseIf Err.Number = 1004 Then
    MsgBox "There is already a PivotTable at that location"
Else
    MsgBox "Error " & Err & " - " & Err.Description
End If


Resume EndOfSub


End Sub
```

Total Titles	Category ▾						
Store ▾	Action	Childrens	Classics	Comedy	Drama	Sci-Fi	Grand Total
Clarkville	22	203	251	345	172	324	1317
Main Street	374	63	203	145	180	324	1289
Northgate	45	320	79	225	287	36	992
West End	310	220	145	296	369	236	1576
Grand Total	751	806	678	1011	1008	920	5174

Figure 10-4: The PivotTable report created by the VBA procedure in Listing 10-3.

Working with PivotTable Fields

All of the fields in a PivotTable report, both visible and not visible, are represented by the PivotField object. If you want to write code to manipulate fields, performing actions such as changing the display format and changing position, you will need to use the PivotField object in code. Tables 10-3 and 10-4 describe the more important properties and methods of this object; then the following sections provide code examples for specific field-related tasks.

TABLE 10-3   IMPORTANT PROPERTIES OF THE PIVOTFIELD OBJECT

Property	Read Only or Read/Write	Description
AutoShowCount	R/W	When AutoShow is enabled for a field, specifies the number of items shown (for example, top 10 or top 5).
Orientation	R/W	Specifies the orientation, or position, of a field. Can be one of the following: xlHidden, xlRowField, xlColumnField, xlPageField, xlDataField.

TABLE 10-4 IMPORTANT METHODS OF THE PIVOTFIELD OBJECT

Method	Description	Return value
AddDataField	Adds a data field to the PivotTable report.	A reference to the PivotField object for the added field.

Creating and Changing Filters

As you learned in Parts III and IV, a filter lets you specify that only some of a field's items are to be displayed in the PivotTable report. To review briefly, an item is an individual data value in a field. For example, the Month field would contain the items Jan, Feb, and so on. To create a filter you are actually hiding or showing individual items by setting the Visible property to False or True. The procedure involves the following steps:

1. Get a reference to the PivotField object that represents the field of interest.

2. Use a For Each statement to loop through all of the items in the field's PivotItems collection.

3. Set each PivotItem object's Visible property to True or False as needed.

The following code example gets a reference to the field named Month in the specified PivotTable report. It then creates a filter that displays data only for the month Jan.

```
Dim pf As PivotField
Dim pi As PivotItem

Set pf = ActiveSheet.PivotTables(1).PivotFields(Index:="Month")
For Each pi In pf.PivotItems
    If pi.Name = "Jan" Then
        pi.Visible = True
    Else
        pi.Visible = False
    End If
Next
```

Removing a filter requires only that you set the Visible property to True for all items:

```
For Each pi In pf.PivotItems
    pi.Visible = True
Next
```

Changing a Field's Position

A field's position — whether it is a row, column, page, or data field — is controlled by the PivotField object's Orientation property. A field can also be hidden, meaning that it is not part of the PivotTable report but is available to be added to the report. These settings are represented by the defined constants xlHidden, xlRowField, xlColumnField, xlPageField, and xlDataField.

To change a field's position you need to get a reference to the field and then set its Orientation property as desired. The following code assumes that the variable pt has been set to refer to the PivotTable report of interest. It then sets the field named Color to be a row field:

```
Dim pf As PivotField
Set pf =pt.PivotFields("Color")
pf.Orientation=xlRowField
```

When a PivotTable report has more than one field in the Row or Column area, the fields have hierarchy beginning with the outermost. In the Row area, for example, the outer field is displayed at the far left and provides the top level of organization of the PivotTable's rows, while the inner field is displayed at the right and provides the lowest level of organization. To change a field's inner/outer position, you set its Position property. A value of 1 specifies the outer field, 2 is the next level, and so on. This addition to the following example sets the Color field to be the outer row field:

```
Dim pf As PivotField
Set pf =pt.PivotFields("Color")
pf.Orientation=xlRowField
pf.Position=1
```

Creating Calculated Fields and Items

A PivotTable report can contain calculated fields and calculated items. To review briefly, a calculated field is a data field whose value is based upon a calculation performed on one or more other fields in the PivotTable report. A calculated item is similar to a calculated field in that it is based on a calculation using an existing data field, but it is not a field; rather, it is an independent item in the report.

Calculated fields are maintained in the PivotTable object's CalculatedFields collection. To create a new calculated field, you call the collection's Add method and pass it the name of the new field as well as the calculation formula. The calculation formula consists of the following parts:

- A leading equals sign.

- The name(s) of one or more existing fields, including other calculated fields.

- The mathematical operators + (addition), - (subtraction), / (division), * (multiplication), and ^ (exponentiation).

- Numerical values.

For example, the formula =Amount*0.07 creates a calculated field that displays 7 percent of the value in the Amount field. Likewise the formula =Commission*Sale creates a calculated field that displays the product of the Commission and Sale fields.

Here is a code snippet that creates a calculated field named Sales Tax that is equal to 5% of the Amount field. Assume that pt is a reference to the PivotTable report of interest:

```
Dim pf As PivotField
Set pf = pt.CalculatedFields.Add(Name:="=Sales Tax", _
        Formula:="Amount*0.05")
pf.Orientation=xlDataField
```

Note the last line of this code, which sets the field to be a data field. This is required if you want the calculated field to be displayed. If you do not do this, the field will be created and will be available for use in the PivotTable report, but it will remain hidden.

A calculated item is associated with an existing field, and you create it by adding to the field's CalculatedItems collection. The syntax for the calculation formula is the same as described for calculated fields. You also specify a caption for the calculated item when you create it. This code adds a calculated item named Next Quarter to the Quarter field, displaying the calculation of 0.9 times the value of the Qtr1 item. Assume that the variable pt is a reference to the PivotTable report:

```
Dim pf As PivotField
Set pf = pt.PivotFields(Index:="Quarter")
pf.CalculatedItems.Add Name:="Next Quarter", Formula:="=Qtr1*0.9"
```

Hide and Show Field Items

Hiding and showing fields is actually a matter of changing their positions. A field is "hidden" when it is not a row, column, data, or page field. You saw how to do this in the section "Changing a Field's Position" earlier in this part. To hide a field, set its position to xlHidden. To show a field, set its position to xlPageField, xlRowField, xlColumnField, or xlDataField.

Using AutoShow and AutoSort

You learned in Part IV how to use the AutoSort feature to sort data in a PivotTable report, and also how to use AutoShow to display only certain values such as the 10 highest. You can also use these features from VBA code.

To enable AutoSort you use the PivotField object's AutoSort method. This method has the following syntax:

```
AutoSort(Order, Field)
```

- Order determines the sort order, either xlAscending, xlDescending, or xlManual.
- Field is the name of the field on which to sort. This must be the unique field name (as returned from the SourceName property) and not the displayed name, which may be different.

The following code sets the field Salesman to sort in ascending order based on the data in the Sales Total field:

```
ActiveSheet.PivotTables(1).PivotField("Salesman") _
    .AutoSort xlAscending, "Sales Total"
```

To enable AutoShow you call the field's AutoShow method. The syntax is as follows:

```
AutoShow(Type, Range, Count, Field)
```

- Type is either xlAutomatic to enable AutoShow for the field or xlManual to disable it.
- Range specifies whether top or bottom items are shown using the constants xlTop and xlBottom.
- Count specifies how many items to show.
- Field is the name of the field to use for determinations. It must be the unique field name (as returned from the SourceName property) and not the displayed name, which may be different.

This example enables AutoShow for the Salesperson field, displaying the top four records based on the value in the Total Sales field.

```
ActiveSheet.PivotTables("Pivot1").PivotFields("Salesperson").AutoShow
xlAutomatic, xlTop, 4, "Total Sales"
```

Part X

Changing a Field's Calculation

PivotTable reports enable you to specify various calculations to be performed by a data field, such as sum and average. You can change a field's calculation using VBA code by setting the field's Calculation property and sometimes the BaseField and BaseItem properties as well.

The Calculation field is set to a defined constant that specifies the calculation. The permitted values are:

- xlDifferenceFrom
- xlIndex
- xlNoAdditionalCalculation
- xlPercentDifferenceFrom
- xlPercentOf
- xlPercentOfColumn
- xlPercentOfRow
- xlPercentOfTotal
- xlRunningTotal

The BaseField property specifies the field that will be used as the base for the calculation.

The BaseItem property specifies the item in the BaseField that will be used for the calculation.

The following code sets the calculation for the field referenced by the variable pf to be the difference from the Jun item in the Month field.

```
With pf
    .Calculation = xlDifferenceFrom
    .BaseField = "Month"
    .BaseItem = "Jun"
End With
```

What About OLAP Data?

Because field calculations for OLAP-based PivotTable reports are defined in the OLAP cube and not in the PivotTable itself, you cannot change the calculation displayed by data fields, either manually or in VBA code. You must modify the OLAP cube itself in order to change a field calculation.

Changing the Display Format of a Field

The display format used for numbers in a field is controlled by the field's NumberFormat property. To change the format you must generate a format string that defines the format. These strings use specific characters, as explained in the following table. (You can find complete details in the Excel online Help.)

Character	Function
#	Defines a character-display position; insignificant zeros are not displayed.
0 (zero)	Defines a character-display position; insignificant zeros are displayed.
. (period)	Indicates the position of the decimal point.
, (comma)	Indicates a thousands separator.
$	Includes a leading dollar sign.
%	Displays number as a percent (for example, 0.08 as 8%).
[xxx] where xxx is Black, Green, White, Blue, Magenta, Yellow, Cyan, or Red	Specifies the text color.
; (semicolon)	Separates sections of the format string. The format specified before the separator is used for values 0 and greater; the format specified after the separator is used for values less than 0.
Other characters such as (and).	As themselves.

Part X

Some examples of format strings and the resulting displays are given in the following table.

Value	Format string	Displayed
123.4	0.00	123.40
123.4	0	123
123456	#,##0	123,456
123456	#,##0.00	123,456.00
123456	$#,###	$123,456
0.095	#.0%	9.5%
0.095	#.000%	9.500%
100000	$#,###.00;	$100,000.00
-100000	$(#,###.00)	$(100,000.00)

You can also control the display format of dates that are part of a PivotTable report. Certain characters in the format string determine how days, months, and years are displayed. These are described in the following table:

To display	Use this code
Months as 1–12	m
Months as 01–12	mm
Months as Jan–Dec	mmm
Months as January–December	mmmm
Months as J–D	mmmmm
Days as 1–31	d
Days as 01–31	dd
Days as Sun–Sat	ddd
Days as Sunday–Saturday	dddd
Years as 00–99	yy
Years as 1900–1999	yyyy

Creating a PivotChart in Code

Creating a PivotChart in VBA code is surprisingly simple. Because a PivotChart is always based on a PivotTable report, all that is required is to create a new chart and then specify the PivotTable as its data source. More specifically, you need to specify the section of the PivotTable report that excludes the page fields, if there are any. The PivotTable object has the TableRange1 property that returns this range. (The TableRange2 property returns the range of the entire PivotTable report, including page fields).

The procedure is as follows:

1. Call the Charts collection's Add method to create a new chart.
2. Call the chart's Location method to specify where the chart will be placed (see below for details).
3. Call the chart's SetSourceData method, passing the TableRange1 property of the PivotTable report as an argument.

The Location method has the following syntax:

```
Location(Where, Name)
```

- Where is the constant xlLocationAsNewSheet, to put the chart on a new worksheet, or xlLocationAsObject, to embed the chart as an object on an existing worksheet.
- Name is required only if you are placing the chart as an embedded object and specifies the name of the worksheet where you want the chart placed.

Here's an example. Assume that the variable pt is a reference to the PivotTable report on which you want the chart based. This code creates a PivotChart and places it on a new worksheet:

```
Charts.Add
With ActiveChart
    .Location Where:=xlLocationAsNewSheet
    .SetSourceData Source:=pt.TableRange1
End With
```

Appendix A

Troubleshooting PivotTables and PivotCharts

PivotTables are a powerful tools and with that power comes some unavoidable complexity. This section covers the more common problems that users encounter when creating and using PivotTables and suggests solutions.

Problems When Using External Data

This section covers problems that you may encounter when a PivotTable is based on external data.

Slow Responses and/or Error Messages

When you are creating a PivotTable based on external data, you may run into problems such as slow response and error messages. Some of these problems cannot be avoided because they are caused by problems with the external database itself or with your network connection to the data. There are, however, some things you can do to avoid or minimize these difficulties.

When your PivotTable report is based on a large amount of external data, laying the report out in the worksheet after completing the PivotTable Wizard can be slow and can sometimes cause error messages to display. Specifically, when you drag a field onto the PivotTable report there may be a delay before the data are retrieved and displayed. Here are some suggestions:

- If you suspect that table layout in the worksheet will be slow, click the Layout button in Step 3 of the PivotTable Wizard and use the Layout dialog box to define the report layout. (Using this dialog box is covered in Part III.)

- If you have started layout in the worksheet and it is slow, click the Always Display Items button on the PivotTable toolbar to turn off data display. When layout is complete, click the button again to turn data display back on.

- If you are still having problems, select PivotTable and PivotChart Report from the Data menu to redisplay Step 3 of the wizard. Then click the Layout button to complete the table layout in the Layout dialog box.

The suggestion in the next section can also help when data retrieval is slow.

Running Out of Resources and/or Memory

When your PivotTable is based on a large amount of external data, Excel may run out of resources or memory. This is simply the result of there being too much data for Excel to handle all at once. It may be possible to get around this problem by defining a page field in your report so that only part of the data is retrieved at one time. (You cannot do this if you are using OLAP source data, however.)

When laying out the report in the Layout dialog box, drag a field to the Page area. Then double-click the Page field to display the PivotTable Field dialog box. Click the Advanced button and select the option Query external data source as you select each page field item.

Even if you are not receiving error messages, this technique can sometimes speed things up when you are accessing large amounts of external data.

You can sometimes avoid running out of memory by opening the Options dialog box for the PivotTable and selecting the Optimize Memory option.

Problems Creating PivotTable Reports

This section covers common problems that you may encounter when creating a PivotTable report.

The Desired Source Report Is Not Listed in the Wizard

When you are creating a PivotTable report from an existing PivotTable report, the desired source PivotTable report may not be listed in Step 2 of the PivotTable and PivotChart Wizard. This is usually because the report is in a different workbook; the wizard lists only the PivotTable reports in the workbook that was active when the wizard was started. You can get around this problem by copying the desired source PivotTable report into the current workbook.

Problems with PivotTable Report Layout and Formatting

This section covers frequently encountered problems with PivotTable formatting and layout.

My Formatting Disappears

Some Excel users are dismayed to see their carefully applied formatting disappear when they refresh the table or change its layout. This can be avoided — usually, at least — as follows:

- For autoformats, make sure the AutoFormat Table option is turned on in the PivotTable options dialog box. (You display the PivotTable Options dialog box by selecting Table Options from the PivotTable menu.)

- For other formats, such as font and color changes, make sure the Preserve Formatting option is turned on (in the same dialog box as above).

The fact is, however, that certain formats cannot be preserved through refreshes and layout changes such as cell borders and conditional formatting.

I Cannot Pivot the Report

If you cannot drag certain fields (or any fields at all) to pivot the report, there are several possible causes.

- If a page field's options are set to Query for external data only when each item is selected, you will not be able to drag that field to the Row or Column areas. To solve this problem, double-click the field, click Advanced, and clear the Disable Pivoting of this Field check box under Page Field Options.

- If the PivotTable is based on OLAP data, certain fields, identified in the Field List by this icon, can be used only as page fields and cannot be dragged to the Data area.

- Other fields, identified by this icon, can be used only as data fields and cannot be dragged to the Page, Row, or Column areas.

- The workbook may contain a VBA macro that disables the ability to drag fields. If this is the case, a cancel symbol displays at the mouse pointer when you try to drag a field.

- If the worksheet has protection turned on, and the Use PivotTable Reports option was not selected when the protection was enabled, you will not be able to modify the report layout.

Problems When Using OLAP Data

This section deals with problems frequently encountered with OLAP data.

The Summary Function I Want Is Not Available

A PivotTable report based on OLAP data is limited to the summary functions defined in the cube file. The OLAP Cube Wizard has a limited number of summary functions, namely Sum, Count, Min, and Max. It does not support the other summary functions such as StdDev and Product. There are two possible solutions:

- If the amount of data is such that your system can handle a standard query (that is, non-OLAP), then create the PivotTable report directly from the external data source rather than from an OLAP cube. You will then have the full range of summary functions available.

- Set up an OLAP server using Microsoft SQL Server OLAP Services. This product offers a much wider range of summary functions than the OLAP Cube Wizard that is part of Office.

Data Present in the Data Source Are Not Available for My PivotTable Report

An OLAP cube does not necessarily contain all of the data in the data source, and a PivotTable based on an OLAP cube is limited to the data in the cube. Depending on how the cube was created, you may be able to modify it to contain the needed data. If, however, the cube was created with the OLAP Cube Wizard in Microsoft Query, you will not be able to add data but will have to redefine a new cube that contains the data.

Appendix B

Excel Version Differences for PivotTables

The PivotTable capabilities of Excel have been evolving over the years as new versions of Office have been introduced. PivotTables in Excel 2000 had essentially all the major features that are present in the latest version of Excel, but there have been some changes in the details since then. The two most recent versions, Excel 2002 (also called Excel XP) and Excel 2003, are essentially identical with regard to PivotTables. This appendix looks at the differences between these versions of Excel and the previous version, Excel 2000.

User Changes

User changes are those that affect the user who is creating and manipulating PivotTables in Excel. The changes in Excel 2002/2003 include the following:

- Dropping a field in the Row or Column area displays the field's items immediately. In the old version you had to drop a field in the Data area before these items were displayed.

- Items in a Row or Column field can be grouped to provide better display of analysis results.

- The PivotTable menu has been reorganized to combine all related commands on one menu. The pop-up menu, accessed by right-clicking, makes the most frequently used commands easily available.

- In a PivotTable that is based on multidimensional data, the page fields enable you to filter on multiple items at once rather than on a single item or on (All).

- Member properties for a multidimensional data source can be viewed (if they exist).

- The GETPIVOTDATA function was improved so that its reference to PivotTable data is maintained despite any changes to PivotTable layout.

Object Model Changes

This section details additions to the PivotTable object model. These changes are relevant if you are writing VBA code to work with PivotTables. There are several new objects and collections:

- The PivotCell object represents a single cell in a PivotTable.

- The PivotItems collection represents all of the items for a single field.

- The CalculatedMember object represents a calculated field or item for a PivotTable based on an OLAP data source.

- The CalculatedMembers collection contains all the CalculatedItem objects for a PivotTable.

In addition, several existing objects and collections have new properties and/or methods. These are detailed in the following table. Some of these methods and properties are discussed in Part X; for others you can find information in the VBA online documentation.

Object/Collection	New Properties	New Methods
Application object	GenerateGETPIVOTDATA	
CalculatedMember object	IsValid	
	SolveOrder	
CubeField object	EnableMultiplePageItems	AddMemberPropertyField
	HasMemberProperties	
	ShowInFieldList	
CubeFields collection		AddSet
PivotCache object	ADOConnection	MakeConnection
	IsConnected	SaveAsODC
	MissingItemsLimit	
	OLAP	
	RobustConnect	
	SourceConnectionFile	
	SourceDataFile	

Object/Collection	New Properties	New Methods
PivotCell object	ColumnItems	
	CustomSubtotalFunction	
	DataField	
	PivotCellType	
	RowItems	
PivotField object	CurrentPageList	AddPageItem
	DatabaseSort	
	EnableItemSelection	
	HiddenItemList	
	IsMemberProperty	
	PropertyOrder	
	PropertyParentField	
	StandardFormula	
PivotFormula object	StandardFormula	
PivotItem object	SourceNameStandard	
	StandardFormula	
PivotTable object	CalculatedMembers	AddDataField
	DataPivotField	CreateCubeFile
	DisplayEmptyColumn	GETPIVOTDATA
	DisplayEmptyRow	
	DisplayImmediateItems	
	EnableDataValueEditing	
	EnableFieldList	
	MDX	
	PivotSelectionStandard	
	ShowCellBackgroundFromOLAP	
	ShowPageMultipleItemLabel	
	ViewCalculatedMembers	
	VisualTotals	

In addition there are some new events. The Workbook object has the new PivotTableOpenConnection and PivotTableCloseConnection events, and the Worksheet object has the new PivotTable update event.

Appendix C

An Excel Chart Primer

Excel's charting abilities are extensive and powerful. When you combine Excel charts with PivotTables, you get PivotCharts, a means by which you can graphically display the data in a PivotTable report. You learned about the PivotChart-specific aspects in Part VI, which assumed that you had some basic knowledge of Excel charts in general. This appendix is provided for those readers whose experience with Excel charts is limited or who want to brush up on the basics. With this information, you will be able to format and customize your PivotCharts exactly as desired.

This appendix does not cover the steps required to create a chart but assumes that you have already created your PivotChart. Nor does it cover changing chart type, which was covered in Part VI.

Formatting Data Series

A data series in a chart represents a related set of values. Usually the values that make up a data set are in a column in the underlying table, although it is possible to have rows of values as data sets as well. In a column or bar chart, a data series is represented by a set of columns (or parts of columns) with the same color and/or pattern. In a line chart it is represented by a line with the same color and symbols. These two types of chart are illustrated in Figures C-1 and C-2.

One Data Series

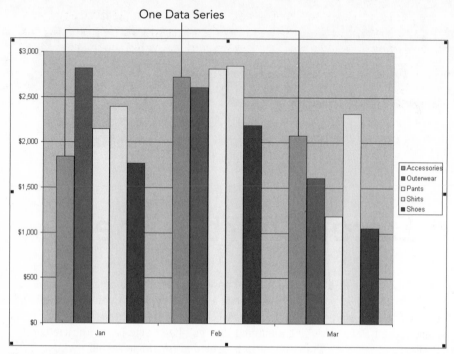

Figure C-1: A data series in a column chart.

Data Series

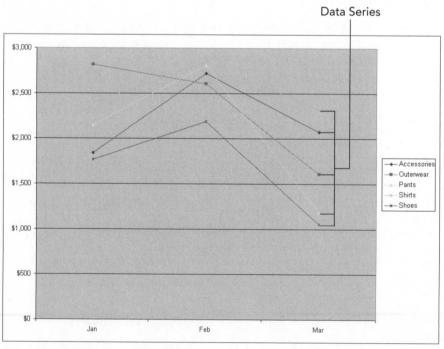

Figure C-2: Data series in a line chart.

You can change the format of a data series in a chart by right-clicking the data series and selecting Format Data Series from the pop-up menu. In the Format Data Series dialog box, the options available to you depend on whether you are working with a column chart or a line chart.

For a column chart, the format options are available on the patterns tab in the dialog box, as shown in Figure C-3. You use them as follows.

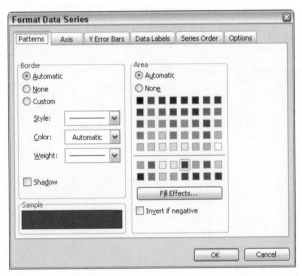

Figure C-3: Formatting options for a data series in a column chart.

In the Border section you specify how the border of each column or bar in the data series will appear:

- **Automatic** — Excel will select the format.
- **None** — No border will be displayed.
- **Custom** — The border will be displayed with the style, color, and weight you select. Click the Shadow option to display a drop shadow.

In the Area section you specify the appearance of the inner part of the column or bar:

- **Automatic** — Excel will select the format.
- **None** — The bar will display no area fill.
- **Color** — Click a color in the palette to select that color.
- **Fill Effects** — Click this button to set advanced area options, including gradient fills and patterns.

Printing in Black and White?

If you will be printing your PivotChart on a monochrome printer, it may be a good idea to format a column chart using patterns rather than colors to distinguish data series. You do this with the Fill Effects button as described above.

If you are working with a line chart, the formatting options for the data series are found on the Patterns tab of the Format Data Series dialog box, shown in Figure C-4.

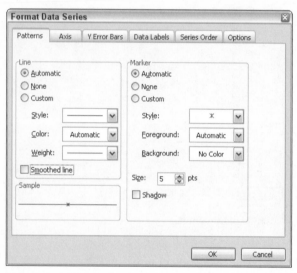

Figure C-4: Formatting options for a data series in a line chart.

In the Line section of this dialog box you specify how the data series line is to appear:

- **Automatic** — Excel will select the format.

- **None** — No line will be displayed between symbols.

- **Custom** — The line will be displayed with the style, color, and weight you select.

- **Smoothed Line** — The line will curve smoothly rather than being straight between symbols.

In the Marker section of the dialog box you select the marker, or symbol, displayed at each data point:

- **Automatic** — Excel will select the format.

- **None** — No symbol will be displayed at data points.

- **Custom** — The symbol will be displayed with the style, foreground, background, and size you select.

- **Shadow** — Each symbol will be displayed with a drop shadow.

Formatting Chart Axes

Most Excel charts have two axes. The vertical axis is called the *value axis* while the horizontal axis is called the *category axis*. Three-dimensional charts have three axes, the *series axis* as well as the other two. These axes are illustrated in Figures C-5 and C-6.

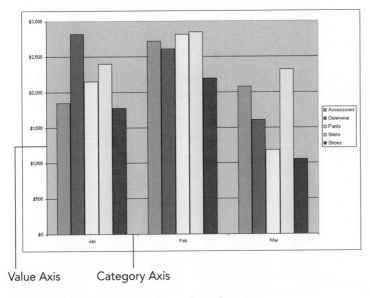

Value Axis   Category Axis

Figure C-5: Most line and column charts have two axes.

To change the format of an axis, right-click it and select Format Axis from the pop-up menu. The Format Axis dialog box has five tabs that give you great flexibility in changing the appearance of an axis.

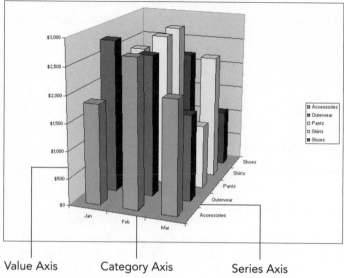

Value Axis   Category Axis   Series Axis

Figure C-6: Three-dimensional charts have three axes.

Scale

The Scale tab offers different options depending on whether you are formatting the value axis or the category axis. For the value axis the Scale tab looks like Figure C-7.

Figure C-7: The Scale tab in the Format Axis dialog box for the value axis.

The axis scale is normally set by Excel to values based on the nature of the data. You can set these values manually by unchecking the Auto box next to a setting and then entering the desired value manually. The available settings are:

- **Minimum** — The lowest value on the value axis.
- **Maximum** — The highest value on the value axis.
- **Major unit** — The distance between major tick marks and labels.
- **Minor unit** — The distance between minor tick marks.
- **Category (X) axis Crosses at** — The axis value at which the category axis crosses the value axis.

The Display units option lets you change the axis display unit to Hundreds, Thousands, Millions, Billions, or Trillions. For example, if you select Thousands, an axis value of 3,000 will display as 3. If you also select the Show display units label on chart option, Excel will display a label — for example, Thousands — next to the axis. Figure C-8 shows the same chart that was shown earlier in Figure C-5, with the value axis display unit set to Thousands.

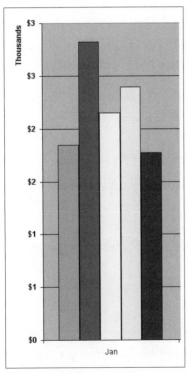

Figure C-8: Using a display unit of Thousands.

- **Logarithmic Scale** — Scales the axis using logarithms. Useful when the data include both very small and very large values.

- **Values in reverse order** — Inverts the value axis so the lowest value is at the top and the largest is at the bottom.

- **Category (X) axis crosses at maximum value** — Places the category axis at the maximum value on the value axis.

For the category axis, the Scale tab looks like what you see in Figure C-9. Because no values are being plotted, fewer axis options are available. These options are mostly self-explanatory and control the crossing of the value axis and the relationship between the categories and tick marks and labels. You can experiment with them to see precisely what effects they have.

Figure C-9: The Scale tab in the Format Axis dialog box for the category axis.

Patterns

The Patterns tab, shown in Figure C-10, controls the axis line and its tick marks.

In the Line section you control how the axis line itself displays:

- **Automatic** — Excel will set the display of the axis line.
- **None** — No axis line will be displayed.
- **Custom** — The axis line will be displayed with the style, color, and pattern you select.

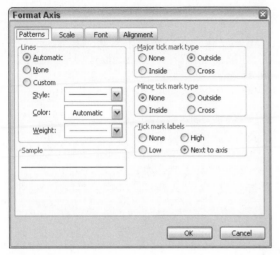

Figure C-10: The Pattern tab in the Format Axis dialog box controls the display of the axis line and tick marks.

On the right side of the Patterns dialog box you control the display of tick marks and tick-mark labels. For both major and minor tick marks you can determine if they are displayed and, if so, where. Note that for a value axis, the distance between major and minor tick marks is determined by the Major unit and Minor unit settings, respectively, on the Scale tab.

Font

The Font tab in the Format Axis dialog box, shown in Figure C-11, controls the font used to display the axis labels (but not the axis title, which will be covered later in this appendix). It is essentially the same as the Font dialog box that you use to format cells in a work-sheet, enabling you to set the font, style, size, color, and other aspects of the text display.

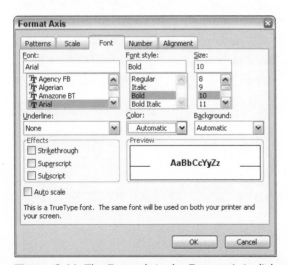

Figure C-11: The Font tab in the Format Axis dialog box controls the font used for the axis labels.

Number

The Number tab is available when you are formatting the value axis. It is shown in Figure C-12. The number formats are the same as those for formatted numerical values in a worksheet — Currency, Percent, General, and so on.

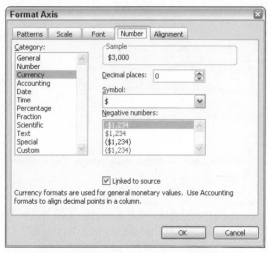

Figure C-12: The Number tab in the Format Axis dialog box controls the display format of numbers on the value axis.

Alignment

The Alignment tab, shown in Figure C-13, controls the angle at which axis labels are displayed. By default the angle is usually horizontal. In the Orientation section you can drag the text icon to the desired angle or enter the desired value in the Degrees box. The Offset option controls how far from the axis the labels are placed.

For example, look at the category axis in the top part of Figure C-14. There is not enough room in the horizontal orientation to display all 12 month names, so Excel defaults to displaying every other one. By changing the label alignment, as shown in the lower part of the figure, you can display all 12 labels.

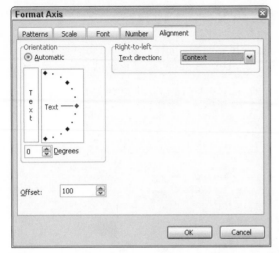

Figure C-13: The Alignment tab in the Format Axis dialog box controls the display angle for axis labels.

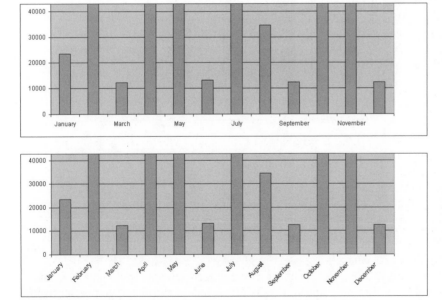

Figure C-14: Using the Alignment setting to display more category axis labels.

Changing Chart and Axis Titles

With a chart you have the option of displaying a title for the chart itself and for each axis in the chart. An axis title is distinct from the axis label, as shown in Figure C-15.

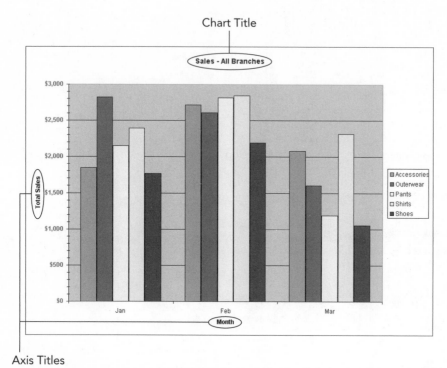

Figure C-15: A chart can display chart and/or axis titles.

To work with titles, right-click the chart and select Chart Options from the pop-up menu. (If this command does not appear on the pop-up menu, try right-clicking in a slightly different position.) The Chart Options dialog box is shown in Figure C-16 with the Titles tab displayed.

On the left, this tab displays a box for the chart title and for each axis in the chart. Enter the desired titles and then click OK. Once a title is displayed on the chart, you can format it by right-clicking the title and selecting Format Title from the pop-up menu. The resulting dialog box lets you specify the font, color, background, and box for the title, among other things. Setting these title options is identical to setting them for an axis, as covered earlier in this appendix.

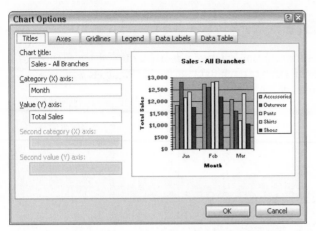

Figure C-16: The Titles tab of the Chart Options dialog box.

The Chart Legend

Excel creates a legend automatically for most charts. The legend, illustrated in Figure C-17, identifies the data series in the chart by color and/or symbol, depending on the chart type.

Figure C-17: The chart legend identifies the data series in the chart.

Some charts, such as those with only one data series, may not need a legend. You can remove it by right-clicking the legend and selecting Clear from the pop-up menu. You can also change the format and location of the legend by selecting Format Legend from the pop-up menu. The Format Legend dialog box has three tabs:

- **Font** — Specifies the font used in the legend.
- **Patterns** — Specifies the color of the legend background and the format of the box surrounding it.
- **Placement** — Controls where on the chart the legend is displayed.

Using Data Labels

Data labels provide a way for you to display text information directly on the chart. Figure C-18 shows an example in which the numerical value of each data series is displayed as a data label. You can also use data labels to display the series and category names.

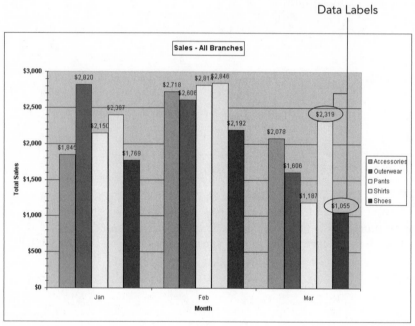

Figure C-18: Data labels let you display text information directly on the chart.

You can set data labels as an option for individual data series. To display them, right-click the data series and select At Data Series from the pop-up menu. Next, select the Data Labels tab in the Format Data Series dialog box. This tab is shown in Figure C-19.

Make selections in this dialog box as follows:

- In the Label Contains section, select one or more items to include in the data label: the value, the category name, and/or the series name. The Percentage and Bubble size options are available only for pie and bubble charts and are not relevant to PivotCharts.

- If you selected more than one item to include in the data label, pull down the Separator list and select the character that will be used to separate the items.

- Select the Legend Key option to include the legend key (symbol or color) in the data label.

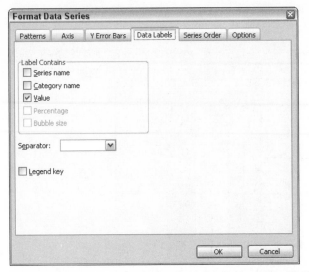

Figure C-19: The Data Labels tab in the Format Data Series dialog box.

You can also set data labels for all data series at once by right-clicking the chart and selecting Chart Options from the pop-up menu to display the Chart Options dialog box. On the Data Labels tab you have the options shown in Figure C-19, but your settings apply to all of the data series.

After you have added your data labels you can format them by right-clicking a label and selecting Format Data Labels from the pop-up menu. The dialog box that appears lets you select font, background, number format, and alignment for the labels. Note that a format applies only to labels for a single data series.

Other Chart Options

In this final section I will mention briefly some other chart options that you may find useful.

Gridlines

A chart can display vertical and/or horizontal gridlines in the background of the chart to provide visual organization and a scale for interpreting the chart data. You can display gridlines at major tick intervals, minor tick intervals, or both. Figure C-20 shows a chart with horizontal (value axis) gridlines at both the major and minor tick intervals.

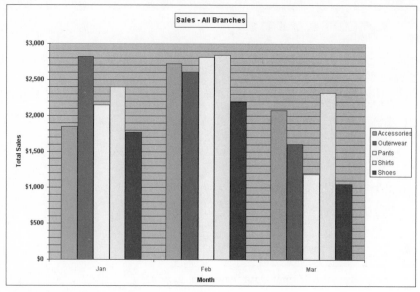

Figure C-20: A chart displaying horizontal gridlines.

To display gridlines, open the Chart Options dialog box, click the Gridlines tab, and then select the gridline options you want. Once gridlines are displayed, you can change their format by right-clicking a gridline and selecting Format Gridlines. The dialog box that appears lets you select the line style and color for the gridlines. It also provides access to the Scale settings for the value axis, which you can use to change the spacing between tick marks (and hence gridlines).

Displaying a Data Table

A data table displays a table of the chart's numerical data under the chart itself, as shown in Figure C-21. You can use a data table when you want to display precise number values as well as the overall trend. Data labels, covered earlier in this appendix, are another way to do this.

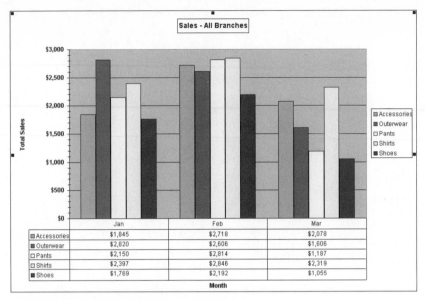

Figure C-21: A chart with a data table displayed.

To display a data table, display the Chart Options dialog box and click the Data Table tab. Select the Show Data Table option to display the data table. Select the Show Legend Key option to include the legend keys (colors, symbols) in the table (as in Figure C-21).

Index

Symbols and Numerics

* (asterisk)
    multiplication operator, 113
    total, marking with, 67
^ (caret) exponentiation operator, 113
, (comma) field format string character, 233
$ (dollar sign) field format string character, 233
= (equals sign)
    formula prefix, 113
    GETPIVOTDATA function shortcut character, 187, 192–193
>= (greater than sign, equals sign) greater than or equal to operator, 208
> (greater than sign) greater than operator, 208
<= (less than sign, equals sign) less than or equal to operator, 208
< (less than sign) less than operator, 208
- (minus sign) subtraction operator, 113
(number sign) field format string character, 233
% (percent sign) field format string character, 233
. (period) field format string character, 233
+ (plus sign) addition operator, 113
" " (quotation marks) function argument delimiters, 185
; (semicolon) field format string character, 233
/ (slash) division operator, 113
3-D PivotChart, 147, 153–157, 161

A

active status
    PivotChart, 13
    PivotTable, 8, 79
Add VBA method, 219
AddDataField VBA method, 222, 224–225, 228
AddFields VBA method, 222, 223–224
addition. *See* total
Application object, 242
asterisk (*)
    multiplication operator, 113
    total, marking with, 67
AutoFilter feature, 19, 209
autoformatting, 66, 70–72, 74–76, 86
AutoShow feature, 105–107, 227, 231

AutoSort feature, 104, 107, 231
average, returning, 95, 97–98, 100, 201, 206

B

background color, 73
Browse dialog box, 21

C

calculated field
    creating, 113–115, 229–230
    deleting, 114
    duration of PivotTable, existence limited to, 113
    editing, 114
    GETPIVOTDATA function, returned by, 187
    metric conversion using, 116–118
    OLAP support, 113, 232
    PivotChart, 145
    total, returning using, 113, 114, 120–122
calculated item, 119–123, 145, 187, 229–230, 242
CalculatedFields collection, 213
CalculatedItem object, 242
CalculatedMember object, 214, 242
CalculatedMembers collection, 214, 221, 242
caret (^) exponentiation operator, 113
category
    field, 123, 140, 143
    grouping category data, 132–135
cell
    border, 67, 101
    calculated item display in, 123
    database cells, counting, 206
    empty cell display, customizing, 68
    field-linked, 73
    formatting, 67, 72, 73
    GETPIVOTDATA function
        generating when cell clicked, 187–188
        referencing cell in, 186, 187–190
    PivotCell object, 242
    referencing, 185, 186, 187–190
    VBA, returning cell value using, 223
Chart Options dialog box, 256–257, 259, 260, 261

continued

continued